Topics on Tradition

Fr. Chad Ripperger, Ph.D.

Dedicated in Honor of All of the Holy Angels

Table of Contents

Abbreviations

The following abbreviations are used in this text along with those abbreviations in use in standard English. Texts of Saint Thomas:[1]

De Ver.	*Quaestiones Disputatae de Veritate*
Meta.	*In Libros Metaphysicorum*
Quod.	*Quaestiones Quodlibetales*
Sent.	*In Quatuor Libros Sententiarum*[2]
SCG	*Summa Contra Gentiles*
ST	*Summa Theologiae*

Other texts:

CCC	*Catechism of the Catholic Church*[3]
OCE	*Catholic Encyclopedia*[4]
CED	*Catholic Encyclopedia Dictionary*[5]
CIC/83	*Codex Iuris Canonici*[6]
SSP	*Summary of Scholastic Principles*[7]

---

[1] All citations from the works of St. Thomas are from *Thomae Aquinatis Opera Omnia*, Issu Impensaque Leonis XIII, edita, Roma: ex Typographia Polyglotta et al., 1882. All translations of St. Thomas are the author's own unless otherwise noted.

[2] Citations from the *Sentences* contain first the book number, then the abbreviation, followed by location within the book.

[3] Editio typica, Libreria Editrice Vaticana, 1997.

[4] The Gilmary Society, New York, 1913.

[5] The Gilmary Society, New York, 1941.

[6] *Code of Canon Law Annotated,* as edited by E. Caparros, M. Thériault and J. Thorn. Wilson & Lafleur Limitée, Montreal, 1993.

[7] Loyola University, 1951.

Introduction

As each new pope is elected after Vatican II, there arise questions in all parts of the Church about his theological stance on this or that, his liturgical views on the Ancient Rite of Mass, his pastoral views, how he will address other religions as well as a variety of other topics. It is hard to imagine that in the past such questions would have been asked about an incoming pope. Each pope is a different man, but what kept them within a certain range of predictability was the Sacred Tradition. What happened? How did the Church get to this state?

This small work is a republishing of many of the articles that I have written in the past as well as a bit more. It is my hope that in republishing this, those who have asked for my articles in the past will now have them available in an anthology.

I am grateful to the *The Latin Mass* magazine for having originally published many of the articles that appear in this book under a slightly edited and different format and for the permission to reprint the articles. I am also indebted to Rod Pead of *Christian Order* for his permission to reprint my articles that appeared in *Christian Order* as well as his excellent editing skills that went into the original articles and are preserved, for the most part, in this book. I thank all of those who reviewed my articles for the sake of editing and input.

Lastly, as an act of devotion, I thank St. Thomas Aquinas whose writing and clarity of thought have proven to be a great source of joy in my pursuit of the virtue of science.

Part I: The Tradition Itself

Chapter 1: The Different Kinds of Tradition

Many in the Church today seem to know very little about tradition. While some traditionalists know a little bit about tradition by reading some of the popular literature, very few have a deep understanding of the nature of tradition and the various kinds of tradition. It is necessary to provide a deeper understanding of the nature of tradition so as to have a clear understanding of our Catholic heritage and to provide a clear path to the full restoration of Catholic tradition in all of its magnificence and glory. As one comes to a deeper knowledge of tradition, his Catholic identity becomes clearer and, at the same time, his appreciation for our Catholic heritage deepens.

I. The Deposit of Faith

Tradition is part of the deposit of faith and is the means of transmission of that very deposit.

> The expression occurs in the two letters of St. Paul (1 Tim. 6:20; 2 Tim. 1:14), in connection with the idea of doctrines of the faith. The "deposit" which St. Paul transmits to his faithful collaborator is the whole of divine revelation (1 Tim. 6:1; 4:6) made up of the dogmas of faith, Christian morals, the sacraments, Holy Scripture, the hierarchical constitution of the Church. The juridical concept of deposit requires that it be not the property of the guardian but of the consignor who has handed it over to him to keep it in a safe state. The "deposit of faith" has come from God and is entrusted to those to whom a special assistance of the Holy Ghost is assured (:2 Tim. 1-14), i.e., to those who succeed the Apostles in their magisterium and in their ministry. Christ has transmitted the deposit whose content cannot be subjected to alterations. ...The Church finds in the "deposit of faith" the riches that she communicates to her children, the arms with which she fights her adversaries...[8]

This definition provides several important points. The first is that the Deposit of Faith is something given (*tradere*) by Christ (God) to the Church or more specifically the Apostles. Second, they are not permitted to change it.

Third, the Deposit of Faith includes several elements, viz. the dogmas of the faith, morals, the sacraments, Holy Scripture and the hierarchical constitution of the Church. It is a common misunderstanding among modern

---

[8]Pietro Parente, *Dictionary of Dogmatic Theology* (The Bruce Publishing Company, Milwaukee, 1951), p.73f.

writers that the Deposit pertains only to the knowledge of the dogmas and morals which Christ taught.[9] This is understandable since many books and treatises on revelation fail to include the sacraments, the hierarchical constitution of the Church and the means of fighting the Church's adversaries as part of the Deposit. The Deposit is what Christ left us. He left the sacraments with the Apostles, principally by means of their reception of the sacrament of Holy Orders. If the sacraments are not part of the deposit of faith which is the essential and intrinsic object of tradition, then the transmission of the sacraments from generation to generation does not enjoy the infallible guaranty of the Holy Spirit. Likewise the hierarchical constitution of the Church as well as the means of fighting the Church's adversaries, such the power of exorcizing the devil, the power to bestow blessings and things of this sort, are passed on by tradition. Therefore, the Deposit is not just knowledge of the teaching of Christ, even though that is an integral part of it.

II. The Nature of Tradition

Tradition is normally divided into oral and written, insofar as the things which are handed on from generation to generation are passed on either in something written (e.g. the Scriptures) or orally (e.g. the transmission of the priesthood by means of the form of the sacrament during ordination). Tradition of the Deposit of Faith, as considered as a fact, is extrinsic to the flux or changes of human things; it does not change intrinsically.[10] This comes from the fact that Sacred Tradition in the Church enjoys God as the cause of its inerrancy and changelessness. Whereas those traditions which come from a human cause, human care and human industry do change. Any kind of tradition, to be an authentic tradition, not merely in the sacred sense but even in the profane sense, is done as a means of passing on what is esteemed as good. Knowledge, works and things, which are worthy to be remembered or passed on, are held in order to be given over to prosperity.

Yet, Sacred Tradition is not only a fact of history, but it is a matter of divine law. The divine law to pass on the tradition was given to the Apostles, when Christ said, "go teaching them all I have commanded you." This law is given with the provision of a special institution (the Roman Catholic Church), constitution of an authentic organ of transmission of the tradition (Church/Magisterium) and the promise of perennial assistance. Without

---

[9]For example, see "The Incommutability of Ecclesiastical Tradition" by D. E. Romanae.

[10]The substance of this article is a summarization of parts of Ludovicus Billot's *De Immutabilitate Traditionis*.

tradition, revelation could not be preserved and subsequent generations could not thereby be saved by the knowledge and means of the Deposit of Faith.

Therefore, Sacred Tradition needs an efficacious medium, by which the things of tradition are passed. An efficacious medium is necessary so that dogma remains incorrupt despite our human condition and so the authentic organ of tradition was instituted by Jesus Christ, viz. the Church, especially the apostolic hierarchy with which He promised to be until the end of time. The tradition is a continual preaching (*predicatio*) from age to age by the apostolic successors under the charism of assistance of the Holy Spirit of the revelation by the Same Jesus Christ and first received orally by the Apostles. The requirement to teach (pass on - *tradere*) the teaching of Christ was manifest when He said "Going therefore, teach ye all nations: baptizing them in the name of the Father and of the Son and of the Holy Spirit. Teaching them to observe all things whatsoever I have commanded you. And behold I am with you all days, even to the consummation of the world."[11] The Apostles are the guardians and faithful dispensers, not inventors of the doctrine of Christ, and the Apostles and successors are to conserve the doctrinal integrity of the teachings of Christ ("teach *all* that I have commanded you"). Therefore, the Apostles and successors are not allowed to substitute Christ's teaching with their own teaching and the institution of the organ of tradition was given an indefectibile charism, viz. Magisterial infallibility. This charism is necessary to know, without doubt, what Christ taught and even Scripture cannot be guaranteed without the continual tradition informing each generation that Scripture is true. The charism of indefectibility applies to all that is contained in the tradition, viz. the teachings (knowledge), sacraments and the organ of tradition itself, i.e. the Magisterium.

The institution of the organ of tradition was not done in any way whatsoever, but in an oral mode which constitutes a perpetual living preaching. This is necessary; it is contrary to what the Protestants argue, viz. that once it was written down, e.g. in Scripture, this sufficed and so the organ of tradition (Magisterium) was not permanent. This is also necessary since, again, we cannot be assured of the truth of Scripture without the organ of transmission. The institution of the organ of tradition is indivisible in itself (rooted in the mark of unicity of the Church) and is always visible (since the Church is a visible institution). Hence, those who cut themselves off from the Church are no longer part of the organ of Sacred Tradition. This is manifest by the fact that schismatics, as a general rule, normally lapse into heresy within one hundred years of their separation from the bark of Peter. Since they have cut themselves off from the organ of tradition which enjoys the charism of infallibility, not only of doctrinal interpretation but also of the

---

[11]Matthew 28:19f.

transmission itself, there is no guaranty that they will pass on the teachings of Christ in their integrity.

Sacred Tradition in the true and Catholic sense is the *regula fidei* or the rule of faith. The concept of tradition as merely a human deed, or only the preaching of Christ and Apostles who alone had Christ's authority is contrary to the teaching of the Church. Here a distinction between the object of faith and the rule of faith must be made. The object of faith is the truth to be believed. The rule is that which contains the truth to be believed and to which we must conform ourselves. In other words, Sacred Tradition is the rule of faith because if one wants to know what the faith believes (object), he looks to tradition (i.e. what the Magisterium has passed on and taught us). This is why tradition is always the principle of judgment for what is to be believed. Those who wish to reject the tradition or wish to stop the passing on of the deposit of faith act contrary to Christ's mandate. Moreover, we are not talking just about what has been taught but what could be clarified and ruled on by the Magisterium since it is part of the tradition. This is why the various distinctions within tradition are important. The distinctions help us to know what can and cannot be changed.

The Protestants and some modern Catholics make Scripture the rule rather than tradition. However, as the rule of faith, Sacred Tradition is, in the temporal order, the order of knowledge and the order of comprehension, prior to Scripture. Tradition is temporally prior since it existed before Scripture, because Christ taught orally and commissioned the Apostles before the Scriptures came into being. Even when the Apostles were inspired in their writing of Scripture, the teaching was first handed on to them by God prior to its writing, since what one writes must first be in the intellect. Sacred Tradition as a rule of faith is always prior to Scripture in the order of knowledge and comprehension as one uses the tradition to interpret Scripture. The Magisterium, which is part of the Tradition, has the right to determine the true meaning of Scripture (a) because the Magisterium was given the authority (rights) and commanded to teach on Christ's behalf. (b) It has been given an infallible charism to avoid error regarding its interpretation of Scripture. (c) It wrote Scripture (i.e. the New Testament). (d) Tradition is temporally prior to Scripture since the Apostles knew what to write before they wrote. Hence, tradition is prior to Scripture in the order of knowledge and comprehension since part of tradition was put to writing which we call Scripture and so if one wants to know what Scripture means, look at tradition from whence it came, i.e. its cause.

At this point, an interesting observation can be recalled by Ludovicus Billot. He says that it was not in Scripture but in tradition that the revealed doctrine was deposited. This follows from the fact that the Apostles were given the teaching prior to its being written. Moreover, Scripture is in the Deposit of Faith, which is given by God to man, so even when written, it is first in the Apostle who passes it on (tradere) by means of writing. The written word is also part of the tradition in the broad sense (to be discussed later). The Magisterium has authority to propose and explicate that which it deems necessary to believe as coming from the revelation of the Apostles. As a result, the Magisterium becomes the proximate and immediate rule of faith, since it passes on the teaching as the official organ of tradition. In other words, if one wants to know what to believe, one looks to the Magisterium.

III. Distinctions

The tradition of the Catholic Church is complex and errors occur in discussions of tradition because of a failure to make adequate distinctions. The authors which discuss tradition provide a variety of ways in which tradition can be distinguished. J.M. Hervé, in his *Manuale Theologiae Dogmaticae,*[12] notes four ways to distinguish tradition. Hervé's first way of distinguishing tradition is by reason of its author. The first kind of author is a divine author and, for this reason, divinely authored tradition is distinguished between Dominical and Apostolic. Dominical tradition constitutes those things which Christ Himself orally taught, e.g. the teaching on the indissolubility of marriage[13] and the precepts of charity.[14] Apostolic tradition is called divino-apostolic since it was promulgated by the Apostles from the dictating of the Holy Spirit. It would appear that the ordination of deacons is part of divino-apostolic tradition.[15] Both of these kinds of tradition proceed from God and therefore are irreformable.

The second kind of author is the Church and Hervé calls the tradition coming from the Church "ecclesiastical tradition."[16] Ecclesiastical tradition is divided into humano-apostolic tradition and mere ecclesiastical tradition. Humano-apostolic tradition are those traditions began by the Apostles which were not divinely revealed. This would include precepts and those things instituted by the Apostles themselves which are not based directly on the

---

[12]Vol. 1, n. 556. All of the various ways of distinguishing tradition are taken from Hervé unless otherwise noted.

[13]Matthew 19:6.

[14]Matthew 22: 37; Mark 22: 30 and Luke 10: 27.

[15]Acts 6:6.

[16]The reader should be aware that the term "ecclesiastical tradition" has varied based upon time of usage and author. We shall address this problem in the last article in the series.

authority of God since they were not revealed. However, they are promulgated indirectly on the authority of God insofar as the Apostles receive their authority from God when promulgating things which are not part of divine revelation. Hervé gives the example of those things which the Apostles promulgated in the various particular churches and which, we may say, vary from church to church. By various churches we do not mean non-Catholic churches since there is only One Church as we profess in the Creed. Rather, the term 'church' here refers to the various rites within the One Church, e.g. the Byzantine rite, the Roman rite, etc. Those things promulgated by the Apostles which are not divinely revealed would be things such as laws regarding fasting and the days of Eastertide. While it pertains to the natural law to obtain the virtue of fasting,[17] which days one ought to fast can be set by different rites within the Church. Hervé observes that these traditions can be modified by the successors to the Apostles.

However, a word of caution should be made. Careful study must be made to obtain a sufficient degree of certitude that a particular tradition started by the Apostles is clearly established as being on the authority of the Apostles alone before any presumption can be made in changing it. Moreover, the longer the humano-apostolic tradition, the greater the cause for a change must be manifest. Therefore, if a humano-apostolic tradition has been in place since the time of the Apostles, only under the gravest of circumstances should it be changed since the will of God is manifest in His approval of the tradition since it remained in place for such a duration. Mere ecclesiastical tradition contains those things instituted by the Church after the time of the Apostles. Some are universal, such as the lenten fast, whereas others are particular, e.g. a local feast.

The next way in which tradition is distinguished is by reason of its object. Hervé divides this method of distinguishing tradition into (1) dogmatic and (2) moral or disciplinary. Dogmatic tradition would include all of those doctrines which are not connected to action but to truth, e.g. it has always been the dogmatic tradition of the Church that Christ is truly present in the Eucharist. The moral tradition would include those moral teachings which the Church passes on, e.g. it has always been a teaching of the Church that adultery is immoral.

The third way in which tradition is distinguish is in relation to Scripture. The first kind of tradition in relation to Scripture is called constitutive tradition. This is tradition in the more restricted sense of the term as pertaining to those things which are taught but not contained in Scripture. Here, Hervé gives the example of the Assumption of the Blessed Virgin Mary.

---

[17]This based on the Thomistic notion that the Natural Law commands all virtues. For a discussion of this, see the author's work *Introduction to the Science of Mental Health*, v. 1, chapter 11 in conjunction with ST II-II, q. 147 (especially a. 3).

The second kind of tradition in relation to Scripture is interpretative tradition. This tradition is when someone gives (*tradit*) the meaning of Scripture. Interpretative tradition is subdivided into inherent tradition and declarative tradition. Inherent tradition is when the meaning of the text from Scripture is clear, e.g. the tradition about the sense of the words "This is My Body."[18] Declarative tradition is when the passage of Scripture is difficult or unclear and the meaning of the text is declared by the Church. The last way in which tradition is distinguished according to Hervé is by reason of time in which some traditions are established for a time whereas others are established in perpetuity.

In connection to the above observations, other authors make further distinctions. Joannes Herrman[19] makes a distinction between tradition taken in the broad sense and tradition in the strict sense. Tradition in the broad sense includes all of those things which are passed on in anyway whatsoever and this even includes Scripture. Then there is tradition in the strict sense which is counter-distinguished from Scripture. This would seem to pertain to constitutive tradition. The import of this distinction is that tradition taken in the broad sense constitutes everything which the Church passes on in any way. The tradition in the broad sense ought to be a homogenous whole. In other words, tradition in the broad sense is a single thing, a totality passed on to each generation. Even though distinctions can be made within tradition, tradition itself has a unity since all of the things of the past are handed to the next generation either in practice, teaching, documents or monuments.[20]

Joseph Wilhelm and Thomas Scannell[21] (henceforth Scannell) make observations and distinctions which provide points of clarification, particularly for us living in an age of confusion regarding tradition. Scannell distinguishes between ecclesiastical tradition and human tradition.[22] Human tradition can only produce human certitude. Human certitude increases and decreases with time and can fail entirely. Ecclesiastical tradition, on the other hand, is human insofar as it is something which is in the hands of men, but it

---

[18]Matthew 26:26 and John 6.

[19]*Institutiones Theologiae Dogmaticae*, p. 528.

[20]What a monument is will be discussed later.

[21]All observations in the remaining part of this article are based upon Wilhelm's and Scannell's work, *A Manual of Catholic Theology*, vol. 1, pp. 71-84. This text was based upon Sheeben's German text "Dogmatik."

[22]Here there is another shift in the meaning of the term "ecclesiastical tradition."

is something far higher than mere human tradition. It is higher because the organ of transmission is Christ's Church which is directed by the Holy Spirit. The value of ecclesiastical tradition does not depend on the number of witnesses as does human tradition, nor does ecclesiastical tradition rely on the person's learning, who passes something on. Rather, the value of ecclesiastical tradition is based upon the rank of the various persons in the Church and the assistance of the Holy Spirit. The Holy Spirit and the rank of the various persons teaching something or passing something on constitutes the basis of certitude of that part of tradition which they pass. The authenticity of the testimony of ecclesiastical tradition remains at every point in the history of tradition. In other words, the ecclesiastical tradition will always be passed on with the assistance of the Holy Spirit until the end of time.

Yet, it must be admitted that the human element in the tradition modifies the perfection of Tradition. While all those things necessary for salvation will always be available to every generation, there can be a break in the ecclesiastical tradition in its continuity and universality in which a temporary partial eclipse of truth is possible regarding the tradition. By this is meant that it is possible for a time that a portion of the Deposit of Faith may not be known and acknowledged by the *whole* Church or expressly and distinctly attested by the leading organs of tradition. The essential integrity, continuity and universality of the oral tradition, as required by the infallibility and indefectibility of the Church and as modified by the imperfections of the human element, are subject to the following laws.

First, nothing can be taught as part of the Apostolic tradition which is not truly part of the Apostolic tradition. Apostolic tradition here means all of those things necessary for salvation which were handed on by God, either in the person of Christ or revealed to the Apostles by God as pertaining to salvation. In this sense, the eclipse of ecclesiastical tradition does not admit of a loss of the passing on of those things necessary for salvation. Each and every generation until the end of time will be handed on all of those things necessary for salvation. This does not mean that everyone in the Church will know everything for salvation, but that the whole of those teachings necessary for salvation will be passed on in perpetuity.

Second, the essential and necessary truths will always be expressly taught, admitted and handed down by the Church. It does not mean that every single pope, bishop, priest or teacher will do so. It merely means that the Church (here Scannell uses the term "Body") as a whole will pass on the whole of the teachings necessary for salvation. It is possible that the truth may become so obscured that not all of the members of the Church will know or profess all of the teachings of the Church.

This teaching is assuring for us in a period of doctrinal obscurity. Even if there is lack of clarity in various parts of the Church regarding the authentic teachings of the Church, nevertheless, those teachings are available.

The unfortunate part of the obscurity is that many faithful are led into error. There can be a variety of factors which can cause the obscurity, but, in either case, the Magisterium must do everything possible to teach with the greatest clarity possible and to seek to pass on the Deposit to every member of the Church by catechetical instruction and to those outside the Church by means of evangelization.

IV: Sources of Sacred Tradition

Scannell[23] divides tradition into oral tradition and documentary tradition; based upon this distinction, he discusses the basis for certitude regarding what we can know from tradition. He observes:

> Only the actual and express Tradition of a truth can be appealed to in proof that it is a matter of Faith. If we can show that at a given time the Tradition was universal this alone is sufficient – continuity is, not absolutely necessary. However, except in cases of an authoritative definition, Tradition, to become universal, requires a long time. Even, when an authoritative definition is given, it is always based upon the fact that the Tradition in question was universal for a long time. Hence the duration for a more or less long period should be proved.

There are two bases of certitude for something from tradition: (1) its duration (if it has always been taught then it is a matter of faith); (2) its authoritative definition. The foundation for holding some truth from tradition is four-fold: (1) If the tradition is universal regarding the doctrine, it is a matter of faith. (2) If it is authoritatively defined, it is a matter of the faith. The authoritative definition is passed on by ecclesiastical tradition and becomes an irreformable and irrevocable part of it. (3) Non-authoritative teachings become part of the tradition and their certitude is based upon the rank of those who teach it, e.g. if several popes have taught something that is more authoritative than say a single bishop. (4) The longer the tradition, the greater the certitude of its truth.

The question of certitude affects the consideration of the various forms or sources within tradition. Some sources have greater certitude than others. The question of sources is important for us as Catholics since we rely on the sources for our knowledge of the Deposit of Faith. Sometimes the sources are called the ways and means by which tradition is safely

---

[23]Joseph Wilhelm and Thomas Scannell, *A Manual of Catholic Theology*, vol. 1, pp. 71-84.

transmitted.[24] The first source is the solemn judgments of the Church which constitute an infallible proof of the truth of some proposition which is to be held as pertaining to the faith. These solemn judgments are part of the documentary tradition of the Church. An example of a solemn judgment would be the definition of the Immaculate Conception by Pius IX. If a Catholic wanted to know what the Church taught on the Immaculate Conception, he could go to the document *Ineffabilis Deus* of Pius IX and read the formal definition. Like all infallible statements, solemn judgments become, as it were, like proper accidents of the Deposit of Faith. In other words, while the Deposit of Faith constitutes the essence of what is passed on in tradition, along with that Deposit are the solemn judgments of the Church. A proper accident is an accident which always accompanies some substance, e.g. rationality is a proper accident of man. Therefore every time one finds a man, one knows that the person has a faculty called reason. We never find a human being without an intellect, even if they do not have use of it. In like manner, the solemn judgements of the Church must always accompany the passing of the tradition since, by virtue of their infallibility, they become inextricably connected to the understanding we have of that element of the Deposit which is clarified in the solemn judgment.

The Holy Father, when meeting the conditions of infallibility laid down by the First Vatican Council,[25] and the bishops when in an ecumenical council, likewise solemnly define or judge some matter of the Faith.[26] We also know that ordinary magisterial teaching, when it is taught by all of the bishops throughout the world, also constitutes an infallible source of Church teaching. This form of infallibility was implied in Pope John Paul II's *Ordinatio Sacerdotalis* (1994). Outside these contexts, we do not have the same degree of certitude when the bishops and pope speak. However, we are still required to give religious assent to the ordinary magisterial teachings of the pope and bishops, even though they do not enjoy the same degree of certitude. For this reason, encyclicals and other documents of the popes are another source of Church teaching.

Yet, infallibility regarding some matter pertaining to the Deposit of Faith is not restricted to the popes and bishops alone. Infallibility is also enjoyed in several other agencies, clearly recognized by the teaching authority of the Church, viz. the *sensus fidelium*, the Fathers of the Church and the Theologians. The *sensus fidelium* is infallible when there is "the distinct, universal, and constant profession of a doctrine by the whole body of the

---

[24] For example, see George Agius, *Tradition and the Church*, p. 185.

[25] Vatican I, *Pastor Bonus*.

[26] See ibid and Vatican II, *Lumen Gentium*, para. 25.

11

simple faithful. This *sensus fidelium* involves a relatively independent and immediate testimony of the Holy Spirit. Although but an echo of the authentic testimony of the Teaching Apostolate [Magisterium], the universal belief of the Faithful is of a great weight in times when its unity and distinctness are more apparent than the teaching of the Apostolate itself."[27] Essentially this means that the Holy Spirit would not allow the entire faithful of the Church constantly (i.e. throughout the history of the Church) to hold to some point of doctrine that is heretical. The appeal to the *sensus fidelium* was used by the Council of Trent in its decree on the Holy Eucharist.[28] Therefore, if we found that every Catholic faithful person held to some doctrine, we would know that it was true. There have been abuses regarding this doctrine in recent times. Because most Catholics have fallen into contraceptive practices, some theologians hold that this is a *sensus fidelium*. But such a position is untenable since the faithful have not constantly held such a position, e.g. prior to the Second Vatican Council, most Catholics believed that contraception was immoral.

    The next infallible source that we can go to are the Fathers of the Church: "When the Fathers of the Church consent on certain doctrines, which evidently belong to the common faith of the Church – and all the faithful believe them – then, that consent of the Fathers shows the divine tradition of those doctrines. It is the same consent of the Universal Church. Consequently, the common consent of the Fathers is infallible, because the Church itself is infallible."[29] The importance of the Fathers and their infallibility has been used and is a constant theme in various documents of the Church as we see in the Council of Orange,[30] Council of Trent[31] and Pius IX in *Gravissimas inter,*[32] among others.[33] It is often said by the popes, that if the Patristics have a consensus regarding a specific doctrine, it is to be held to be of the faith. While not everything that the Patristics say is infallible, nevertheless, the Patristics constitute a specific source of knowledge regarding

---

[27]Scannell, vol. 1, p. 73.

[28]Denz.1637/874.

[29]Agius, *Tradition and the Church*, p. 240.

[30]Denz. 370/173; 396/199

[31]Denz. 1600/843a; 1692/905.

[32]Denz. 2855/1672.

[33]For a fuller listing, see Denz. *Index systematicus* under A7ad.

those things which pertain to the faith.

The next infallible source is the Theologians. Obviously given our current historical context, this needs clear explanation. Herve[34] observes that we are not talking about a single theological school or theologian, but the whole of the scholastic theologians. During the medieval period, there were varying theological schools, e.g. the Dominican, the Franciscan, etc. If there was a consensus of the various theologians in these schools regarding a particular point of dogma, that teaching was held to be of the faith. When the term *Theologians* is used, it should not be confused with the generic (lower case) *theologians*. The term "Theologians" refers to a specific group of men, viz. those theologians of the various scholastic schools from the twelfth century until the middle of the eighteenth century (roughly during the years of 1100 to1750).[35] Pius IX in *Tuas Libenter*[36] says that we are to hold those teachings as pertaining to the faith not only the decrees of the councils but the universal and constant consensus of the Catholic Theologians. Here we see the two criteria for the infallibility of those things held by the Theologians, viz. that it must be (1) constant and (2) universally held by those theologians during that historical period. To put this teaching in context, Scannell observes

> Although the assistance of the Holy Ghost is not directly promised to Theologians, nevertheless the assistance promised to the Church requires that He should prevent them as a body from falling into error; otherwise the Faithful who follow them would all be led astray. The consent of Theologians implies the consent of the episcopate, according to St. Augustine's dictum: "Not to resist an error is to approve of it - not to define a truth is to reject it.'"

We must be clear that this teaching does not extend to the theologians today. While some theologians try to stake a claim for themselves in this regard, this does not enjoy the support of Church (papal) teaching. The fact that the consensus of the Theologians of that period holds such weight indicates the Church's mind regarding the theological work of that period. While modernists today systematically reject anything that occurred in the medieval period, such a mindset is contrary to the mind of the Church. The Church

---

[34]J.M. Hervé, *Manuale Theologiae Dogmaticae* (Berche et Pagis, Paris, 1929), v. 1, P. 557.

[35]Herve, ibid.

[36]Denz. 2879/1683. See also Gregory IX, *Ab Aegyptiis* (Denz. 824/442); Sixtus IV, *Romani Pontificis provida* (Denz. 1407 [no corresponding old #]).

holds the work of that period, particularly that of St. Thomas, in the highest regard.[37]   Many traditional scholars maintain their intellectual balance precisely by immersing themselves in the writings of the Fathers of the Church (particularly in the area of Scripture) and the Theologians, again, particularly St. Thomas.

The various creeds promulgated throughout the life of the Church constitute an unerring source of what we believe as Catholics. Many of them were promulgated by Ecumenical councils and enjoy infallibility. The creeds are broken down into the various articles of faith which are propositions which formulate what we believe. These are important for us as Catholics because they are a constant reference point and principle of judgment regarding what we hear and see in the Church.

Perhaps one of the best sources for Catholics regarding what pertains to the traditional teaching of the Church is found in catechisms, particularly the Catechism of the Council of Trent, sometimes called the Roman Catechism. This Catechism constitutes a norm for all subsequent catechisms, even the *Catechism of the Catholic Church*.[38]   The Roman Catechism is important since it is the first major catechism promulgated by the Magisterium. While there were lesser catechisms (lesser meaning in size not necessarily in importance) in the Church, such as the Didache, the Roman Catechism is an ordinary magisterial document which lays down the essentials of the faith. Since the essentials of the faith do not change, subsequent catechisms must always be understood in light of the Roman Catechism regarding the essentials of the faith. Another catechism not well known but clear in its presentation of the faith is the Catechism which Pope St. Pius X published.

We begin to see the various sources which we can use to know what the Church has traditionally taught. We can go back to the catechisms which the Church has officially promulgated, especially the Roman Catechism. We can take up the official documents of the Church, not just the ones since Vatican II, but all of the prior magisterial documents. We can read the Fathers of the Church, many of whom are saints. We can read the Theologians, particularly St. Thomas, who provide clear explanations and defenses of our beautiful faith. These sources are rich and multitudinous. They are an almost inexhaustible source of the Catholic Faith. Since some aspects of them are infallible, they too become like proper accidents to the Deposit of Faith and

---

[37] See Leo XIII *Aeterni Patris*, CIC/17, CIC/83; Pius V bull *Mirabilis* which is the declaration of St. Thomas as a doctor the Church; the evident use of St. Thomas at the Council of Trent; Pius X's *Pascendi*, et al.

[38] Why this is the case will be seen in subsequent parts of this article regarding how we are to look at modern documents in light of tradition.

therefore must always be passed on to subsequent generations. Even if one generation, due to moral or doctrinal depravity, neglects these sources, they can be still be accepted and propagated by subsequent generations since these sources are their patrimony.

The depth of the tradition of the Church is gloriously manifest in what the Church calls *the monuments*. The monuments are among the richest aspects of our tradition and the visible part of the monuments constitutes much of the tradition which your Sunday Mass goer knows and sees. Monuments constitute an important source of our knowledge of the faith and our Catholic patrimony. A monument, in most cases, is something which creatures create by the work of their own hands, e.g. St. Peter's Basilica. Sometimes monuments are supernaturally given, yet received by a creature, e.g. the Rosary. Monuments proceed from faith and may even incorporate divinely given or taught teachings. The composition or creation of some monuments enjoys the guidance and direction of the Holy Spirit: "divine providence did not leave the Church without irrefragable documents to show the world that she is the greatest work in creation. ...It is still more evident through the ancient monuments of Christian Art."[39] Because the monuments proceed from a Catholic Faith and since they are often commissioned or written by the Church herself, they constitute a manifestation of the teachings of the Church. Therefore, we as Catholics can look to these monuments as signs and, in some cases, formulations of what we are to believe.

The monuments are of different kinds and for the sake of grasping the richness of our Catholic heritage and patrimony in this regard, we should consider the different kinds of monuments. The Church documents (such as encyclicals, exhortations and the like), the writings of the saints, the Patristics and Theologians are monuments. The first kind of monument, however, that we want to discuss is the various liturgies and rituals written, promulgated or approved by the Church. This would include the various missals and rituals of the sacraments promulgated by the popes. Every missal ever promulgated by a pope which is organically developed and true to the Catholic faith (tradition) constitutes a source of knowledge for what we believe as Catholics. They also constitute a manifestation of that faith insofar as the faith approves of specific forms of worship of which God Himself has preordained certain elements, e.g. in the Mass, the words of consecration. Yet, this kind of monument is highly important. It was always conceded that if a feast was in the liturgical calender for a long period of time, the existence of the saint of the feast or the event of the feast itself took on greater certitude the longer it was part of the calendar.

The monuments are sacred objects and their passing from one

---

[39] George Agius, *Tradition and the Church*, p. 223. Much of this section is taken from Agius' work.

generation to another constitutes a sacred act. It is a good and holy thing to pass on the monuments to subsequent generations. Conversely, the destruction of a monument or its modification was tolerated in the past only when a greater or more perfect monument was erected or promulgated. In the context of the liturgy, this meant that missals were updated to augment the calendar of feasts to accommodate the newly canonized saints and/or to make minor changes so that the worship of the Church became more perfect. Wholesale modifications in the past would have been considered by saints as an act of impiety, because the sweeping modification blocks or denies the perfection of the form of worship and feasts of saints (when removed) to the subsequent generations. It is impious because wholesale modification presumes that prior saints were not adequately directed by the Holy Spirit in the compositions of the prayers of the Mass and no saint would dare to presume to affect the liturgy passed to him by his ancestors to such a degree, particularly because the reverence he would have regarding the guidance of past saints by the Holy Spirit. To presume to block the passing of a monument, not by perfecting it which is actually a part of authentic tradition, but by modifying it in such a way as to deny many of the elements in that monument, is to presume that one is greater than one's ancestors, as we discussed above. Great care had to be taken so as not to deny God's providential care of the Church manifest throughout history.

The various sacred objects made for liturgical use such as vestments, altars, chalices, etc. are also monuments testifying to the truths of faith. The sacred books containing the various rites of the Church constitute a true source of knowledge for us. We can learn about the faith in the prayers contained in these rituals as well as the Church's understanding of how the sacred realities, such as the sacraments, were to be treated and properly adorned with ritual. Since all of these things manifest the faith in various degrees, they constitute a true form of learning for the faithful. This is why the promulgation of a rite is so important, as is evidenced in the phrase *lex orandi lex credendi.* Because the ancient rituals manifest the faith and the Church's moral code in practice, the ancient rituals are always something by which subsequent rituals are judged. Every rite which manifests the faith of the Church, thereby teaches the faith; therefore, we judge the subsequent rituals by these rites. No matter how much some modern theologians and ecclesiastics wanted the Old Mass to go away, the fact is that even if, God forbid, its use were to completely die out, the ancient rite of the Mass would still remain a principle of judgment regarding the new rite of Mass.

Another form of monument in the area of liturgy are the various rituals of the Church, e.g. the *Rituale Romanum.* The various rituals teach us a great deal about our Catholic faith and their use constitutes a living out of the Catholic faith. For instance, the blessing of Holy Water tells us a great deal about our Catholic faith regarding the use of sacramentals. It also teaches us about how we are to live. The Old Rite of blessing of water exorcized the salt and water prior to the blessing, making the holy water efficacious in driving out the demonic. Hence, we know that part of the Church teaching is that we should use sacramentals to ward off the demonic, not in a superstitious manner but in a manner proceeding from devotion and faith. These liturgical monuments affected and shaped culture and were often the foundation and basis of the culture itself (since culture comes from *cultus*). The fact that there has been a collapse in the use of various rituals of the Church, the sacraments, etc., is a direct cause of the collapse of Catholic culture. There are a whole host of rituals and blessings contained in the Roman Ritual and Catholics would fare well to use them frequently.

This is why parents should come to knowledge of the various blessings in the Roman Ritual and not only ask them for their own benefit, but they should teach their children to ask for these various blessings and sacramentals. While it is true that the official organ of tradition is the Magisterium of the Church, the fact is that, in the concrete, much of the tradition is passed from one generation to another through the hands of parents to their children. It is the parents who are the first catechists of the children and therefore pass on the teachings to their children.[40] It is the parents who teach their children the way of living a Catholic life by use of the sacraments, the sacramentals, the blessings, etc. It is the parents who normally purchase prayer books for their children and teach them the basic prayers which each Catholic should know. The prayer books themselves are kinds of monuments and are part of the Catholic tradition.

Para-liturgical rituals are also important for us as Catholics since they manifest what we believe. For instance, the Stations of the Cross (not only as a physical entity which falls under Christian art but also as a form of prayer and devotion) tell us that we believe that Christ was crucified, died and was buried. The Stations of the Cross also tell us something about the devotional life that is proper to a Catholic, i.e. one knows that this form of devotion is a good and wholesome form of Catholic devotion. Another para-liturgical act is Benediction which teaches us the majesty, the grandeur, the reverence and worship due to God, both in the order of knowledge and in our own behavior.

The next category of monuments is Christian art which manifests the glory of the Church and of God. There are different kinds of art, among which are physical churches. Most traditional Catholics know of the experience of having their senses and minds lifted to God by entering a magnificent church. Magnificent comes from the two Latin words *magnus* and *facere* which means literally to do something great. The construction of these churches is and was a great work. These churches, their form and structure, their layout, tell us

---

[40] Pope St. Pius X, *An Exhortation on Catechetics to Catholic Parents and Teachers*, no. 3.

something about the faith of those who constructed those churches. The architectural styles themselves are part of the monumental tradition and should continue to be used even today. In magnificent churches, the sanctuary is clearly marked off from the rest of the church and elevated to show the primacy of its status. The sanctuary tells us that we are in a heavenly court, since when Christ Who is in heaven becomes present in the Eucharist, the sanctuary becomes the heavenly court of God. We also learn our own place with respect to God by the lowly place we take as the faithful in relation to the heavenly court represented by the sanctuary.

The monumental tradition with respect to churches is very important for the stability of the Catholic faith of those who attend Mass in the churches. Since the monument often manifests some aspect of faith, to modify the monument requires great care. Since monuments manifest our faith, like the liturgy, if the monuments are modified too much, one can be left with the impression that the faith has changed. Since the construction of these kinds of monuments is a manifestation of the devotion, charity and faith of those who construct them, to radically modify them without a sufficient reason is, again, against piety. While, at times, some physical monuments such as these must be reverently dismantled because their physical life has come to an end, nevertheless, they should not be gutted or destroyed even when their physical life has come to an end. While it may be necessary to reverently deconsecrate and dismantle a church to avoid sacrilege because of disuse of the church and therefore its decay, nevertheless this should only be done when necessary. If the monument is constructed in right faith, there is no reason to radically change it unless one is augmenting the beauty and glory of the church. This is not done by gutting the church, taking out the statues, sledge hammering the high altars and things of this sort. This type of behavior has been associated in the Church with the heresy of iconoclasm, as we saw during the Protestant revolt because of the loss of their faith. For the Protestants to irreverently treat monuments was not only unjust to God but it was a sin against charity to our neighbor.

Monuments are the general patrimony of the Church under the care of specific individuals, but those specific individuals do not have the right to destroy these monuments since they belong to the general patrimony of the Church. Such destruction is a kind of robbery in which subsequent generations are robbed of monuments which would ennoble their spirit and lift their minds and hearts to God. It is a kind of robbery of God who deserves worship in suitably appointed churches. Monuments of this sort strengthen the faith of those who see them and instruct them in the teachings of the Church by the various statues and saints depicted there.

This brings us to the next form of Christian art which is sculpture and paintings. Christian art, like many of the physical monuments, are a "visible part of that assistance, with which the Holy Spirit helps the Church to keep

18

intact the Deposit of Faith and not fall into error."[41] In the catacombs of St. Priscilla, there is a famous fresco entitled "Fractio Panis" which dates to the first half of the second century. This fresco clearly represents the Sacrifice of the Mass indicating that the Mass was taking place very early on in the Church. The myriad of pictures and statues of Our Lady clearly represent doctrinal teaching, such as those icons which contain words such as "theotokos" or bearer of God indicating that Our Lady is truly the Mother of God.

Paintings and sculptures often contain symbols which are also monuments since the symbols represent some spiritual reality. The two keys given to St. Peter represent the two powers of orders and jurisdiction.[42] They are bound together with a red cord indicating that their proper usage should not be separated from each other. The Church often uses symbols to draw our minds to God and to teach us about the spiritual realities, e.g. IHS which, we often see, are the first three letters in Jesus' name in Greek. The symbolism on liturgical items enriches the liturgy and adds to its mystery. The stripping of religious symbolism from liturgical items reduces the beauty, splendor and mystery of the various rites of the Church. This has had a direct impact on the laity in their spiritual lives insofar as this stripping of the monuments has lessened the mystery in the minds of the laity and so they tend to treat liturgical items with less reverence.

Other monuments include epitaphs written on the tombs of saints and the faithful, many of them centuries old, giving testimony to the unchanging faith shared by our ancestors. These manifestations of the faith of our fathers move us to reverence for those who lived before us and passed on this faith in an uninterrupted tradition even to the present day. We see the necessity in having reverence for our ancestors since they were the instruments by which the things of tradition are passed to us. Out of reverence for this sacred action of tradition and for those who had the faith and performed this action insofar as they are the instruments of God, we must treat their remains, their works (monuments) and their tombs with great respect. This is why monuments such as crypts, sarcophagi, and tombs must be treated with great reverence and never defiled.

While the number and kind of monuments are virtually inexhaustible, only partially discussed here, one last area of monuments is of great importance for the sake of our discussion. We have already referred to sacramentals in the discussion of monuments, but a greater exposition is in order. Many of the sacramentals in use by the faithful come from a

---

[41] Agius, *Tradition and the Church*, p. 225.

[42] It should be noted that thre has been different meanings ascribed to the symbols of the keys of St. Peter, e.g. the spiritual temporal authority of the Church, etc.

supernatural origin, e.g. the Miraculous Medal and the Scapular were given to us by Our Lady. Another great monument is the Rosary, again given to us by Our Lady. There are certain monuments which should not be altered as to their nature or structure because of the divine or supernatural origin. Man should not presume to be able to improve a monument which was given to us by someone possessing the beatific vision. Yet, other monuments instituted by the Church herself or approved by the Church herself are highly important. The rite of blessing holy water has already been mentioned in this regard.

The last area of tradition which we shall discuss is pious tradition. While pious tradition does not provide for us the same degrees of certitude as the other forms of tradition, nevertheless, pious tradition is often rooted in the faith of Catholics throughout the ages. One example of pious tradition is the belief of some that Adam and Eve are in heaven. It is not a dogma of the faith and we are not required to believe it, nevertheless, it is a pious tradition.

The tradition of the Church is very broad and deep. One individual is incapable of exhausting all aspects of the tradition. The Catholic tradition is a source of knowledge which a person can spend his entire life studying and contemplating. The Catholic tradition is a source of Catholic life insofar as every Catholic can make use of the various aspects of tradition to lead a fully imbued Catholic life. Catholic tradition provides depth to one's spiritual life when it is lived as fully as we are capable.

V: Difficulties

There are a few areas regarding the discussion of tradition which have posed some difficulties in recent years and a discussion of these problems would help greatly to provide clarity to how tradition itself is to be understood. The first area that needs to be addressed is the use of the term "ecclesiastical tradition." In the course of the articles, we have seen that this term has been used in different ways. It was noted that ecclesiastical tradition is divided into humano-apostolic tradition and mere ecclesiastical tradition. Humano-apostolic tradition is one which is started by an Apostle but which is perpetuated in the Church. Mere ecclesiastical tradition contains those things instituted by the Church after the time of the Apostles. An example of the lenten fast was given as an example of a mere ecclesiastical tradition. Ecclesiastical tradition was also used as counter-distinguished from human tradition. Human tradition is based upon human industry and testimony alone whereas the value of ecclesiastical tradition is based upon the rank of the various persons in the Church and the assistance of the Holy Spirit. In this use of the term "ecclesiastical tradition," the term indicates all aspects of tradition within the Church that enjoy the assistance of the Holy Spirit and therefore is more inclusive than any one distinguished part of tradition. Sometimes the "term ecclesiastical" tradition is counter-distinguish from divine tradition. In this case, ecclesiastical tradition is all of those things which are not intrinsic to the Deposit of Faith, but which form the heritage and patrimony of the work of previous generations graciously passed on by the Church to subsequent generations whereas divine tradition are all of those things intrinsic to the Deposit of Faith. In this case, not everything of the ecclesiastical tradition is changeable since infallible magisterial judgments would be part of the ecclesiastical tradition. However, the infallible magisterial judgments must always accompany the understanding we have of those parts of the Deposit of Faith to which they pertain. When the term "ecclesiastical tradition" is used in this sense, it means that there are also parts of the ecclesiastical tradition which can be changed since they are not irreformable or infallible.

One last use of the term "ecclesiastical tradition" is that which is contained in the second council of Nicaea and which has caused some misunderstandings among those not giving precise interpretations to the council. In this council, the term "ecclesiastical tradition" is used and the use of the term includes both written and unwritten tradition which the council summarizes as resting upon the decrees of the ecumenical councils that went before it and so it would include infallible definitions. The council also included in reference to ecclesiastical tradition the monuments and a good part of the discussion of the council is about icons. The inclusion of relics in altars is also included under ecclesiastical tradition and the lack of doing so is condemned as a novelty. Therefore, how the second council of Nicaea uses the term "ecclesiastical tradition" appears to include virtually all aspects of tradition.[43] From this, we must be certain that when we read an author or a source such as the second council of Nicaea, we must be very clear about *how* the author uses the term "ecclesiastical tradition" so that we do not misinterpret what the author is conveying. This is particularly important since authors in the last one hundred years or so have used the term "ecclesiastical tradition" in a different way than is used in the second council of Nicaea. This does not mean that the use of the term is false as long as the meaning of the term is clear in the author's use and he does not assume the use of the second council of Nicaea and contradict what the council has condemned.[44]

---

[43]In relation to the various things included in the term "ecclesiastical tradition" in the Second Council of Nicaea, see David Palm's work, "A Question of Novelty: Why Tradition Rejects it".

[44]This was the error of committed in the article "The Incommutability of Ecclesiastical Tradition" by D. E. Romanae. He criticized this author based upon the use of the term "ecclesiastical tradition" from the second council of Nicaea when this author was not using it in that way. This error coupled with the error on his

The second council of Nicaea also has an anathema which is often misunderstood, even by traditionalists. The canon reads as follows: "If anyone rejects any written or unwritten ecclesiastical tradition of the Church, let him be anathema."[45] Sometimes this is interpreted to mean that if someone holds that changes can or should be made to something that is capable of being changed, they are subject to this anathema. Such an interpretation, in the opinion of the author, oversteps what is being stated in the anathema and it is a denial of the very reality of ecclesiastical history. As to overstepping what the anathema means, it would be better to interpret the anathema with two principles in mind. The first is that certain teachings and parts of the tradition are permanent and irreformable, e.g. the teaching that Jesus Christ has two natures (one human, one divine) and the fact that holy orders is passed on in an uninterrupted tradition even to this day. As to the second principle, it should be stated in the manner prior discussed. It was stated: "No matter how much some modern theologians and ecclesiastics wanted the Old Mass to go away, the fact is that even if, God forbid, its use were to completely die out, the ancient rite of the Mass would still remain a principle of judgment regarding the New Mass." Not only is a person bound to accept all parts of the Deposit of Faith and all of the irreformable doctrines declared by the councils and popes, but one is also bound to accept the teaching contained in and the legitimacy of all monuments and teachings of the Church which do not contain novelty or contradict the teachings of the Church. This means that if one were to reject the Ancient Rite as evil or heretical, he would be subject to this anathema.

However, acceptance of all of the tradition (which the anathema requires) does not exclude an acceptance of legitimate change within those parts of the tradition which can be subject to change. What can and cannot change, we shall see in a moment, but as long as a change is not a novelty and as long as those making the change have the authority to do so and provided they do not reject the legitimacy of what went before them, they do not incur this censure. Ecclesiastical history is a good example of what is being stated here. In St. Peter's Basilica underneath the high altar, there is the tomb which tradition tells us is the tomb of St. Peter. On that tomb, around 150 or so a small funeral monument to St. Peter was built, sometimes called the "Trophy of Gaius." Later, a church was built over the tomb by Constantine and the tomb was enclosed in a marble monument in the center of the apse. Then in 1506, Pope Julius II order the construction of the basilica as we see it today which meant that the monument of the prior church was partly dismantled

_____

understanding of Deposit of Faith led to the remaining errors in the article.

[45]Second Council of Nicaea, Anathema 4: "Εἴ τις πᾶσαν παράδοσιν ἐκκλησιατικὴν ἔγγραφον ἢ ἄγραφον ἀθετεῖ, ἀνάθεμα ἔστω"

and the church which was built over the prior church. It is not possible for us to apply the anathema of the second council of Nicaea to Pope Julius II who built the modern day St. Peter's. Many parts of Rome contain histories similar to this, such as the Church of San Clemente. Even in the United States, there are accounts in which churches (monuments) were reverently dismantled and more magnificent churches were built. We also know for a fact that the liturgy, even in the Roman Rite, has under gone organic changes over the course of centuries. In fact, the current Tridentine Rite is itself a reformed rite, and it is a fact that the rite was changed. We would not want to accuse Pope St. Pius V of incurring this anathema since he changed the Roman Rite. Being open to change does not necessarily (although it can) mean one rejects the prior tradition. One should not be open to any kind of change whatsoever, but only the right kind of change when change is truly called for or necessary.

Therefore, what traditionalists need to realize is that some things in the tradition can be changed and an orthodox Catholic needs to know what can and cannot be changed. Obviously, the Deposit of Faith and the infallible and irreformable teachings cannot be changed, period. In those aspects of tradition that can be changed, the change is based upon the very *nature* of that aspect of tradition. In other words, there are different principles which govern how different aspects of the tradition may be changed. In relation to monuments, it was noted that they were only changed when there was some perfection or augmentation of the monument. But even monuments differ. Churches and their interiors were changed only when they were beautified, perfected or augmented, unless, as was noted, reverent dismantling of the church was required to avoid sacrilege. Rituals, which are monuments, have different principles which governs their change. They should only be changed when (a) the change is truly organic so that a ritual is not composed out of thin air and which has a true connection to the prior rituals and (b) the ritual will more perfectly express the faith as well as the composition of the prayers better express the intention of the Church and are therefore more efficacious before God.

Ordinary non-infallible magisterial teachings are classified as reformable. This must be understood, however, as a class and not necessary as applicable to all ordinary teachings. An ordinary non-infallible magisterial teaching could be changed under the following conditions: (1) the prior ordinary magisterial teaching does not take into account some aspect of the tradition or some aspect of the Deposit of Faith. In other words, the principles from which the teaching (conclusion) is drawn are at variance with the tradition or Deposit of Faith. (2) Ordinary magisterial teaching can be changed if the principles do not include sufficient data for the conclusion and later reflection by the Magisterium indicates the opposite conclusion *must* follow. If the opposite conclusion does not of necessity follow, the prior teaching should remain in place until further reflection clarifies the issue. (3)

Those teachings which were taught as part of the ordinary non-infallible part of the tradition should only be changed by a more authoritative pronouncement, otherwise two contradictory ordinary magisterial teachings are left at the same authoritative level. Prudentially, these ordinary magisterial teachings should normally only be changed by infallible pronouncements, such as was the case with the Immaculate Conception where centuries of debate by some theologians was put to an end. (4) The longer the tradition of an ordinary magisterial teaching, the less likely is its change possible. (5) When a change is made to an ordinary non-infallible magisterial teaching, the Magisterium has a grave obligation due to the virtues of prudence, justice and charity, either to clearly manifest where the error in the prior ordinary magisterial teaching lie and/or to pronounce the new teaching infallibly. These are necessary so to leave all possibility of doubt excluded from the minds of the faithful since the Magisterium has a grave obligation before God to protect and promote the faith of all of the members of the Church. Given these principles and given that in the past the Magisterium took great pains to ensure that their teaching was coherent with the tradition, very few ordinary magisterial teachings would be subject to change. This is why the Church has always required the faithful to give religious assent to the ordinary magisterial teachings. It is religious assent because the assent is not absolute since in this class of teachings some could be reformable. However, that does not mean each and every one within the category of reformable teachings are in fact reformable.

Some monuments, while being changeable, ought never to be changed. This follows from two principles, viz. (1) some sacramentals have a supernatural origin and (2) the piety and devotional practices associated with the sacramental should be as fixed as possible to provided the faithful with fixed understandings of God and the saints. The only time a sacramental which has a supernatural origin should be changed is when a supernatural agent indicates the change to be done.

Over the course of centuries, the principles governing the change of certain aspects of tradition have been developed. We cannot go into all of them here since such a task would constitue a book on its own. Yet, no changeable part of the tradition should be changed except when change is going to increase the faith of those who receive the tradition. In other words, the faith of the members of the Church is a constant principle that must *always* guide the change. Here we recognize that two practices should be avoided. The first is changing things unnecessarily and contrary to authentic Catholic principle. Second, experimentation should be avoided. There is no reason for experimentation, for example, in the liturgy if the development is organic and truly augments the perfection of the liturgy. If there is a question about its effect on the members of the Church or if there are questions about its efficacy in the eyes of God, then the liturgy is not the place for to test it.

The liturgy should not be a "testing ground" for methods of worshiping God since to do so runs the risk of adversely affecting people's faith which the Magisterium has a grave obligation to protect and it runs the risk of offending God. On both accounts, to do experimentation goes contrary to the integral part of the virtue of prudence of caution.

One should not be left with the idea that change should occur on a regular basis. One should not be closed to authentic change which perfects our worship, increases the glory of the monuments and gives greater precision to the orthodox teachings of the Church. Yet, caution must likewise be observed so that one does not fall into novelties.

VI: Novelty

Novelty is that which is opposed to tradition since novelty by nature supplants or contradicts the tradition. Novelty is bad because it breaks the continuity of tradition. Since our salvation depends upon tradition, continuity in tradition by which the means of salvation are passed on from generation to generation and to as many people as possible is imperative. Moreover, the continuity of tradition ensures that each generation will inherit the wealth of patrimony of the saints.

One of the best writers on the topic of novelty is St. Vincent of Lerins in his work the *Commonitorium* written in 437 A.D. St. Vincent provides the following principle to begin the discussion of novelty in a text we saw before:

> In the Catholic Church itself, great care must be taken, that we hold that which has been believed everywhere, always, and by all. For this is truly and properly Catholic, which, as the force and notion of the name declares, almost all universally comprehend. But this at last becomes consent, if we follow the universal antiquity. Moreover, we follow universality in this way: if we confess that one true faith, which the whole Church throughout the world confesses; such is it with antiquity, if from those senses we in no way depart from what is manifest by our holy ancestors and fathers celebrated; so also it is the same with consent, if we adhere to the definitions and beliefs of all or almost all priests and doctors in that same antiquity.[46]

---

[46] St. Vincent of Lerins, *Commonitorium*, para. II: in ipsa item Catholica Ecclesia magnopere curandum est ut id teneamus quod ubique, quod semper, quod ab omnibus creditum est. Hoc est etenim vere proprieque catholicum, quod ipsa vis nominis ratioque declarat, quae omnia fere universiter comprehendit. Sed hoc ita demum fiet, si sequamur universitatem antiquitatem, consensionem. Sequemur autem universitatem hoc modo, si hanc unam fidem veram esse fateamur quam tota per orbem terrarum confitetur ecclesia; antiquitatem vero ita, si ab his sensibus nullatenus

St. Vincent essentially establishes that the principle of judgment about what we are to believe is that which we have received from "our holy ancestors and fathers." In effect, it is tradition, i.e. that which has been handed on to us, which constitutes what we are to believe. For there is no aspect of what we believe as Catholics that was not passed on to us from those who went before us.

> For that holy and prudent man knew that to admit the notion of piety is nothing other than that everything is received by faith from the fathers and consigned by the same faith to the sons and [piety is] not our religion, which we want, that leads but more that which leads must be followed, for it is proper to Christian modesty and gravity not to pass on his own beliefs to those who come after him, but to preserve what has been received from his ancestors. What then was the issue of the whole matter? What but the usual and customary one? Antiquity was retained, novelty was rejected.[47]

Tradition requires that we accept what is given to us and pass it on intact without passing on our own teaching. Catholic tradition does not admit of a Hegelian view that things must always change and cannot help but change. Rather, the Catholic tradition holds that those things necessary for salvation will not change even until the end of time.

When novelty arises, confusion ensues:

> Not only from the example of Photinus but also Apollinaris do we learn the danger of eccleasiastical temptation and at the same time we warn by observering to diligently keep custody of the faith. For he gave rise to great burning and great agitation among his disciples; the Church's authority drawing them one way, their master's influence the opposite; so that, wavering and tossed hither and thither between

---

recedamus quos sanctos majoros ac patres nostros celebrasse manifestum est: consensionem quoque itidem, si, in ipsa vetustate, omnium vel certe pene omnium sacerdotum pariter et magistrorum definitiones sententiasque sectemur.

[47]St. Vincent of Lerins, *Commonitorium*, para. VI: Intelligebat etenim vir sanctus et prudens, nihil aliud rationem pietatis admittere, nisi ut omnia, qua fide a patribus suscepta forent, eadem fide filiis consignarentur, nosque religionem non, qua vellemus, ducere, set potius, qua illa duceret, sequi oportere, idque esse proprium christianae modestiae et gravitatis, non sua posteris tradere sed a maioribus accepta servare. Quis ergo tunc universi negoti exitus? Quis utique, nisi usitatus et solitus? Retenta est scilicet antiquitas, explosa novitas.

the two, they did not know what to choose.[48]

One of the effects of novelty, i.e. heresy, is that it tends not to clarify what the Church has always believed but to confuse the faithful. "In the Church of God the teacher's error is the people's trial, a trial by so much the greater in proportion to the greater learning of the erring teacher." This applies not only to priests or confessors but also to members of the Magisterium. If a member or some members of the Magisterium deny or contradict a traditional teaching of the Church, great confusion will affect the faithful until the teaching is reaffirmed with clarity. We may say that if a pope were to do so, as in the case of Pope John XXII discussed above, it would cause the greatest of confusions since it is the office of the papacy above all that is to guarantee the clarity of what is taught in the Church and the continuity of the tradition.

What then are the principles by which one can detect whether something is a novelty? St. Vincent observes that when something is passed on, beginning with the ancestors and coming to our own day, "this rather should be the result,--there should be no discrepancy between the first and the last."[49] The core teachings of the tradition should remain the same from the time of the death of the last Apostle until now. Therefore, if there is any contradiction between what the tradition has *always* held and the new teaching, the teaching is a novelty and is to be rejected.

This applies whether it is a matter of principle or of conclusion. When it is a matter of principle, the new teaching will contradict some formally defined teaching or some part of the creed, e.g. if one were to say that Christ became reincarnated and did not resurrect, that would be contrary to the line of the Creed which states that "He rose from the dead." Therefore, Christological reincarnation would be a novelty. When it is a matter of conclusion, a conclusion from the novelty would contradict some traditional teaching of the Church. For example, if someone were to say that Christ did not know He was God, the conclusion would be that He did not know that He was the savior since only God can save.

Another way of determining whether a teaching is a novelty is when it is a teaching that has never heretofore been taught, i.e. it is a completely

---

[48] St. Vincent of Lerins, *Commonitorium*, para. XI: Neque solum Photini sed etiam Apollinaris exemplo istius Ecclesiasticae tentationis periculum discimus, et simul ad observandae diligentius fidei custodiam commonemur. Etenim ipse auditoribus suis magnos aestus et magnas generavit augustias; quippe com eos huc Ecclesiae traheret auctoritas, huc magistri retraheret consuetudo; eumque inter utraque nutabundi et fluctuantes, quid potius sibi seligendum foret non expedirent.

[49] Ibid., c 23: consequens est ut primis atque extremis sibimet non discrepantibus.

new doctrine. Here we are not talking about valid conclusions drawn from traditional teachings, but one which has no real connection as such to the teachings. For example, if one were to assert that there is an eighth sacrament, one would know that this teaching is a novelty.

Authentic development of doctrine always provides a clearer understanding of the constant teachings of the Church. Novelty does not, as we saw in the quote above from St. Vincent. Therefore, one of the ways of knowing that a teaching is a novelty is if it leads to greater confusion among the faithful. While this is not a hard and fast rule, since sometimes abstract but valid conclusions in theology can leave some faithful who are not very knowledgeable or intelligent confused, nevertheless, a novelty never begets clarity of intellectual vision regarding the teachings of the Church.

Another way to know whether something is a novelty is to see the effect it has on the spiritual lives of those who follow the novelty. If the new teaching makes people holier, more than likely it is an authentic development, e.g. St. John of the Cross' doctrine on detachment is a greater clarification of the teachings known since the time of Christ or even before. Those who follow St. John's teaching become holier. But a novel teaching will tend to adversely affect one's spiritual life. For example, if one were to propose that the Precious Blood should be poured down the sacrarium or back into a jug containing wine rather then reverently consumed, this would be a sacrilegious practice, a novelty, and harmful to people's faith in the Real Presence and harmful to them spiritually. So if the teaching is a clarification, it will help people to lead more Catholic lives than before, whereas if it is a novelty, it will erode people's spiritual lives.

St. Vincent provides another principle to determine whether something is a novel teaching and that is when the terminology changes, i.e. the people use new words.[50] Great care must be taken regarding this principle, however, for there have been times in history when new words were introduced which actually clarified the teaching, e.g. the word *transubstantiation* was a term "coined by the theologians of the 12th century (Magister Roland [who later became Pope Alexander III] about 1150, Stephen of Tournai about 1160, Petrus Comestor 1160-1170."[51] This term greatly clarified the reality of the change of substance in the Eucharist. But, at other times, authors will introduce new terms which actually reflect a heretical mind. For example, the term "transsignification" was a theological term introduced which denied that there is a substantial change in the Eucharist but merely a change in meaning to those attending Mass. We must also be on guard against those who change the meaning of traditional terms to

---

[50] See Ibid., c. 24.

[51] Ludwig Ott, *Fundamentals of Catholic Dogma*, p. 379.

something which is heretical. For example, some have changed the meaning of the term "revelation." Traditionally, public revelation ended with the death of the last Apostle. Today, some theologians use the term "revelation" to mean an on going manifestation of God to man or an on going process by which man comes to a better understanding of himself which is contrary to the continuity of the tradition and the very nature of revelation.

St. Paul in his first epistle to Timothy (6:20) says " O Timothy, guard the Deposit, avoiding profane novelties of words and oppositions of science falsely so called."[52] Those introducing novelties will often use pseudo-science in order to undermine the traditional teaching so that there is no opposition to the introduction of the novel teaching. They will use a false science or a false conclusion from a science in order to contradict some teaching of the tradition. For example, the use of Darwinian evolutionary theory is often used as a means of undermining the traditional teaching of all men descending from Adam and Eve and the doctrine of Original Sin. The novel teaching is called polygenesis and it was condemned by Pius XII.[53] The scientific foundations for Darwinian evolution are clearly in question and there is question as to whether it is truly scientific as a theory.[54]

These are some of the means by which one can know whether a teaching is a novelty or not. Even though we must be on guard against novelty, we must also accept the clearly traditional understanding that over the course of time, members of the Church have given greater precision to the expression of certain doctrines through theological endeavors. Moreover, the rejection of novelties does not of itself reject the possibility that the changes mentioned are not possible. What rejection of novelties does mean, however, is that (a) the members of the Church, particularly the Magisterium, must be on guard against heresy/novelty and (b) changes must follow authentic Catholic principles.

Development of teaching is possible only when it is homogenous, i.e. what is believed by our fathers is the same as what we believe today. While we might have a more precise expression of some doctrine, such as in the teaching of the term "transubstantiation," what the Fathers and Doctors of the Church believed before is identical to what we ought to believe today. Homogenous development also means that any conclusions which a

---

[52]Translation is by the author from the Vulgate: "O Timothee depositum custodi devitans profanas vocum
novitates et oppositiones falsi nominis scientiae."

[53]Pius XII, *Humanae Generis*, para. 37.

[54]There is a whole host of literature available on this question, but for an example, see Michael Behe, *Darwin's Black Box*, Touchstone, New York, 1996.

theologian may draw from the Deposit of Faith must follow logical rules. The conclusions cannot assert what is denied in the premises. For example, one cannot assert that since God is all merciful (premise), He could never damn anyone to the eternal punishment of hell (conclusion) since one of the principles or teachings of the Church is that God is also infinitely just (premise), which requires that should someone die in the state of mortal sin, he should be condemned for his sin (conclusion). Greater precision in the method of theology helps one to see with greater clarity the same truth as that truth held by our ancestors. Just as better glasses help one to see what one saw before with greater clarity, so greater precision over time has helped the members of the Church to see the truth of what has been revealed. If the glasses one wears blurs what one sees or changes what one sees (such as in the case of rose colored glasses), one should take off those glasses and don a pair that will help him to see better. In like manner, when one finds himself in a period of novelty, the novelty can obscure his intellectual vision and so he must return to the the constant teaching of the Church, i.e. to tradition in order to have a greater grasp of the truths of the faith. Theological development should not cause one to reject the faith, but move one to a more firm assent to the truths that are revealed.

True intellectual advance is only possible by the handing on of tradition, not only in theology but in all fields of science. If the prior generation had never passed on to the current generation any of the knowledge they had of the empirical sciences, we would not enjoy the knowledge in the empirical sciences that we do today. In like manner, in theology, we must stand on the shoulders of our predecessors and use the advances that they made so that we can continue the advance. If we do not do so, we run the risk of intellectual stagnation and ignorance. The virtue of faith will help us to see the greatness of our forefathers and the theological work that they did, such as St. Thomas, St. Augustine and all of the Doctors of the Church. When tradition is rejected, one rejects the work that was already accomplished, the homogenous development is rejected and our understanding of the faith is lessened. Therefore, the science of theology can only advance when theologians stand on the theological work and accomplishments of the saints and build upon that work.

This is why we must look at the Deposit of Faith through the eyes of the past. While it is possible for theological precision to increase our understanding of some aspect of faith and the Church has defined doctrines which gives greater clarity and which settles disputes, that judgment is still done by looking back to the tradition for the foundation of those judgments. The eyes and direction of one's sight remain the same, the glasses improve our vision.

Western culture is in a decline, not only in the Roman Catholic Church but also outside of it. The foundation of western culture was the tradition of the Catholic Church; it is the thing which made western civilization great. But that foundation has been rejected and so the culture, having lost its foundation, is now crumbling. If we are ever to stop the implosion of Western civilization, we must, as a generation, continue and propagate the tradition of the Roman Catholic Church.

VII: Recouping the Tradition

We must return to the tradition. Each and every generation has an obligation to accept the tradition since the knowledge and means necessary for salvation is only passed on by means of the tradition. We therefore come to a point where we can
discuss what we can do to recoup the tradition. The means to recoup the tradition can be generally understood as merely "embracing one's Catholic patrimony." Yet, what we should do concretely depends on a person's state in life, since a priest can do more than a layman.

As for the clergy, there are a number of things which they can do. The first thing they can do is to realize that the very notion of the priesthood involves tradition. This is not only because Holy Orders is passed on by an uninterrupted tradition, but because the very function of a priest is to be a vehicle of tradition. The priest, before he is ever ordained, must realize that it is his function and duty to pass on the traditional teachings of the Church, to employ and care for the monuments of the Church and to pass on and make available the means of salvation for the faithful. It is not his place to substitute his "ideas" or teachings in place of the traditional teaching. It is not his place to make the rituals (monuments) a constant novelty. Rather, it is his place to accept what has been given to him in his intellectual formation (provided his formation is sound) and at his ordination and pass those things on to those under his pastoral care.

In order to do this effectively, we may suggest the following which he can do to be an effective means of tradition. The first thing he can do is begin offering the Ancient Rite of Mass. Even if he thinks pastoral necessity requires that he offers the New Rite of Mass, he is still free to offer the Ancient Rite of Mass at least privately.[55] Furthermore, he is permitted to offer the Ancient Rite of Mass publically. As he offers the Ancient Rite consistently and with devotion, he will more than likely find that a traditional mind set will supplant any novel notions he may have, even if this takes some time. He can read authors on the liturgy which will give a traditional perspective, such as Fr.

---

[55] See the three documents: motu proprio *Ecclesia Dei* of July 2, 1988, the Apostolic Letter *Summorum Pontificum* July 7, 2007 and the Instruction *Universae Ecclesiae* April 30, 2011.

Nicolas Gihr whose work *The Holy Sacrifice of the Mass* will provide him with traditional principles by which he can understand the Mass as well as his priesthood. The priest must recognize that the essential function of a priest is to offer sacrifice and not to sit in committee meetings or to facilitate people's emotions. The priest can ask his bishop if he can fulfill his obligation to pray the office by using the Breviary in force in 1962. While it is longer and more burdensome as to time and degree of concentration required, the benefits are inestimable. Many priests who have switched to the older Breviary have experienced a change in their spiritual life.

As Pope John XXIII observed in his encyclical *Veterum Sapientia*, "The Latin language, which we can truly call catholic having been consecrated through constant use by the Apostolic See, mother and teacher of all the churches, must be considered 'a treasure... of Incomparable value', and a door which leads into direct contact with the Christian truths handed down by tradition and with the documents of the teaching of the Church." It is a fact that a vast majority of the patrimony of the Roman Rite is bound up with the Latin language. Modern priests who lack a knowledge of Latin are cut off from a large portion of their patrimony. While many of these documents and writing of the Fathers and saints have made their way into translation, many have not. On an academic note, it is not possible to engage in serious historical and theological research without a knowledge of Latin. Therefore, one of the things that a priest can do to make the connection to his heritage is to learn Latin.

Next, he can study the traditional teachings of the Church. This is done principally by studying the Magisterial documents throughout time and not just in the last forty years. He can study and read the saints, particularly St. Thomas, St. Augustine, the Fathers of the Church, the Theologians, etc. No priest today can (a) be a traditional priest or (b) remain traditional, except in the rarest of circumstances, without study. Priests who suffer from intellectual sloth are doomed to intellectual ignorance. They will be ignorant of the tradition and will expose themselves to being led by those in error since they will not have the intellectual wherewithal to combat novel ideas. This indicates that the future of the traditional movement and of the priesthood lies in recouping its intellectual moorings. Holiness is not enough even though it is absolutely necessary. Priests should not presume, even if they have been priests for some time, that merely offering the Ancient Rite of Mass will suffice for them. Tradition is a package deal, a homogenous whole that they must accept and come to know so that they can pass on the riches of tradition to the faithful. To want to be traditional, i.e. "traditional intentions," are not enough; knowledge is necessary.

A traditionally minded priest who has a firm grasp and knowledge of the basics of tradition will have a greater depth and repertoire from which to preach than one who is ignorant of the tradition. Preaching today is generally flat, uninformative, lacking conviction and practicality in the spiritual life. This is the direct result of the pastoral and spiritual having been divorced from the dogmatic. The pastoral life of a priest, part of which is preaching, is directly affected by how a man thinks. *Agere sequitur esse* as we say in Latin; "action follows upon being." If a priest is not traditional, if he has no historical or doctrinal depth which tradition provides, his preaching will not have depth.

The priest can begin to foster traditional pious practices in himself and in the faithful. He must do them himself since the pious practices provide a means for him to form his own mind and to provide grace by which he can be holy. As a vehicle of tradition, he should teach and set up pious practices in his parish, such as Forty Hours Devotion, Eucharistic adoration and saying of the Rosary (e.g. before Mass on Sundays). He should be sure to have the traditional Stations of the Cross, at least during Lent. Since a priest should strive for more than the mere minimum requirements of the Church, he should come to knowledge of traditional ascetical practices and engage in them.

He should come to knowledge of the traditional schools of spirituality and he should know the basic mechanics of the spiritual life as formulated and refined by the saints and doctors of the Church throughout time. Such books as *Spiritual Theology* by Jordan Aumann, *The Spiritual Life* by Fr. Adolphe Tanquerey and *The Three Stages of the Interior Life* by Fr. Reginald Garrigou-Lagrange provide a beginning in this regard. Just because he has been preaching about spiritual matters for years, a priest should not assume that he has a traditional understanding of the spiritual life until he has read the masters on the subject. Moreover, he must follow their advice and live a life according to the traditional spiritual doctrines so that these traditional teachings become a very part of his spiritual life and psychology. The priest should come to knowledge of the traditional forms of architecture, Christian art and music and other physical monuments. This will provide him with a knowledge necessary to protect and perfect the monuments entrusted to his care according to a traditional mind rather than a novel mind. These are just a few things that he can do to begin to be a receptacle and a propagator of the tradition.

For the laity, there are a number of things which they can do and we have already suggested some already. They, being the proximate means by which their children receive the tradition, can and ought to buy traditional catechisms. These catechisms can be a reference source for the family and they can be the means by which the children are taught the tradition. If parents want their children to pass on the tradition, they must realize their children will only do so if they receive it from someone and normally the children receive the tradition from the parents. For those parents who want a more detailed catechism, they can purchase *The Catechism Explained* by Francis Spirago.

Next, parents can learn and teach their children the traditional Catholic prayers, such as acts of faith, hope and charity. This comes about in two ways. (1) They can teach their children from books they buy for them. (2) They must pray the prayers together with their children. Tradition is not merely a thing passed on from one generation to the next. The act of tradition, i.e. the act of passing on our Catholic heritage, also begets a set of habits in which the person who develops these habits is always seeking to know the tradition, to live it and to pass it on. Our current generation is in the habit of novelty and that is why the tradition is so difficult for many of them because tradition is not just a thing but an action, a way of living. This way of living is manifest in traditional prayer, morals and spiritual life.

One of the principal ways in which parents can ensure the passing of the tradition to their grandchildren is to make sure that their children are reared and formed in the proper understanding and the living of the moral and theological virtues. Traditional Catholicism has always rested upon a core code of conduct which we call morals. The Church has always held that certain things are morally right and certain things are morally wrong. Parents must teach their children the traditional morality otherwise the tradition will be blocked. This follows from the fact that dissolute living finds moral principles and principles in general repugnant since they are seen as a way of taking away a person's freedom and appetitive license. If a child is taught virtue and lives virtuously, the sweetness and joy of virtue will help him to lead a principled life and so he will recognize the need to conform himself to the principles passed on by tradition. If he is immoral, he will more than likely reject the tradition. A collapse in morality in any culture or society is always accompanied by a rejection of authentic tradition.

Parents can also buy and read books which will inform them about the Catholic faith. This provides them with the knowledge necessary to form their children. The books will also be available for the children as they get older to read for themselves. A traditional Catholic family should always have a modest sized library, determined by the financial means of the family, which serves as a source of knowledge and inspiration for those in the home. It provides an external sign for those in the house that we must conform ourselves to the tradition and not the tradition to ourselves. The parents, depending on the degree of their knowledge and education, can go back to the sources of tradition as we have mentioned, such as magisterial documents and writings of the saints. They should also be sure to have some hagiographical texts which provide them and their children with examples of saints who led lives of purity and holiness.

By obtaining these books, one is claiming one's patrimony. Our patrimony and tradition is not something lost. They are not something to which we go back unless we have personally abandoned them. Rather, it is a matter of accepting them. Our Catholic patrimony is available if we are willing to accept it and pass it on to the next generation. Yet the laity must recognize that the default position into which people fall is theological error. In other words, there seems to be a general atmosphere of theological and philosophical error, both among many members of the Church and in society so that unless one is put in contact with the tradition or accepts it on his own, he will naturally fall into error. Today, it seems that the default error is modernism and so unless one is deeply rooted in the faith by being knowledgeable and committed to the tradition, more than likely that person will fall into the error of modernism.

Culture is often influenced by art and so parents must adorn their home with Christian art. If their children see the art which is placed throughout the house, they will see that Catholic tradition is part of life. This practice will have a direct impact on the catechetical/intellectual formation of the child. The parents themselves must lead a traditional Catholic life. If they can, they should attend a valid and licit traditional Mass and have their children receive the sacraments according to the traditional rites. If their children go to the Ancient Rite of Mass, it will have a formative effect on the children. If the children see the parents engaging in traditional prayer and pious devotions, this will teach the children how they are to lead their own lives. Parents must pray traditional prayers and engage in traditional pious practices with their children. This is one of a principal ways in which tradition lives.

One simply cannot exhaust the different ways in which parents and clergy can recoup their heritage and patrimony. By seeking knowledge of and living a life imbued with tradition, parents and clergy will pass on that heritage to their children. By doing so they partake in the sacred act of tradition and by doing so, like any other sacred act, they can gain merit in heaven by doing so. All of us are obligated to engage in passive tradition, i.e. the act of receiving the Sacred Tradition from those who go before us. All of us are obligated to lead lives in congruity with tradition and for some that means that they must engage in active tradition, i.e. the act of passing on what is given to them, each according to his own measure. But like any other sacred act, we depend upon the grace and providence of God, Who is the very Author of that tradition. We pray, therefore, for God to grant to the members of the Church the grace to receive willingly and to pass on zealously, the glory, the magnificence, the wonder which is the sacred Catholic tradition.

Part II: Subversion of the Tradition

Chapter 2: Operative Points of View[1]

In 1996, a group of friends had lunch in Rome at the Czechoslovakian college. One of the priests who offers Mass according to the New Rite was a bit dumbfounded. He had written an article in which he had discussed certain aspects of the liturgical reform. His puzzlement came from the fact that the traditionalists had attacked his article and he could not understand why. A seminarian, who was a traditionalist, said to the priest, "we agree that something has to be done about the liturgy, but we do not agree on *what* should be done." Traditionalists[2] and neo-conservatives[3] often find each other mystifying and the reason for this has to do with the relationship each position holds with respect to ecclesiastical tradition.

A. Tradition

In classical theological manuals, textbooks and catechisms, the word "tradition" was given a twofold meaning:

---

[1]This chapter first appeared as an article in the March 2001 edition of *Christian Order.*

[2]The term "traditionalist" has two different meanings. The first is the heresy condemned by the Church i.e. a philosophical/religious system which depreciates human reason and establishes the tradition of mankind as the only criterion for truth and certainty. This heresy denies the ability of reason to know the truth and so it must be gained through tradition alone. It is different from the current movement in the Church which clearly recognizes the ability of reason to know the truth but which sees the good of the tradition of the Church and would like to see it re-established.

[3]The term "neo-conservative" refers to those who are considered the more conservative members of the Church. More often than not, they are those who hold orthodox positions, but they would not assert that it is necessary or a good idea to reconnect with ecclesiastical tradition. The prefix "neo" is used because they are not the same as those conservatives in authority in the Church right before, during and after the Second Vatican Council. The current conservatives, i.e. the neo-conservatives, are different insofar as the conservatives of that earlier period sought to maintain the current ecclesiastical traditions which were eventually lost. Obviously all of these labels have a certain inadequacy, but since they are operative in the current ecclesiastical climate, we will use the terms here in order to denote certain theological and philosophical positions. It should be noted, however, that the term "liberal" is often misleading. Many "liberals" are, in fact, unorthodox and do not believe what the Church believes. One can legitimately be a liberal, if and only if, one upholds all of the authentic teachings of the Church and then in matters of discipline or legitimate debate, one holds to a more lenient view. But often liberalism is merely another name for what is really unorthodox.

- The first signification of the term "tradition" was taken from its Latin root word which is *tradere*, which means "to pass on".[4] In this sense, the word tradition refers to all of those things which are, in any way, passed on from one generation to the next. This would include all of the divine truths which the Church passes on to the subsequent generations in any way[5], including the Scriptures.[6]

- The second sense or more restrictive sense of tradition refers to a twofold division within that which is passed on and not written down,[7] viz. **divine tradition**[8] and **ecclesiastical tradition**.[9]

Divine tradition is that tradition which constitutes one of the sources of revelation, i.e. a source of our knowledge about those things which were revealed to man by God. This means that divine tradition is intrinsic to the Deposit of Faith, which constitutes all of the divinely revealed truths necessary for salvation and passed on by the Church in an uninterrupted tradition. Since it is intrinsic to the Deposit of Faith, this form of tradition is sometimes called intrinsic tradition, a prime example of which is the magisterium of the Church and the sacraments since they were established by Jesus Christ and passed on

---

[4]Tanquerey observes (*Synopsis Theologiae Dogmaticae*, vol. I, p. 635) that the word *tradere* comes from "trans" and "do" (*dare*) which literally means to give across or to give over.

[5]See ibid.

[6]The irony of Protestantism is that while rejecting tradition, it, in fact, employs tradition in order to pass on from one generation to the next the Scriptures and its teachings about the Scriptures. This leads one to conclude that the Protestants were not so much against tradition as such. Rather, they were (are) against *Catholic* tradition.

[7]In this case, Scripture is distinguished from tradition as Scripture is written, whereas tradition, in the stricter sense, refers to those things passed on which were not written down.

[8]Divine tradition is further divided according to dominical tradition (that which was given directly by Our Lord while on earth) and apostolic tradition (that which the Apostles passed on under the inspiration of the Holy Spirit).

[9]Tanquerey, op. cit., p. 636f and Christian Pesch, *Praelectiones Dogmaticae*, vol. I, p. 397f.

and will be passed on until the end of time.[10]

Ecclesiastical tradition is all of those things which are not intrinsic to the Deposit of Faith, but which form the heritage and patrimony of the work of previous generations graciously passed on by the Church to subsequent generations for their benefit. Because it is extrinsic to the Deposit of Faith, ecclesiastical tradition is also called extrinsic tradition, examples of which include the Church's disciplinary code as set out in canon law and non-infallible teachings of the ordinary magisterium. This would include those things contained in Apostolic exhortations and encyclicals in which infallibility is not enjoyed, e.g. Pope Leo XIII in *Immortale Dei* asserts that the Church is a perfect society.

Because God Himself entrusted the Deposit of Faith to the Catholic Church, the Catholic Church is inherently traditional. Since all men by nature desire to know[11]),the Church cannot help but develop an ecclesiastical tradition. Once man was given the Deposit of Faith, he naturally reflected upon the Deposit resulting in a greater understanding of it. That understanding was then passed on. This also means that the Church herself would pass judgment upon the Deposit in magisterial acts[12] and these magisterial acts become part of the ecclesiastical tradition. The ecclesiastical tradition, therefore, was formed over the course of time i.e. in the life of the Church throughout the twenty centuries of its existence.

Ecclesiastical (or extrinsic) tradition developed according to two principles:

- The first principle, was the Deposit of Faith itself. The members of the Church used the teachings within the Deposit to develop schools of spirituality, Church discipline and legislation, as well as all of the other things which pertain to ecclesiastical tradition. Since the teaching of Christ must govern the life of the Church, it was necessary for any authentic extrinsic tradition (e.g. Canon Law) to be consistent

---

[10]Vatican I, *Pastor Aeternus*, chpt. 2 (Denz. 1825/3058).

[11]Aristotle, *Metaphysics*, Bk. I, chpt. 1 (980a22

[12]This indicates that one must distinguish between that which pertains to the Deposit and that which does not. The Church sometimes passes judgment on the Deposit of Faith in order to clarify the teaching contained within the Deposit for the good of the Church, e.g. when Pius IX declared the Immaculate Conception of Our Lady. Other magisterial acts are merely extrinsic to the Deposit of Faith and do not necessarily point to anything within the Deposit, but which may be connected to the Deposit in some way. This would include some ordinary magisterial acts as well as matters of discipline. However, more is contained in ecclesiastical tradition than just the acts of the magisterium.

with those teachings. Anything that was contrary to the teachings contained in the Deposit caused the Church great affliction but over time it was cut off from the life of the Church[13].

- The second principle was the nature of man. Since Scripture itself tells us a great deal about man and as philosophical systems advanced in an understanding of the nature of man, especially in the medieval period, the extrinsic tradition was fashioned based upon the knowledge of that nature. Furthermore, it was known to be a wounded nature, i.e. one affected by Original Sin and so the extrinsic tradition was designed to aid man in his condition. For example, many schools of spirituality and rules of the religious orders were designed in order to help man overcome his proclivity to self-will and concupiscence in order to conform himself to the ideals taught within the Deposit. Those who fashioned the extrinsic tradition were often saints who were guided and helped by divine aid in establishing some custom or aspect of the extrinsic tradition which was passed on to subsequent generations. The extrinsic tradition came to form a magnificent patrimony and heritage of all Catholics.

B. Subversion of Extrinsic Tradition

As the Modernist crisis grew under the impetus of modern philosophy, the extrinsic tradition was eroded and subverted due to several factors. The first was a change of view about the nature of man. With the onslaught of rationalism[14], then empiricism[15] and later Kantianism[16] and other

---

[13]Here we have in mind those who develop heterodox teachings of their own (heresies), spiritualities and customs which are contrary to the teachings of the Church.

[14]Rationalism is any one of the views that attribute excessive importance to human reason. Often rationalists hold that all of our knowledge is innate, i.e. we already have all our knowledge within ourselves from the beginning and that knowledge is not acquired by means of the senses.

[15]Empiricism is a system which holds that the sense knowledge is the only form of knowledge. Empiricists do not hold that there is anything beyond the material or if there is anything beyond the material, we are incapable of knowing it because our only form of knowledge is sense knowledge.

[16]Kant held that we are incapable of knowing things in themselves, i.e. we do not really know things outside of ourselves. He held that any experience we have is received according to a priori categories which are in the mind and which impose

modern innovations about the nature of man, the Thomistic view, i.e. the realist view of man, was supplanted. At first, this occurred outside the Church and was kept at bay by formal teaching within the Church which maintained a proper view of man. The Protestants, not having an intellectual heritage, quickly succumbed to the modern philosophies. As the Modernist crisis spread within the Church and the curiosity and fascination with modern philosophy grew, the view of man held by Catholics began to change in the latter part of the nineteenth century and during the twentieth century.

Rationalism also changed how man viewed revelation. Since rationalists do not believe that one can come to true intellectual knowledge by means of the senses, then that which pertained to the senses was systematically ignored or rejected. Since revelation is something introduced into sensible reality[17], revelation came under direct attack. Moreover, if one is cut off from reality, then one is locked up inside oneself and so what pertains to one's own experience becomes paramount. After Descartes,[18] came Spinoza[19] who systematically attacked the authenticity of oral tradition regarding the Scriptures[20] and through his philosophy he began to change

---

structure and order on our experiences. As a result, man is essentially cut off from knowing anything in reality because his mind changes the experience according to these categories.

[17]When Christ was on earth, He used sensible signs that we could see and hear. He used sensible signs in order to teach us about spiritual realities which are not physical or material.

[18]Rene Descartes lived from 1596-1650. He was a rationalist who began his philosophy by systematically doubting the truth of the senses and so his philosophy starts in the intellect rather than in reality.

[19]Benedict Spinoza lived from 1632-1677. He held that there was one thing and only one thing, viz. God and all of us are merely part of God. Since God was eternal and did not change, then what we see in the world is not really changing. Spinoza used the phrase "Deus sive Natura" which employs the inclusive "or" (sive) in Latin to show that God and nature were the same thing. This notion that God is nature and nature is God is the intellectual foundation for the current New Age movement in the West and it was also partly responsible for the eroding of the notion of God's transcendence. Spinoza was excommunicated by the Jews because of the incompatibility of his views with Judaism.

[20]David Laird Dungan in his text *A History of the Synoptic Problem* recounts how Spinoza developed the historical/critical exegetical method and from that point on, Scripture studies began to deteriorate outside the Catholic sphere. Later, these same problems enter into the Church with the uncritical adoption of the same methods.

people's view of the world. As empiricism rose, the view of man as simply a material being led to fixing man's meaning in the "now" or always in the present. Since for the empiricist, man's meaning is found in what he senses and feels, this led eventually to a lack of interest in the past since the past as such (and future for that matter) cannot be sensed nor fulfil our sensible desires.[21] With the advent of Hegel,[22] the intellectual groundwork was laid for a wholesale lack of interest in and distrust of tradition. With the scepticism of Spinoza about the sources of Scripture,[23] coupled with the Hegelian dialectic, the past (including all forms of tradition) was now outmoded or outdated and tradition was to be distrusted. As a consequence, those who wanted to impose some religious teaching based upon tradition or history became suspect.

At the same time in which the intellectual underpinnings for trusting tradition collapsed in the minds of modern intellectuals under the impetus of modern philosophy, a growing immanentism[24] arising from three sources[25] became entrenched.

---

[21] What this means is that if someone is only interested in what is sensibly pleasing or if they lead their lives according to their sensible appetites, they will not be interested in the past because the appetites are not interested in the past as such.

[22] G.W.F. Hegel lived from 1770-1831. He, like Spinoza, held that there was one thing and only one thing. But the difference between Hegel and Spinoza was that Spinoza held that this one thing was static and did not change, whereas Hegel held that this one thing was in a constant state of flux. This one thing went from an original state, sometimes called a thesis, to its opposite which is sometimes called an antithesis. Then there is the merger of the two opposites within the one thing and that becomes the synthesis and the synthesis becomes the thesis in the next series of perpetual changes. This process was called the dialectic and it indicated that things were constantly advancing. Hence, the past became irrelevant.

[23] See Laird, op. cit.

[24] Immanentism is a philosophy which holds that anything of importance is contained within the individual, i.e. the individual becomes the measure or standard by which things are judged. "Immanent" comes from the two Latin words "in" and "manere" which means "to remain in." Immanentism essentially holds that exterior reality is not important except to the extent that we can express ourselves in it. What is really important is that which is within ourselves.

[25] There are actually more than three but these three are particularly important.

- The first was Kant, who, through an epistemology[26] which was founded on Cartesian and empirical scepticism of the senses,[27] left one locked into one's own mind, logically speaking[28]. This meant that everything is within oneself or one's own mind which means that man's experiences are essentially immanent, i.e. they are within or remain within himself.[29]

- The second source of immanentism was the location of the theological experience within the emotions and this was done by Friedrich Schleiermacher.[30] For Schleiermacher, religion was primarily an expression of piety and piety is found only in the emotions. Religion could not be satisfied with metaphysical treatises and analysis, i.e. a rational approach to religion; rather, it had to be something emotional. This led to the immanentization of religion since piety or religious experience was something within the individual. We often see this today: people expect the liturgy to be conformed to their emotional states rather than they conforming themselves to an objective cult, which conforms itself to God.

---

[26]Epistemology is the branch of philosophy in which we investigate how man knows the world around him.

[27]Descartes starts his *Discourse on Method* with a systematic doubt about everything which cannot be known with certitude. Since, for him, the senses can be deceived, he doubted them. The problem is that the senses put us into contact with reality and if we cut ourselves off from reality by doubting our senses, there is no epistemological foundation for being able to know reality. The empiricists held that we only know our sensations and not the things which correspond to those sensations. Hence, all we know is sense knowledge but not necessarily things outside of ourselves.

[28]Etiene Gilson in his various epistemological works demonstrated that Transcendental Thomism was untenable. Transcendental Thomism is a philosophical system in which the epistemology of Descartes is merged with Thomism. Gilson showed that once one accepts the *cogito* of Descartes (i.e. the beginning point of his epistemology, viz. one begins in thought and not in reality first) one is not able to get back to reality. In this respect, Gilson's works are of particular importance today.

[29]As this is transposed to the domain of theology, since one cannot know things outside of oneself, then God must speak to one directly through one's conscience or some interior experience. This Kantian notion provided the intellectual foundation for the Protestant's theory of the subjective religious experience.

[30]His work *On Religion* is where this finds a full expression.

- The third source which led to immanentization and therefore provided an intellectual foundation for acceptance only of the present and a rejection of the past was the work of Maurice Blondel.[31] Blondel held that:

> "modern thought, with a jealous susceptibility, considers the notion of *immanence* as the very condition of philosophizing; that is to say, if among current ideas there is one which it regards as marking a definitive advance, it is the idea, which is at bottom perfectly true, that nothing can enter into a man's mind which does not come out of him and correspond in some way to a need for expansion and that there is nothing in the nature of historical or traditional teaching or obligation imposed from without that counts for him..."[32]

> For Blondel, only those things which come from man himself and which are immanent to him have any meaning. No tradition or history has any bearing upon his intellectual considerations unless it somehow comes from himself.

These three sources of immanentism as they influenced the Church during the waning of an intellectual phase of Modernism in the 1950s and early 1960s[33]

---

[31] Maurice Blondel lived from 1861-1949.

[32] "Letter on Apologetics" as found in the article by Peter J. Bernardi, "Maurice Blondel and the Renewal of the Nature/Grace Relationship," *Communio* 26, p. 881.

[33] The heresy of Modernism has occurred in four phases. The first was the initial phase which began around 1832 when it was called liberalism until the beginning of the First Vatican Council in 1869. The second phase was the intelligentsia phase in which it began to infect the Catholic intelligentsia more thoroughly and this occurred from 1870 to 1907 at which time Pope St. Pius X formally condemned Modernism. Then from 1907 until about 1955 to 1960, the underground phase occurred in which the Modernist teachings were propagated by some of the intelligentsia in the seminaries and Catholic universities, though quietly. Then, in the latter part of the 1950s, a superficial phase began in which the intellectual energy was exhausted and what was left was the practical application of the vacuous teachings of Modernism which occurred during the period in which the Second Vatican Council was in session and persists until this date. Vatican II was the catalyst or opportunity seized by the past and current superficial intellectuals who teach things contrary to the teachings of the Church.

provided the foundation for a psychological break from tradition *as a norm*. As Peter Bernardi observes, Blondel was "working at a time when the Church was just beginning to become conscious of a certain break in its tradition"[34]. The work of Blondel and the influx of the other modern philosophical points of view, which were antithetical to the ecclesiastical tradition,[35] had a drastic impact on Vatican II.[36] By the time Vatican II arrived, all of the intellectual foundation was in place for a systematic rejection of all of the aspects of ecclesiastical tradition.

In summary: Blondel and others, under the influence of modern philosophy, thought that modern man could not be satisfied with past ways of thinking. They provided an intellectual foundation upon which the Church, with a Council as a catalyst, could "update" itself or undergo an *"aggiornamento"*.[37] With the foundations for the extrinsic tradition having been supplanted, the extrinsic tradition was lost. In other words, since *the view of man had changed* and since *the view of the Deposit of Faith was subjected to a modern analysis*, the extrinsic tradition, which rested upon these two, collapsed. We are currently living with the full blown effects of that collapse.[38] The members of the Church today have become fixated on the here and now and the past traditions are not only irrelevant but to be distrusted and even, at times, demonized.

C. "Magisterialism" and Positivism

This has had several effects on the members of the Church. The first is that those things, which pertain to the extrinsic tradition and do not touch upon the intrinsic tradition, are ignored. This manifests itself in the fact that

---

[34]Ibid., p. 806.

[35]Blondel, in fact, wanted to go back to an earlier tradition and ignore the tradition which was passed on to him. This essentially meant that Blondel and other Modernists wanted to get away from medieval traditions which begot the Mass of Pius V and go back to earlier traditions because they were congruent with the immanentized experiences of modern man.

[36]Bernardi observes this but in a positive way in loc. cit.

[37]This was John XXIII's word for updating the Church.

[38]That is we are living with the full effects of the superficial stage of Modernism. For example, unlike previous generations there are no great theologians; theological discourse and writing in scholastic journals lacks the depth afforded the subjects that were given to it, even just fifty years ago, and there seems, in general, to be a lack of intellectual advancement of the science of theology.

some ecclesial documents today do not have any connection to the positions held by the magisterium prior to the Second Vatican Council. For example, in the document of Vatican II on ecumenism, *Unitatis Redintegratio*, there is not a single mention of the two previous documents which deal with the ecumenical movement and other religions, viz. *Satis Cognitum* by Leo XIII or *Mortalium Animos* by Pius XI. The approach to ecumenism and other religions is fundamentally different from the approach of the Vatican II document or *Ut Unum Sint* by Pope John Paul II.[39] Moreover, the problem is not just with respect to magisterium prior to Vatican II but even with the magisterium since the Council.[40]

This type of behaviour coupled with the modern philosophical encroachment into the intellectual life of the Church and the bad theology

---

[39]While the current magisterium can change a teaching which is under non-infallible ordinary magisterial teaching, nevertheless, when the magisterium makes a judgment in these cases, it has a moral obligation due to the requirements of the moral virtue of prudence to show how the previous teaching was wrong or to be understood differently by discussing the two different teachings. However, this is not what has happened. The magisterium since Vatican II often ignores previous documents which may appear to be in opposition to the current teaching, leaving the faithful to figure out how the two are compatible, e.g. as we see in *Mortalium Animos* and *Ut Unum Sint*. This leads to confusion, infighting within the Church as well as the appearance of contradicting previous Church teaching without explanation or reasoned justification.

[40]For instance, the Congregation for the Doctrine of the Faith (CDF) in 1975 (*Declaration on Certain Questions Concerning Sexual Ethics*) asserts the following regarding masturbation: "The main reason is that, whatever the motive for acting this way, the deliberate use of the sexual faculty outside normal conjugal relations essentially contradicts the finality of the faculty." This indicates that regardless of one's intention or motive, the act is in itself gravely immoral. Then in the *Catechism of the Catholic Church*, a definition is given which seems to allow for different intentions to modify whether such an act is evil or not: "Masturbationis nomine intelligere oportet voluntarium organorum genitalium excitationem, ad obtinendam ex ea veneream voluptatem," i.e. "by the name masturbation it must be understood as the voluntary excitement of the genital organs to obtain from it veneral pleasure." The last part of the definition therefore includes in the act of masturbation a finality, viz. "to obtain from it venereal pleasure." This appears to contradict the prior teaching of the Church as well as the teaching of the CDF. If one does not do it for the sake of pleasure, does that mean that it is not masturbation? For example, if one does it for the sake of determining one's fertility, does this justify it? One can rectify the situation by arguing that when it is done for the sake of pleasure it is an instance of masturbation, but that the actual definition is what the Church has always held. Clearly, however, this example is testimony to how careless the magisterium has become in its theological expression.

resulting therefrom has led to a type of "magisterialism".[41] Magisterialism is a fixation on the teachings that pertain *only* to the current members of the Magisterium.[42] Since extrinsic tradition has been subverted and since the Vatican tends to promulgate documents exhibiting a lack of concern regarding some of the previous magisterial acts, many have begun ignoring the previous magisterial acts and listen only to the current magisterium.

This problem is exacerbated by our current historical conditions. As the theological intellectual community began to unravel before, during and after Vatican II, those who considered themselves orthodox were those who were obedient and intellectually submissive to the magisterium since those who dissent are not orthodox. Therefore, the standard of orthodoxy was shifted from Scripture, intrinsic tradition (of which the magisterium is a part) and extrinsic tradition (which includes magisterial acts of the past, such as Pius IX's *Syllabus of Errors*), to a psychological state in which only the *current* magisterium is followed.

Neo-conservatives have fallen into this way of thinking i.e. the only standard by which they judge orthodoxy is whether or not one follows the current magisterium. Traditionalists, as a general rule, tend to be orthodox in the sense that they are obedient to the current magisterium, even though they disagree about matters of discipline and have some reservations about some aspects of current magisterial teachings which seem to contradict the previous magisterium (e.g. the role of the ecumenical movement). Traditionalists tend

---

[41] The term is the author's own designation for this phenomenon.

[42] To be more precise, one may say that magisterialism is a disregard or rejection of the remote rule of tradition while still holding to the necessity of following the current members of the Magisterium. There has been some criticism of the use of the term neo-conservative in which it is observed that they are not really conserving the tradition of the Church. To this criticism, we must concede that in many respects, it is true. The neo-conservatives are conserving, ironically, more faithfully than all others, the changes in the Church since the second Vatican Council. The traditionalists want the tradition to be restored and the changes to be reversed which are not in congruity with the tradition. The liberals want to advance the changes even further. Whereas it is often the "neo-conservatives" which are trying to maintain the changes brought about as a form of "loyality and obedience" to the members of the Magisterium as well as, in some cases, a question of orthodoxy. Some have therefore began calling them "neo-Catholics" but that term also has its difficulties. It is hard to see how an intellectual position which favors current teachings of members of the Magisterium *against* the remote rule (e.g. religious liberty as taught by the second Vatican Council which was formally condemned by Pope Leo XIII in *Libertas Praestantissimum*) can be construed to be Catholic in the sense that the Fathers would understand. Perhaps, for that reason, since neither term fully captures their position, their position should be refered to as the magisterialist position.

to take not just the current magisterium as their norm but Scripture,[43] intrinsic tradition, extrinsic tradition *and* the current magisterium as the principles of judgment of correct Catholic thinking. This is what distinguishes traditionalists and neo-conservatives i.e. their perspectives regarding the role of ecclesiastical tradition and how the current magisterium relates to it.

Inevitably, this magisterialism has led to a form of positivism.[44] Since there are no principles of judgment other than the current magisterium, whatever the current magisterium says is *always* what is "orthodox." In other words, psychologically the neo-conservatives have been left in a position in which the extrinsic and intrinsic tradition are no longer included in the norms of judging whether something is orthodox or not. As a result, whatever comes out of the Vatican regardless of its authoritative weight, is to be held, even if it contradicts what was taught with comparable authority in the past. Since non-infallible ordinary acts of the magisterium can be erroneous, this leaves one in a precarious situation if one only takes as true what the current magisterium says. While we are required to give religious assent even to the non-infallible teachings of the Church, what are we to do when a magisterial document contradicts other current or previous teachings and one does not have any more authoritative weight than the other? It is too simplistic merely to say that we are to follow the current teaching. What would happen if in a period of crisis, like our own, a non-infallible ordinary magisterial teaching contradicted what was in fact the truth? If one part of the magisterium contradicts another, both being at the same level, which is to be believed? Unfortunately, what has happened is that many neo-conservatives have acted as if non-infallible ordinary magisterial teachings (e.g. the role of inculturation in the liturgy as stated in the *Catechism of the Catholic Church*) are, in fact, infallible when the *current* magisterium promulgates them. This is a positivist

---

[43]Neo-conservatives as a general rule accept Scripture and give it a rather prominent place. But Scripture along with intrinsic tradition are not that much of a norm for them except insofar as the current magisterium asserts the necessity for following them as a matter of orthodoxy.

[44]Positivism is a philosophical system in which one regards only the sensible, the particular (singular) experience, as real and holds that only the knowledge of such facts is certain because only they can be (physically) verified. This would mean any reality which is not physical is to be denied. Positivists tend to hold that legislation does not have to be founded on any other principle than the mere fact that a given authority promulgates it. Since tradition or past history is not something tangible, it is ignored.

mentality.[45]

D. Collective Amnesia and Mutual Suspicion

As the positivism and magisterialism grew and the extrinsic tradition no longer remained a norm for judging what should and should not be done, neo-conservatives accepted the notion that the Church must adapt to the modern world. Rather than helping the modern world to adapt to the teachings of the Church, the reverse process has occurred. This has led to the neo-conservatives being overly concerned about politically correct secular matters. Rather than having a certain distrust of the world which Christ exhorts us to have,[46] many priests will only teach something from the pulpit as long as it is not going to cause problems. For example, how many priests are willing to preach against anti-Scriptural feminism? The fact is that they have adopted an immanentized way of looking at what should be done, often from an emotional point of view. And this coupled with political correctness has incapacitated ecclesiastical authorities in the face of the world and within the Church herself where the process of immanentization, with its flawed understanding of the nature of man and his condition as labouring under Original Sin, has severely undermined discipline. Even those who try to be orthodox have become accustomed to softer disciplinary norms, which fit fallen nature well, resulting in a lack of detachment from the current way of doing things and a consequent reluctance by neo-conservatives to exercise authority - precisely because they lack the vital detachment required to do so.

All of the aforesaid has resulted in the neo-conservatives rejecting the extrinsic tradition as the norm. This is why, even in "good" seminaries, the spiritual patrimony of the saints is virtually never taught. Moreover, this accounts for why the neo-conservatives appear confused about the real meaning of tradition. Since it is not a principle of judgment for them, they are unable to discuss it in depth. In fact, they ignore extrinsic tradition almost as much as the "liberals." Even when neo-conservatives express a desire to recover and follow the extrinsic tradition, they rarely do so when it comes to

---

[45]Many of the things which the neo-conservatives do are the result of implicitly adopting principles which they have not fully or explicitly considered. Many of them would deny this characterization because they do not intellectually hold to what, in fact, are their operative principles.

[46]The world which God created is not to be despised because it is evil but because it is a good, i.e. because it is good we can become attached to it rather than God and, as a result, it can lead us to moral ruin. This requires us to live in the world but be detached from it. Sometimes the term "world" is also taken to include man and his moral corruption due to sin.

making concrete decisions.

It now becomes clearer why there is a kind of psychological suspicion between neo-conservatives and traditionalists: they have fundamentally different perspectives. The neo-conservatives have psychologically or implicitly accepted that extrinsic tradition cannot be trusted, whereas the traditionalists hold to the extrinsic tradition as something good, i.e. something which is the product of the wisdom and labour of the saints and the Church throughout history. For this reason, the fundamental difference between neo-conservatives and traditionalists is that the neo-conservative looks at the past through the eyes of the present while the traditionalist looks at the present through the eyes of the past. Historically, the *mens ecclesiae* or mind of the Church was expressed through the extrinsic tradition. That is to say that the Church, since it receives both its teaching from the past and the labour of the saints and previous magisterium by tradition, always looked at the present through the eyes of the past. In this, she looked at the present not as man under the influence of modern philosophy looked at the present,[47] but through the eyes of her Lord Who gave her His teaching when He was on earth (i.e. in the past). Only at the time of Christ, is it possible to look authentically at the past through, what was then, the eyes of the present, since Christ was the fulfilment of the past. But once the work of Christ became part of history and He ascended into heaven, we must always look back to Christ and to our tradition for an authentic understanding of the present.[48]

This fundamental shift in perspective has left the traditionalists with the sense that they are fighting for the good of the extrinsic tradition without the help of and often hindered by the current magisterium. Liturgically, traditionalists judge the *Novus Ordo* in light of the Mass of Pius V and the neo-conservatives judge the Tridentine Mass, as it is called, in light of the *Novus Ordo*[49]. This comes from the Hegelianism which holds that the past is

---

[47]In fact, this seems to be the theme which is warned against by the magisterium prior to Vatican II.

[48]As the dictum says, he who does not study history is bound to repeat it. This is because if you do not look at the present through the experience or eyes of the past, you will not take heed of the lessons learned by past generations. Furthermore, man's identity is determined in part by the history from which he comes. As a result, we do not fully understand ourselves and our circumstances without knowing where (historically) we came from.

[49]This has caused many a traditional priest problems. Even when they are discussing liturgical matters with those who uphold the teachings of the Church, they are often faced with criticism of the Old Mass based upon principles which govern the New Mass. It is difficult even to discuss it coherently when the accepted principles or premises of those holding different views are fundamentally at odds.

always understood in light of the present, i.e. the thesis and antithesis are understood in light of their synthesis. This leads to a mentality that newer is always better, because the synthesis is better than either the thesis or the antithesis taken alone. Being affected by this, the neo-conservatives often assume or are incapable of imagining that the current discipline of the Church may not be as good as the prior discipline. There is a mentality today which holds that *"because it is present (Hegelianism), because it comes from us (immanentism), it is necessarily better."*

Furthermore, neo-conservatives love the Church and have a strong emotional attachment to the magisterium which causes them to find it unimaginable that the Church could ever falter, even with regard to matters of discipline. Like the father who loves his daughter and therefore has a hard time imagining her doing anything wrong, neo-conservatives have a hard time conceiving that the Holy Spirit does not guarantee infallibility in matters of discipline or non-infallible ordinary magisterial teaching. Traditionalists, confronted by a Church in crisis, know that something has gone wrong somewhere. As a result, they are, I believe, more sober in assessing whether or not the Church exercises infallibility. That, allied to their looking at the present through the eyes of the past, helps the traditionalists to see that the onus is on the present to justify itself, not the past.

The dominance of Hegelianism and immanentism also led to a form of collective ecclesiastical amnesia.[50] During the early 1960s, there existed a generation which was handed the entire ecclesiastical tradition, for the tradition was still being lived. However, because they laboured under the aforesaid errors, that generation[51] chose not to pass on the ecclesiastical tradition to the subsequent generation as something living. Consequently, in one generation, the extrinsic tradition virtually died out. By the late 1960s and early 1970s, seminary and university formation in the Catholic Church excluded those things which pertained to the ecclesiastical tradition. Once the prior generation had chosen this course, not to remember and teach the things of the past, it was never passed on and so those whom they trained i.e. the current generation, were consigned to suffer collective ignorance about their patrimony and heritage.

A further effect of what we have considered is that no prior teaching is left untouched. In other words, it appears as if more documentation has been issued in the last forty years than in the previous 1,960. Every past teaching, if the current magisterium deems it worthy of note to modern man,

---

[50] This can also be asserted of the customs, morals and culture in the secular sphere.

[51] This is, of course, a generalization. Not everyone of that generation agreed with the course of action that their own generation was taking.

is touched upon anew and viewed through the lens of the present day immanentism. The impression is given that the teachings of the previous magisterium cannot stand on their own and so they must be given some form of "relevance" by being promulgated anew in a current document. Moreover, the current documents often lack the clarity and succinctness of the prior magisterium,[52] and, with relatively few exceptions, are exceedingly long and tedious to read in their entirety. As a result, the frequency of the documents taken together with their length have eroded their authority because, as a general rule, people simply do not have the emotional or psychological discipline to plough through them.

Conclusion

The differences between traditionalists and neo-conservatives are rooted in their respective attitudes to extrinsic or ecclesiastical tradition. Even if a neo-conservative holds notionally[53] that the extrinsic tradition is of value, nevertheless in the daily living of his life and in his deliberations, he simply ignores a large portion of it, if not completely. But there is hope, even outside the circles that hold to tradition. Many of the young, even those in neo-conservative seminaries, are no longer weighed down by the intellectual baggage which afflicted their counterparts in the previous generation. Because they have been taught virtually nothing about religion, they lack a perspective that might influence them negatively in favour of one particular view of extrinsic tradition. Many of them are eager to learn the truth and do not have any preconceived ideas about the current state of the Church. As a result, if they are provided with or are able to arrive at the knowledge of their patrimony, many of them seeking it out on their own, then we can be assured of a brighter future. But this requires knowledge of the problem and the willingness to adopt or connect to the extrinsic tradition by embracing it as something good. It is unlikely that the role of ecclesiastical tradition will be sorted out soon, but we can hope that its restoration is part of God's providential plan.

---

[52]What this means is that there is a certain restlessness today in the Church and its members cannot seem to leave things in the past alone. Perhaps this is due to their perspective which holds that the past, i.e. the extrinsic tradition, was inherently inadequate.

[53]In philosophy, a distinction is made between notional and real assent. Notional assent is when the person may make an intellectual judgment that something is true, but it does not really determine his action or thinking. Real assent is when a person makes an intellectual judgment about the truth of some matter and actually lives and thinks according to it.

Chapter 3: Immanentism and the Ecclesiological Devastation[54]

It is likely that the average layman has heard but possibly not grasped, that the current ecclesiastical crisis consists, not in a crisis of theology, but in a crisis of philosophy that has caused a loss of faith and in turn, devastation in theology. This chapter will deal with arguably the most foundational and important part of modernism-what has come to be known as the principle of immanence. We may define the principle of immanence as "a philosophical position which holds that the first thing one knows is self and that all our knowledge of external reality is judged in light of self." Many people, who study modernism, e.g. by reading the papal encyclical *Pascendi* and the Syllabus of Pius IX, know that living immanentism has been condemned. But their understanding of that principle is often vague and unclear. Yet, a clearer understanding of the principle of immanence will afford the Catholic layman a profound understanding of the current state of the Church. This chapter will provide a short presentation of the principle of immanence, apply it to various aspects of theology that are affecting the Church, and finally present solutions so that we ourselves do not fall into the very problem against which we are fighting.

A. The Principle of Immanence

Our discussion of the principle of immanence will be admittedly brief and inadequate for anyone looking for a thorough overview. On the other hand, for some readers the first part of this chapter will seem quite difficult. The reader is urged to follow along as closely as he can, in order better to understand the conclusions we draw later. Let us begin with a distinction between the immanent and the transcendent. In the traditional or scholastic use of the terms, immanent is defined as "present in an operation within; indwelling: as, God is immanent in all things by his power, knowledge, and authority."[55] Transcendent, on the other hand, means "so excellent that [it] surpasses the limits of created perfections and is really distinct from creatures."[56] With these two classical definitions, God is seen as both

---

[54] Originally published in *Latin Mass Magazine*, Winter 2007

[55] Wuellner, *A Dictionary of Scholastic Philosophy*, p. 133.

[56] Ibid., p. 310.

immanent in His causation, since the cause is always present to the effect,[57] as well as transcendent in His existence, which means that God is really distinct from created things. Immanence can also mean "living, originating in and remaining within the agent as a perfection of the agent."[58] For example, we see this when we perform a moral action: the defect of sin or virtue is caused by the action which remains in us. In this discussion of immanence, we shall not normally be using the term in these classical but valid senses. Rather, we shall be using it in the modern sense of the term, which will become clear as we proceed.

In order to give a basic outline of the genesis of the principle of immanence, which has impacted theology so drastically, we need to consider some of the points advanced in the philosophies of Descartes, Kant, Schleiermacher, Feuerbach and Blondel.[59] Most modern scholars hold that the principle of immanence began with René Descartes (1596-1650).[60] Descartes, in his *Discourse on Method*, began with a systematic doubt of anything that was not absolutely certain.[61] This led him to doubt the senses, since the senses can deceive us. He gave the example of a stick, which when placed in water appears to bend because of the refraction of light. The observer knows that the stick has not actually become bent but his senses report that it is. Consequently, the senses, according to Descartes, could not be trusted. This systematic doubt is the foundation for the Cartesian philosophy (that is, the philosophy of Descartes) and all modern philosophy which flows from it.

---

[57]This is known as the principle of simultaneity. See Wuellner, *Summary of Scholastic Principles*, p. 18, #45.

[58]Wuellner, *A Dictionary of Scholastic Philosophy*, p. 133.

[59]It is not possible to give a full treatment of the development of the principle of immanence throughout modern philosophy within the space of this chapter. For a full account, see Cornelio Fabro, *God in Exile: Modem Atheism from its Roots in the Cartesian Cogito to the Present Day*.

[60]For example, see Fabro, *God in Exile*, passim. Jacques Maritain in *Three Reformers: Luther, Descartes, Rousseau* asserts that the principle of immanence began with Luther. While it must be conceded that Luther was an immanentist, he was an informal immanentist. His teaching lacked any systemization and was expressly opposed to reason. In this sense, he cannot be said to be a formal immanentist in the sense that his immanence was rooted in systematic thought, for it was not. It would be more accurate to say that Luther provided a "spiritual" or psychological ambience in which immanence could flourish. But historically the actual intellectual foundation of the principle of immanence that affects Western civilization belongs to Descartes.

[61]René Descartes, *Discourse on Method*, part II.

Descartes went on to observe:

> But immediately upon this I observed that, whilst I thus wished to think that all was false, it was absolute necessary that I, who thus thought, should be somewhat; and as I observed that this truth, *I think, therefore I am* [*cogito ergo sum*], was so certain and of such evidence, that no ground of doubt, however extravagant, could be alleged by the skeptics capable of shaking it, I concluded that I might, without scruple, accept it as the first principle of the philosophy of which I was in search.[62]

This passage contains something of great importance: the beginning and founding of his philosophical reflection on himself. The first thing of which Descartes is certain and which he knows is himself, rather than extramental (outside the mind) reality reported to him by his senses. This point of departure in his philosophical reflection deviated from the Thomistic understanding that knowledge first begins in the senses, that from sensible knowledge we proceed by abstraction to intellectual knowledge, and that by this process we come into contact with reality. Descartes inverted the process by first founding knowledge in oneself and then trying to establish that knowledge of extramental reality is not false or unreliable. Ultimately, if one accepts the *cogito*, i.e. the principle that the first object of knowledge is self (stemming from systematic doubt), one is cut off from reality and being.[63] After Descartes, modern philosophy, having adopted the *cogito* as a principle, vacillates between trying to get back to reality and trying to make thought identical with reality.[64]

Immanuel Kant (1724-1804), accepting the Cartesian *cogito* and the Humean critique of causation,[65] developed an understanding of epistemology

---

[62] Ibid., part IV, 63. The italicized section has been changed by this author from, "I think, hence I am," to "I think, therefore I am" in order to bring it into congruity with the common way in which this passage is quoted.

[63] Fabro, *God in Exile*, passim but especially p. 1063 and p. 1066. Gilson makes this part of the theme of his book *Thomist Realism and the Critique of Knowledge*.

[64] Fabro, *God in Exile*, part X, passim.

[65] Hume's critique of causation effectively cuts one off from reality. According to Hume there is no cause of one thing to another but only a constant conjunction of one event with another. Iin other words, we may not conclude, when 1) one billiard ball strikes another and 2) makes the second one move, that a necessary connection exists between the two occurrences, but simply that the two occurrences have merely been correlated consistently with each other. This view isolates one intellectually

(a branch of philosophy that investigates the origin, nature, methods and limits of human knowledge) that led him to the following conclusions. Kant labeled the thing-in-itself, i.e. the thing in reality, the *noumena*, and said it was inaccessible to human understanding and knowledge. But he went on to say that we did have some kind of experience of the noumena, called the *phenomena*. Our experience of the phenomena did not penetrate to the essence of the noumena, and thus we were still unable to reach the real. However, man does have an *a priori* knowledge of things as well as his experience or phenomena. What is important in this whole discussion is the phenomena, i.e. human experience. In later philosophical systems, this experience will become the focal point in the discussion about God.

Kant brought full reflection to bear on this notion of being cut off from reality. Kant argued that neither ontological[66] nor cosmological[67] arguments for God's existence worked. Cosmological arguments for God's existence argue from something in reality (such as order in the universe[68]) to God as its cause. But Kant rightly understood that, if one accepted the Cartesian *cogito*, i.e. if one was cut off from reality, there would be no way to prove God's existence on the basis of reality outside the mind.

The next philosopher we need to consider is Friedrich Schleiermacher (1768-1834). As reflection upon religion developed increasingly from the Kantian understanding of epistemology, the focus became the experience, the phenomena or various aspects of the phenomena. Schleiermacher observed:

> Your feeling is piety, insofar as it expresses, in the matter described, the being and life common to you and to the All. Your feeling is piety insofar as it is the result of the operation of God in you by means of the operation of the world upon you. This series is not made up either

---

from reality since there is no causal connection between the knowledge in one's intellect and what one senses in reality, for the senses are not necessarily being acted upon in a causal way by some exterior object. See David Hume, *An Inquiry Concerning Human Understanding*, ch. VII.

[66]See Immanuel Kant, *Critique of Pure Reason*, p. 331-59. This criticism of the ontological argument was foreseen by Saint Thomas Aquinas in ST I, q. 2, a. 1, a. 2. Ontological arguments try to argue from a concept of God to the reality of God, which Kant rightly pointed out does not work. Simply because one has something in his mind does not mean that it actually exists in reality. So it is an illicit logical move to proceed from thought to reality without having first received it from reality. In other words, just because one thinks God exists does not mean that He actually, i.e. in reality, exists.

[67]See Kant, *Critique of Pure Reason*, p. 331-59.

[68]See ST I, q.2, a.3.

of perceptions or of objects of perception, either of works or operations or of different spheres of operation, but purely as sensations and the influence of all that lives and moves around, which accompanies them and conditions them. These feelings are exclusively the elements of religion, and none are excluded. There is no sensation that is not pious, except it indicate some diseased and impaired state of the life, the influence of which will not be confined to religion. Wherefore, it follows that ideas and principles are all foreign to religion... [I]f ideas and principles are to be anything, they must belong to the knowledge which is a different department of life than religion.[69]

This passage indicates that for Schleiermacher religion was merely a matter of feeling, and any kind of feeling, insofar as one could experience God in it, could be part of religion. But Schleiermacher also created a division between an intellectual approach to religion and religion itself. He went on to observe:

From within, in their original, characteristic form, the emotions of piety must issue. They must be indubitably your own feelings, and not mere stale descriptions of the feelings of others, which could best issue in a wretched imitation....[70] The sum total of religion is to feel that, in the highest unity, all that moves us in feeling is one; to feel that aught single and particular is only possible by means of this unity; to feel, that is to say, that our being and living is a being and living in and through God.[71]

This passage indicates that in matters of religion it is not other people's emotions that are important but your own. In the final analysis, it is not the place of anyone else to tell you what to believe, what to think[72] or how to feel in relationship to God or religion. Rather, the place of any religion would be to facilitate these emotions or feelings in relation to God.

Ludwig Feuerbach (1804-1872) began to reflect on what all this meant in relationship to man, particularly in the realm of psychology. If we could not

---

[69]Friedrich Schleiermacher, *On Religion*, p. 45f.

[70]Ibid., p. 48.

[71]Ibid., p. 49f.

[72]In ibid. (p. 62), Schleiermacher says that one looks for no rule outside oneself.

know anything outside of ourselves and if we could not prove God's existence (as Kant had shown), then the only thing that was left was man.[73] Feuerbach observed, "If, for example, feeling is the essential organ of religion, the nature of God is nothing else than the expression of the nature of feeling."[74] God was therefore "pure unlimited, free feeling."[75] Feuerbach then went on to describe how man, in taking these ideas and feelings about God, projected them into beings independent from himself. If one accepts the Cartesian/Kantian epistemology and Kant's critiques of the proofs for the existence of God, discussions about God or religion are really discussions about man and his feelings. In this sense, Feuerbach observed that religion is really anthropology, i.e. man looks at some perfection in himself and then projects it out to a god which he thinks exists independently of himself. While we might think Feuerbach is unsound in his thinking, if one accepts the Cartesian *cogito* this is one of the conclusions: atheism (i.e. there is no God but only man projecting perfections or thoughts about God into reality). In contrast to Feuerbach's line of thinking, there were some who, having a religious mind were uncomfortable with the final atheistic outcome of the *cogito*. Among these was Maurice Blondel (1861-1949), who sought to give a defense or an apologetic for religion in view of the modern philosophies. Blondel first observed that the old forms of apologetic, which were ultimately scholastic (referring to the philosophy articulated by the Latin Fathers, Aristotle and his commentators - especially Saint Thomas Aquinas) in nature, did not work for modern man, for the general movement of modern thought had turned more and more against it.[76] Blondel essentially rejected the scholastic approach to religion and placed himself within the context of the modern philosophical approach to God:

> In a phrase which must be explained but which indicates at once the seriousness of the conflict, modern thought, with a jealous susceptibility, considers the notion of immanence as the very condition of philosophizing; that is to say, if among current ideas there is one which it regards as marking a definite advance, it is the idea, which is at bottom perfectly true, that nothing can enter into a

---

[73]Feuerbach, *The Essence of Christianity*, xxxv.

[74]Ibid., p. 9.

[75]Ibid., p. 10f.

[76]Blondel, *The Letter on Apologetics and History of Dogma*, p. 150. It would be more accurate to say that the scholastic arguments or forms of apologetic do work for man whether he is modern or not, although they do not work for modernist man.

man's mind which does not come out of him and correspond in some way to a need for development and that there is nothing in the nature of historical or traditional teaching or obligation imposed from without which counts for him, no truth and no precept which is acceptable unless it is in some sort autonomous and autochthonous.[77]

For Blondel, the point of departure was the notion of immanence or, we may say more appropriately, the principle of immanence. What this means is that, in the context of the philosophical history from which it derives, to proceed philosophically in the discussion about religion one must first begin with self:

For our idea of transcendent truths or beings, whether real or imaginary is always immanent in so far as it is our own; and before we can pronounce upon the significance of what we are thinking it is important to decide what in fact we are thinking; that is, we must go over the whole series of our inevitable ideas and their necessary implications apart from the mutilations or partial restrictions which the superficial intervention of our reflexive decisions seems to bring about when we are preoccupied with moral and ontological problems. The method of immanence, then, can consist in nothing else than in trying to equate, in our own consciousness, what we appear to think and to will and to do with what we do and what we think in actual fact... And its special business is to criticize all of phenomena which make up our inner life, each one in the light of others, to adjust them, to study the connections between them, to show all their implications, to discover what principles are presupposed by thought and by action, to define on what conditions we may ascribe reality to the objects or the means of salvation which are inevitably conceived by us, to study (for example) our idea of God, not just as God, but insofar as it is our necessary and effective thought of God.[78]

For Blondel, even the discussion about God and the transcendent[79] was subject to the method of immanence. One judges the things of God and the transcendent based upon one's own experience. The final conclusion is that all of religion becomes subject to the self. In the above passage, we italicized the word "decide" because Blondel was influenced by Kant's stress on the

---

[77]Ibid., p. 15lf.

[78]Ibid , p. 156f. (Emphasis mine.)

[79]Ibid.

primacy of the practical reason or moral will.[80] This reduces religion to choice, i.e. we decide what we believe. That follows from the principle of immanence. (Later we shall see that this leads to a heavy emphasis on action in relation to religion.) For Blondel, truth was not the adequation of intellect with thing (adaequatio intellectus et rei);[81] rather it was adequation of intellect with life.[82] In other words, the truth does not consist in our knowing reality and conforming to that objective reality (in religious terms, in our conforming ourselves to the Deposit of Faith). Rather, we must decide what we believe and conform our lives to that. In the end, truth is merely a consistency between what one believes and how one acts. We now come to a crucial, highly debated point that must be addressed. There are those who assert that Blondel, while holding to the method of immanence, did not succumb to the doctrine of immanence, which was condemned by Pope Saint Pius X. Some hold that the condemnation did not apply to Blondel because he proposed a method of immanence rather than the doctrine of immanence.[83]

Again, the method of immanence, the approach to being through critical reflection on the subject, could easily be converted and had in fact been converted into a doctrine of immanence, asserting that nothing exists outside human consciousness or that the statement that anything so exists is devoid of meaning. There remained therefore the problem of pursuing the method of immanence while avoiding the doctrine or principal of immanence.[84]

The doctrine or principle of immanence starts in the Cartesian *cogito* and asserts that human thought is the principle of judgment of all things that exist:

> This is far from the metaphysics of Christian Philosophy, for it begets the principle of immanentism, the idea that the activity of human consciousness stands at the root of being and hence of value. Human thinking feels itself independent of and ontological reality is given from the higher Source of existence and indeed conceives of itself as

---

[80]Copleston, *A History of Philosophy*, vol. IX, p3 229.

[81]See Saint Thomas Aquinas, *Quaestiones Disputatae de Veritate*, q. l.

[82]Blondel, *L' Action Essai d'une critique de la vie et d'une science de la pratique.*

[83]For example, see Copleston, op. cit., p. 232f.

[84]ibid, 2p. 27.

the creator of being and value.[85]

The principle of immanence essentially states that the first thing we know is ourselves and that all our knowledge of external reality is judged in light of self. Blondel wished to avoid this, since he knew that it led to Kant's rejection of the proofs for God's existence and ultimately to atheism, and that this was contrary to what the First Vatican Council had stated regarding what we could know about God's existence.[86] Blondel then asserted the necessity of following the method of immanence and was careful not to assert the doctrine or principle of immanence. The difficulty, however, lies in the analysis of the term "method." Method is a mode of proceeding insofar as the method determines how one proceeds. But method is an action, i.e. a series of intellectual reflections, and according to a Thomistic analysis, actions always implicitly contain the end towards which they are directed. In scholastic moral theology, this is called the *finis operis*, i.e. the end of the action or work. In order for the action to achieve the end, it must be proportioned and directed to the end. This direction towards the end is the end of the action itself or the *finis operis*. The end is often called the principle of the action for it is that which is first in the order of intention, i.e. one first conceives the end and then sets about seeking a means to achieve the end. When we apply this notion to the method of immanence, we recognize that the method contains within itself the end towards which the method is ordered. Since Blondel stated that he would rigorously apply the method of immanence,[87] the immanence must be fleshed out in order for us to understand precisely where it is heading. Blondel observed that the method of immanence was confined to determining the dynamism of our experience and that this was the very condition of modern philosophy in its intransigent independence.[88] Since it is the person's own experience and not reality that constitutes the foundation of the method, the doctrine or principle of immanence is contained implicitly in the method of immanence, since the method terminates (ends) in self. While Blondel would

---

[85]Chervin and Kevane, *Love of Wisdom: An Introduction to Christian Philosophy*, p. 236.

[86]See *Filius Dei*. The First Vatican Council dealt with certain aspects of modernism that were starting to make their way into Catholic thought at the time. Among other things it treated the proofs for God's existence and what we can know about God through the natural light of reason. It also dealt with the authority of the Church.

[87]Blondel, *The Letter on Apologetics and History of Dogma*, p. 156.

[88]Ibid., p. 159.

assert that this is not the case and that he does not wish to follow where the principle of immanence leads, nevertheless, he is still subject to the principle of immanence in his adoption of the method of immanence. His methodology will not lead one outside one's own thought, for as we have noted above, once one cuts oneself off from reality, i.e. once one accepts the *cogito*, the final trajectory is atheism.

As we noted earlier, some have asserted that the condemnation by Pope Saint Pius X involved a different kind of immanence, and therefore the condemnation does not apply to Blondel. Yet, what Pope Saint Pius X describes in *Pascendi Dominici Gregis* in paragraph seven is the doctrine of immanence, which contains the rejection of the proofs for God's existence and natural theology; the explanation for these things "must, therefore, be looked for in man."[89] While some say that the condemnation of immanentism is strictly with respect to vital immanence or religious immanence, in fact what is being condemned is the principle of immanence, i.e. basing the judgment of things that pertain to revelation or religion within man himself.[90]

To be sure, the Pope did not condemn Blondel by name. However, the condemnation of a man's thought is not based upon whether he is named or not but whether the philosophical or theological position he holds has been condemned. We also concede that Blondel "made it clear enough that he had no intention of identifying God with the immanent idea of God."[91] This is why the discussion of Blondel is so difficult: because his method from the foregoing analysis indicates that it contains implicitly the principle of immanence, even though he denies that it contains that principle.

B. Conclusions Drawn from the Philosophy of the Principle of Immanence

In the prior article, we discussed the philosophical aspects of the principle of immance. From that discussion, we begin to see certain conclusions which are drawn from the principle of immanence. Based upon the principal of immanence, one is inevitably led to atheism;[92] there is no God

---

[89]Pope Saint Pius X, *Encyclical Pascendi Dominici Gregis*, para. 7.

[90]Cf. ibid., paras. 13, 19, 20, 22 and 37.

[91]Copleston, loc. cit. See Blondel, *The Letter on Apologetics and History of Dogma*, p. 157.

[92]Fabro, *God in Exile*, passim. Fabro observes that the principle of immanence is the nucleus of modern atheism but we may also say it is the inner nucleus of modernism. Since each person differs by disposition and therefore will choose or decide what he is to believe based upon how he feels and since everybody feels

or, in the case of Feuerbach, man is God,[93] which just means there is no God outside of man; in other words, there is no God. If one adopts the principle of immanence, it is inconsistent or contradictory to assert that there is a God. On a practical level, one ends up an atheist, as we shall see in regards to the application of the principle of immanence to theology.

Adoption of the principle of immanence, since it cuts one off from reality, leads to a philosophy which is no longer founded on being[94] or reality. As Billot points out, truth is the adequation of intellect and thing (being/ reality); the principle of immanence, since we cannot know reality or are cut off from reality, destroys the foundation of absolute truth.[95] The principle of immanence inevitably leads to relativism and subjectivism. While it is possible to be a relativist and subjectivist prior to one being an immanentist, once one is an immanentist and the foundation of truth is destroyed, truth becomes relative or subjective or, as in the case of Blondel, truth is merely the adequation of what one believes with how one behaves, i.e. one is consistent in his own life.

Furthermore immanentism ultimately destroys or denies the transcendent.[96] Due to the fact that immanentism locks one inside one's own thought and cuts oneself off from reality, one cannot ultimately know God or the transcendent since the transcendent is above and beyond oneself and all one ultimately knows is himself and his own thought. This will have a horizontalizing effect within the context of religion insofar as religion will be about man and lack any sense of the sacred or the transcendent.[97] Moreover, it will lead to another rather strange conclusion. If one follows Schleiermacher's assertion that the experience of the divine occurs within emotion, the outcome of this will be that one will think what God wills or wants is the same thing as what "I" feel or what "I" want.

---

differently, it will lead to every form of heresy. Since modernism is a synthesis of all heresies, we may conclude that the principle of immanence is the inner nucleus of modernism.

[93] Fabro, *God in Exile*, p. 593.

[94] Fabro, *God in Exile*, p. 59.

[95] Billot, *De Immutabilitate Traditionis contra Modernam Haeresim Evolutionismi*, p. 128.

[96] Fabro, *God in Exile*, p. 1062.

[97] Fabro observes (op. cit., pp. 1082ff) that immanentism leads to secularization.

But religious consciousness cannot imagine God's will except as being in relation to mine. Much more necessary than the "personality" of God is the real presence of God's will in mine, our actual and literal satisfaction in common: this is the ideal principle of immanentism.[98]

In theology, this will lead to a psychological situation in which people cannot imagine the will of God being at variance with their own. Here we are not talking about an intellectual analysis of what God wills based upon some manifestation, e.g. in created reality or in revelation. Rather what it means is that the whole of the religious endeavor will become subject to the person's will: what he wants makes good religion. But we are forced to recognize one other thing about human psychology as laboring under the effects of original sin and that is very often our will merely follows our appetites, feelings or emotions. Therefore, religion will descend into feeling, as we saw with Schleiermacher.[99]

Yet there is one other aspect of immanentism that must be addressed and that has to do with immanence leading to self-actualization.

For when the act of knowing is posited as the ultimate beginning, it has no other truth than that of its naked self-positing and self-effectuation.[100]

Actually, the sole foundation of the *cogito* is the *cogitare* [to think], the act of consciousness (of mind) in its own self-actualization, which cannot and ought not to be mediated by any content (object) but only by itself in the historical experience that impels it.[101]

Thus has Nietzsche carried the principle of immanentism back to its ultimate origin which is also at the definitive term: if the *cogito* is the principle of being and being is the becoming of consciousness, then the *cogito* is identified with the *volo* [I will], which is no mere abstract willing nor yet a willing of self annihilation. Rather it is a willing of the actualization of the Superman who is to take the place left vacant by God.[102]

---

[98]Ibid., p. 773.

[99]Cf. Fabro, op. cit., p. 576.

[100]Fabro, *God in Exile*, p. 1062.

[101]Ibid., p. 1071.

[102]Ibid., p. 879. See also ibid., pp. 129, 786 and 1084.

These passages from Fabro unpack a certain aspect of the Cartesian *cogito*. Once one starts in thought and cuts oneself off from reality, the only thing left is self-actualization. Historically, this develops along the line that since there is no God and one is cut off from reality, then the only thing that is left is for one to help oneself to the degree possible and this comes in the form of self actualization. Rather than God aiding the person to overcome imperfections and to strive for perfection, what is left is for one to self-actualize.

C. Theological Fallout

What one thinks about the created order affects how one understands God's interaction with that created order and how we can know anything about God. This is another way of saying that one's philosophical understanding of the created order affects, determines and limits one's understanding of theology. When modern philosophical thinking is applied to theology, serious problems result. In order to see how damaging modern philosophical thinking is to theology, we will consider various disciplines within theology.

The first area that we want to consider is dogma or doctrine. Due to the fact that the Cartesian *cogito* cuts one off from reality and since revelation is something introduced into sensible reality, one is effectively cut off from revelation (which would occur in sensible reality). This effectively means that if there is to be a revelation, it must be shifted from objective reality (what Christ and Our Lord revealed to us) to the interior, i.e. inside the self. In this respect, the self becomes the principle of judgment regarding theological matters since the only way one can have revelation is if God reveals to one interiorly. As we saw with Schleiermacher, this ends up reducing theology (what he calls piety) to feeling or emotion. Yet in order to have this emotion, there must be some kind of experience and, following the Kantian way of thinking, God affects the phenomena, i.e. my experience, and so religion gets reduced to experience. Yet since one's experience is constantly changing, what one thinks about God will change, not based on new knowledge gained from reality, but based upon self.[103] In the context of theology, this means that whatever is taught to one from outside of the person is modified, based upon

---

[103]This is why the principle of immanence is even more foundational than the Hegelian dialectic. Since our interior lives are constantly changing, my judgment about God will constantly change. Hence, the principle of immanence virtually contains the Hegelian dialectic.

the person's experience.[104] This is why tradition within the context of modern philosophy only makes sense insofar as what is passed to someone else is modified based upon that person's interior life or experience and then that is what is passed on from one person to the next. This is why Blondel makes the following observation: "For the way in which theology has in the past legitimately interpreted the facts, while nourishing itself upon them, will teach us the normal way by which the sacred deposit develops, by which it will always adapt itself to the course of history."[105] For the modernist or immanentist, the idea of an infallible, guaranteed and unchanging Deposit from the time of Christ to the end of history is unthinkable. But this is also why modern ecclesiastics cannot comprehend why traditionalists do not accept their modifications of the Deposit which they have received. Furthermore, because they think that the Deposit changes with the passing from each person to the next, they cannot imagine going back to what others consider to be an unchanging Deposit. This leaves the entire discipline of theology in a constant state of flux from one generation to the next. In the end, this is the destruction of the authentic form of sacred tradition.

The theological fallout of this is immense. Since what is passed on is modified by each person and since each person judges what he received based upon himself, this opens the door for every kind of error and heresy. Since each person has different dispositions, habits, virtues and vices and since we are affected by original sin which leaves us with a darkened intellect, disordered wills and weakness intellectually as well as morally, if we apply all that to the Deposit of Faith, it will become the synthesis of all heresies. It is the synthesis of all heresies, not because every single person is completely erroneous about all aspects of the Deposit of Faith, but because each person will adapt the Deposit based upon himself. Once self, i.e. the principle of immanence, becomes the principle of judgment of theological matters, people

---

[104]Kant held that the mind imposed categories on the person's experience and so it was necessary to strip away these categories to the degree possible in order to get as closely as possible to the noumena (the thing in itself/reality). Phenomenology, which is a method of describing one's experience in order to get as closely as possible to the noumena, develops from this. However, we are compelled to agree with Fabro that phenomenology leads to atheism arising from immanentism since it proceeds from the Cartesian and Kantian epistemologies and therefore never really gets to the thing in itself but merely terminates in an interior reflection on one's experience. A full discussion of this is not possible within the context of this chapter. However, for a discussion of this topic see Fabro, *God in Exile*, pp. 5, 940-2, 1066 and 1071f.

[105]Blondel, *The Letter on Apologetics and History of Dogma*, p. 224.

will choose[106] what fits them.

Furthermore, since the principle of immanence terminates in self-expression, it is not possible to force everybody into the same church, since not everybody has the same form of self-expression. This is why the modern form of ecumenism is such an integral part of the immanentists' mind set. Since each person has a different experience of God, it is not appropriate to force each person to convert to Catholicism. The finality of modern form of ecumenism is not conversion but mutual understanding through dialogue and encouraging others to live well according to their own experience or faith. This is done in order to enhance each person's experience of God by coming to knowledge of the other person's experience of God. This is why the following words of Fabro are so compelling:

> But they [the Magisterium] are often quasi-paralyzed, and the avalanche of progressivists is isolating and boycotting them. The progressivists in fact present themselves as the authentic interpreters, having the capacity to "carry forward" the project of *aggionamento* proposed at Vatican II. But the traditional theologians accuse them of returning to *Gnosis*, to *betrayal* of the salvific message, mediating the "surrender to the world" and the adhesion to Protestant concepts and "libertinism" in the camp of dogma and morals. The progressivists, on the other hand, ridicule the condemnations of Vatican I, of *Pascendi* of St. Pius X and of *Humani Generis* of Pius XII... and they affirm that Vatican II had made a clean break with the tradition, which liquidated definitively the principle of authority, introducing the charismatic principle; glorified, the modernists proclaim the unlimited religious liberty, ecumenism and unconditioned theological pluralism, accepting secularism and the demythologization...[107]

This quote is so poignant because of the fact that already in the 1960s and 1970s it was clear to sound Thomists, theologians and philosophers that the

---

[106] It is important to recall that once the *cogito* is accepted, what is left is choice or act of the will in self-expression.

[107] Cornelio Fabro, *L'Avvenura dell Teologia Progressista*, p. 19 [translation mine]. It is unfortunate that this text has appeared only in Italian at this time. Other than his text *God in Exile,* it is perhaps one of the best texts on Modernism written. Cf. ibid., p. 31. As a side note, the writings of Fabro have enjoyed very little circulation in the post-Vatican II academic circles. This may be due to the fact that he is one of the best Thomists and philosophers in the last century as well as to the fact that he had a keen insight into the influences of modernism in the Church. It may also be due to the fact that he came to his peak intellectually and in his writing at a time when Thomism was being rejected.

modernists viewed Vatican II as a clean break from the tradition. One difference which we are seeing today, perhaps due to their sensitivity to this criticism of cutting themselves off from the tradition, is the rewriting of history and even the tradition itself in light of the immanentist/modernist principles.

The principle of immanence causes a loss of the sense of Catholicity, not only because it rejects an unchanging Deposit, but because it rejects the universality of the Church since immanentism is rooted in the individual. Catholicism can appeal to all men because it proposes for belief an unchanging Deposit to which all men can conform themselves. This is why the members on the modern Church are so disunified, because the modernists do not conform themselves to a single object, i.e. the Deposit of Faith, and so there is no principle of unity among them.1[108]

The principal of immanentism (this can be said of modernism in general) destroys the intellectual rigor of theology. Since the principle of immanence results in the descending of intellectual reflection into one's own personal experience and towards one's own emotion or piety *a la* Schleiermacher, the discussion of theological topics degenerates into self-expression, self-will and self-emoting. Furthermore, intellectual rigor is nothing other than the intellect conforming itself with precision to the object of study. Since we are cut off from the object of study, intellectual rigor collapses. This is why some have noted that there do not seem to be any great theologians in our time.

In the area of moral theology, we find ourselves in agreement with Billot, who says that the principle of immanence or modernism destroys the foundation of morality.[109] As he points out, since they destroy the foundation of absolute truth (adequation of intellect with thing) since we cannot conform ourselves to the thing because we are cut off from it, we cannot conform ourselves to the Natural Law or the Divine Positive Law which is known through Revelation. The Natural Law requires us to study the thing[110] and Revelation is known in sensible reality and we are cut off from them based upon the principle of immanence. Since God's Will and Law are known by means of sensible reality, the principle of immanence sets up a morality

---

[108]This will also become important in the discussion of charity.

[109]Billot, *De Immutabilitate Traditionis contra Modernam Haeresim Evolutionismi*, p. 128ff.

[110]Morality gets separated from metaphysics since one cannot know reality. Cf. Ibid., p. 128f.

independent of God.[111] Morality becomes what the individual chooses it to be, which is just another way of saying in the area of morality, cafeteria Catholicism is acceptable. Eventually this leads the immanentists to assert that objective value, i.e. what is objectively good (or we may even say evil), is unknowable.[112]

This is why someone who is an immanentist who has an "experience" of God is said to be a religious person, even if they do not adhere to the moral code of Catholicism. Religion is allowed without any duties or transcendent sanctions,[113] i.e. religion and discussions of religion are allowed in the public forum as long as there are no denials in relation to specific forms of behavior. It is forbidden to tell someone that a specific form of behavior is immoral. On the other hand, since one's experience of God reveals to the person God Himself, if one has a good experience of some kind of behavior which he engages in, then that becomes the Will of God. We get a certain pleasure out of doing our own will. Therefore, whatever one does or wants is the Will of God. God's Will is "my" will, which is a basic way of saying that whatever I will is the same as the Will of God. This means that all morality becomes a matter of what one chooses it to be.

But since God ultimately *is* known by means of reality and people have a general understanding that God forbids some things and allows others, with some immanentists, God is denied in order to guarantee man's freedom.[114] This is based upon the principle that God would forbid the person to do something and so he must deny God in order to continue in his freedom. This is the thinking and the psychology behind practical atheism which is often the result of the principle of immanence.

On the pastoral level, immanentism destroys common sense. Since common sense is the general ability to grasp what a thing is, this can only be done by putting oneself in contact with reality. Since the principle of immanence cuts oneself off from reality (i.e. what the priest does pastorally is based upon the immanentist principle, i.e. himself), he does not base his pastoral activity on what is objective. Since the principle of immanentism often degenerates into the person simply following his appetites or emotions, pastoral activity descends into the emotional.

---

[111]Billot, *De Immutabilitate Traditionis contra Modernam Haeresim Evolutionismi*, p. 136.

[112]Ibid., p. 145.

[113]Fabro, *God in Exile*, p. 263. Fabro observes that the sanctions will be exclusively immanent ones.

[114]Ibid., p. 26.

Since the emotions find discipline, mortification and self-denial disagreeable, the principle of immanence drastically affects discipline. In the consideration of objective reality and looking at the Deposit of Faith in which God reveals to men the effects of original and actual sin, we come to realize man's dire need of mortification, fasting, self-denial, etc. But adhering to the principle of immanence causes a certain effeminacy or weakness, since immanentists will not want to do anything disagreeable or arduous.[115] As a result, the traditional discipline of fasting and of penance is rejected because it is viewed as too difficult, too harsh or not understanding of modern man. Of course, we all recognize that modern man is unruly and out of control and, if any generation needs more discipline, it is this one.

Furthermore, as Fabro noted above, the principle of authority gives way to a charismatic principle. People who adhere to the principle of immanence seek out not an authority figure who will tell them what to do and what not to do, but someone who will "tickle their ears"[116] or make them feel good. As a result, people will begin parish shopping by going from parish to parish to find the priest who suits their disposition. The traditional discipline, in which people had to attend Mass within their home parish unless there was a sufficient reason, is rejected.

Another phenomenon which we see in relationship to the reign of the principle of immanence in the last 50 to 60 years has to do with the term "pastoral theology". In the past, the term "pastoral theology" referred to the administration of the sacraments as well as having a connection to spiritual theology in which one knew the means to aid others in growing in holiness and the saving of their souls. There has been a subtle shift, grasped by observing titles of old manuals of pastoral theology[117] and then also observing the newer manuals of pastoral theology.[118]

Yet what is even more subtle is the intellectual foundation for the shift. The principle of immanence cuts us off from reality and so instead of conforming ourselves to God which is what the old pastoral theology manuals

---

[115]Psychologists observe that homosexuals are solipsistic and as long as the principle of immanence reigns among the some of the members in the Church, they will never address the problem of homosexuality. See Gerard J.M. van den Aardweg, *Battle for Normality: A Guide for (Self-)Therapy for Homosexuality*, passim.

[116]2 Tim. 4:3: "For there shall be a time, and they will not endure sound doctrine; but, according to their own desires, they will heap to themselves teachers, having itching ears."

[117]For example, see Davis, *Moral and Pastoral Theology*.

[118]The titles are numerous but one can observe the shift occuring in the 1940s and 1950s.

understood, we concern ourselves with our experiences. This is simply another way of stating that pastoral theology has descended into psychology. Since experience is something which occurs within the psychological faculties of man and now pastoral theology is about psychology, we want to know how the psychological faculties can be manipulated to maximize the experience people have. This will have a direct impact on the understanding of the liturgy.

Closely connected to this topic is how spiritual theology has been affected by the principle of immanence. If discipline, i.e. mortification, is no longer accepted as an integral part of one's spiritual life, then ascetics is changed based upon the self. This leads ultimately to the rejection of suffering and penance and a pursuit of those things which give us a good experience. This is defined by the spiritual writers as spiritual gluttony and it is one of the reasons why many forms of modern spirituality are simply immersed in spiritual gluttony, such as the charismatic renewal and the like.

Yet without a life of penance and mortification one is bound to spiritual tepidity or lukewarmness:

> As soon as a person begins to live in tepidity, he seeks himself in everything, he continually looks for what will give pleasure, he surpasses the sensual in seeking his own comforts, and his self-love, not being weakened by being bestowed on exterior objects, concentrates itself on himself and applies itself entirely to thinking out a nice comfortable life. It is easy to see that a soul in this state, insensible to the most terrible truths of salvation, and still more insensible to the most striking proofs of the love which Jesus Christ has for us, is too far from the dispositions necessary for the devotion to the Sacred Heart of Jesus Christ to draw any fruit from it.[119]

In one sense, tepidity is the cause of self-love or the principle of immanence insofar as tepidity moves one to want to conform spiritual things to himself so that they are not difficult. But in another sense self-love or the principle of immanence is the cause of tepidity. Since we have been affected by the disorders of original and actual sin, if we conform our spiritual lives to ourselves, then we will conform ourselves to the weakness and the malice that flows from the effects of sin. This is why anybody who is overly self-conscious is bound to spiritual tepidity.

It is here that we must regrettably reflect upon the statement made by Maritain in his book on integral humanism:

---

[119] Croiset, *Devotion to the Sacred Heart of Jesus: How to Practice the Sacred Heart Devotion*, p. 114.

Let us say that these primarily theological knowledges sufficed for the Middle Ages. They enveloped a very powerful psychology, but not in the modern sense of the word: for it was from the point of view of God that all things were regarded then. The natural mysteries of man were not scrutinized for themselves by a scientific and experimental knowledge. In short, the Middle Ages were just the opposite of a reflex age: a sort of fear or metaphysical modesty, and also a predominant concern to see things and to contemplate being, and to take the measures of the world, keep the gaze of medieval man turned away from himself.[120]

Maritain goes on to assert that an integral humanism requires man to look upon himself. This criticism of the medieval age is rooted in a fundamental misunderstanding of the spiritual life. The metaphysical modesty of the Middle Ages was based upon a realization that God is the center of the universe and that towards which all things are ordered, even man. That meant that in order to study created things, one always had to view them in light of God to have the fullest understanding of those created things. For this reason, even man, when reflecting upon his own interior life, always did it *sub specie Dei aut sub ratione Dei* [under the aspect of God or the perspective of God]. So the perspective of the medieval age was based on an authentic metaphysical understanding. However, Maritain's criticism of this metaphysical modesty, while not necessarily proceeding from an immanentist principle, fuels the immanentist mind set.

It is precisely here that we must discuss one of the major fallouts of immanentism. In an article this author made the following observation:

> Charity does not merely consist in love of God and love of neighbor, but in the love of God and the love of neighbor *for the sake of God* (*propter Deum*). One's neighbor is not loved for his own sake but for the sake of God and God constitutes the formality, i.e. the perspective taken on one's neighbor. Hence, the virtue of charity is ultimately about God, even when one loves one's neighbor for the sake of God. ...We must not forget that God is goodness itself and so it is proper for God to love Himself. We are not goodness itself, but are only good by virtue of the fact that we participate in some way in God's goodness. Therefore, our love should not rest on ourselves but upon God, Who is the source of our own goodness. For God, to love everything for His own sake is right order; for us to love other things only insofar as we love ourselves is disordered, because we are not goodness itself;

---

[120]Maritain, *Integral Humanism: Temporal and Spiritual Problems of a New Christendom*, p. 10.

God is.[121]

The order as established by the principle of immanence causes one to order all things to self and is diametrically opposed to the order established by charity. As a result, within the Church the principle of immanence has destroyed charity in all aspects and all levels.[122] While God is continually sanctifying the members of the Church[123] and therefore while there is some charity, it is very rare except among those who are ardently adhering to the traditional schools of spirituality.

Maritain's statement, if followed, nullifies advance in the spiritual life, because when one looks at oneself for the sake of oneself and not under the aspect of God, the terminus or finality of that action is self and not God. Since the spiritual life is about advancing toward perfect union with God, it requires one to put oneself aside and look to God alone:

> It [the soul in advancing spiritually] has become too a great extent oblivious of self and its own concerns, and begins to be more occupied with the interests of God Whom it loves. It is not that it is obliged to make efforts to leave self out of count or to forget self; but preoccupied as it is, about God, it ceases without observing it, to think about self at all. The absence of self-consciousness, the characteristic of that childlike simplicity that Our Lord demands as a condition of entrance into intimacy with Him, develops with the growth of charity; this want of self-consciousness precludes to a great extent the necessity of that active and positive oppression of self which constituted the chief work of the soul in the two previous stages. The acquisition of simplicity does away with the necessity of self repression – for self is no longer assertive. According as this self-

---

[121] *The Latin Mass* (Summer 2006).

[122] Our Lord predicted that in the end times, "because iniquity hath abounded, the charity of many shall grow cold" (Matthew 24:12).

[123] This is part of the Mark of the Church of Holiness. Immanentism causes a loss of faith in or adherence to the Marks of the Church. It destroys Catholicity by rooting everything in the individual and therefore detracts from the universality of the Church. It destroys faith in or adherence to the Mark of Unicity, again by rooting everything in the individual rather than some external objective criteria. It destroys faith in or adherence to Apostolicity, as we see among some traditionalists who reject the perpetual succession of the papacy. Finally, it destroys faith in or adherence to the Mark of Holiness insofar as it rejects the notion that Christ established a Church to which they must belong in order to be sanctified and saved and whose moral code they must follow.

consciousness disappears there is developed a consciousness of another kind – namely, a growing realization of the great truth that one is not a mere isolated individual but forms part of the great mystical organism in the life of which the individual shares the Catholic sense is gradually replacing the individual sense.[124]

As one advances in the spiritual life, his mind set becomes more Catholic in the universal sense. But even more foundational, he becomes more focused on God and turns from self.

The principle of immanence conjoined with self-love deceives people into thinking their spiritual life is better than it is. This is one of the reasons why today people think they are more spiritually advanced than people in the past. Self-love and the principle of immanence destroy the motivation to take on the sorrow of mortification and the inclination from God by grace to mortification and purification and advancement in holiness are at variance with the principle of immanence. Those who labor under the mentality of immanentism often delude themselves into thinking that God does not demand great things of them or great sanctity and so they neglect their spiritual life. On the other hand, they often think they will have a very high place in heaven without doing anything to merit it. If they do advance spiritually, they want to be filled with consolations and sweetness, again because they are spiritual gluttons. They judge themselves to have very few defects. This is based upon the fact that we get a certain pleasure from thinking about self and so we think we are better than we are.

In addition to this disorder of the principle of immanence and its relationship to the order of charity, we also see that instead of peace in the soul which arises from charity, the interior life as well as common life deteriorate. The immanentist is often miserable interiorly because his desires are never satisfied by his life or by others. His emotional life is virtually uncontrollable; this is based upon the fact that his emotional life does not follow the order of reason, which is conformed to the order of charity which sees God as the sole object of affection. Once God becomes the sole object of affection, the emotional life becomes quiet and interior peace takes over.

D. Spiritual Fallout

The spiritual writers tell us that there are three things that are the source of temptation: the world, the flesh and the devil. The pivotal area of temptation is the flesh because the world and the devil act upon the flesh. Immanentists make themselves the principle of judgment and not some

---

[124]Leen, *Progress through Mental Prayer*, p. 97f.

74

external reality, such as God. As a result, they do not conform themselves to God or exterior things. This means that the life of temptation is far more difficult for them because they will tend to follow whatever the world or the devil impress upon them, i.e., what the devil and the world cause in their experience, so long as it feels good.

Another consequence of immanentism is the extreme difficulty one has advancing in the life of prayer. There are nine levels of prayer and most people never get beyond the first two levels. This is because prayer is difficult and is therefore disagreeable to experience in our passions except for those who have advanced to a certain degree. Immanentists simply will not pray because it is a negative experience.

Immanentists also suffer from pride, thinking themselves better than they are because they are intoxicated with a good feeling that comes from thinking about themselves and basing their actions upon themselves. Immanentists generally like people who like them, yet they hate people who are selfish. The Saints, on the other hand, were often the exact opposite: they preferred the people who hated them.

Finally, we will finish a reflection on the spiritual life by considering the following quote from Garrigou-Lagrange:

> Self-will thus defined is the source of every sin. For this reason St. Bernard says: "take away self-will, and there will no longer be any hell." Self-will is particularly dangerous because it can corrupt everything. Even what is best in man becomes evil when self-will enters in, for it takes itself as its end instead of subordinating itself to God. If the Lord sees that it [self-will] inspires a fast, a penance, a sacrifice, he rejects them as pharisaical works accomplished through pride in order to make oneself- esteemed. Without going that far, we must admit that we cling greatly to our own will. Occasionally we hold to our way of doing good more than to the good itself; we wish it to be done, but by ourselves and in our way. When this egoism becomes collective, it may be called *esprit de corps*, a corruption of family spirit; it is the source of a great many unpleasantnesses, partialities, defamations. Sometimes a certain group wishes to promote a good work, or it hinders one from being developed. It is like wishing to smother a child who seems to be one too many, when as a matter of fact it may become the honor of the family. Evidently such a course of action can only displease the Lord.[125]

---

[125] Garrigou-Lagrange, *Three Stages of the Interior Life*, vol. 2, p. 151.

What can be said of the spiritual life can *mutatis mutandi* be applied to the liturgy.

This sort of damage has been done by all the stunted forms of religious practice in every environment of human history, both outside and (unfortunately!) Sometimes inside of Christianity, as often as they twist or bend religion to personal whims.[126] Immanentism leads to self actualization and self-expression, and the liturgy becomes the place of self-expression or actualization. In effect, the liturgy becomes subject to personal whims of those who perform it. This is why options have become so integral and important to modern liturgy, since they allow the liturgy to be tailored to the person's own disposition.

According to Feuerbach, religion is about man[127] since religion is merely anthropology. The liturgy constitutes the principal form of religious action and the Holy Sacrifice of the Mass above all. Consequently, the liturgy becomes focused on man. This is why the readings are now in the vernacular; why there are, at times more people in the sanctuary than in the nave of the church; and of course, it almost goes without mentioning, why the altar orientation is towards man. Moreover, since pastoral theology has degenerated into psychology, the liturgy is now viewed through the psychological lens. This is why the liturgy in many places now seeks to facilitate people's experience and emotions, i.e. to make them feel good. Yet in order to know what makes people feel good, you have to apply psychology and, since modern psychology rules the day, the liturgy becomes subject to modern psychological techniques. For example, no liturgical action is done which might hurt women's feelings. As a result, women are allowed into virtually every aspect of the liturgy, save the priesthood alone. Those who object are often labeled as having psychological problems, which is a way of merely dismissing them without really dealing with their objections.

Yet, the liturgy is not entirely without governance from the Church, even though at times it might appear to be so. This is stated with the recognition that the old Rite of Mass is controlled and heavily regulated by most of the bishops. Catholicism is the religion which is diametrically opposed to immanentism, and since immanentism is what rules the day in the minds of many ecclesiastics, the governing principle in the liturgy and even the common life within the Church is: "anything but Catholicism." Those who are in control determine what is considered acceptable in the liturgy, which on one level is the way it should be. On another level, given the aforementioned principle, it means that what is considered acceptable in the liturgy is only that which those in control consider acceptable in the liturgy. Given the

---

[126]Fabro, *God in Exile*, p. 52.

[127]Cf. Fabro, *God in Exile*, p. 263.

historical context, it means that what is acceptable in the liturgy is only that which appeals to the mindset of those whose formative period in their own lives terminated just prior to or during the 1960s. This is why the liturgical development within the Church is in a "time warp", to use a modern phrase. Because the liturgy was changed in the 1960s,[128] those who control the liturgy came to intellectual fruition just prior to or during the 1960s. As a result we now have a liturgy which is stuck in the 1960s: the music is from the 1960s; the liturgical principles and trajectory are from the 1960s (i.e. headed towards ever greater familiarity between members of the congregation and the priest, lacking propriety and modesty, hallmarked the 1960s); the vestments are from the 1960s; the church architecture is from the 1960s. Once the liturgy becomes subject to historical conditions and fails to transcend them in its governing principles, the liturgy will be stuck in the age in which it was formed.

One of the beauties of the old Rite of Mass is that it's liturgical principles and actions transcend any particular time or moment in history. Even if they come from a particular time period, they nevertheless transcend that time in history. This actually brings us to another aspect of the immanentist/Hegelian understanding of the liturgy. One of the common errors within the church today is the notion that, if one can discover the historical moment of the liturgical change, one necessarily understands the nature of the content of the liturgical change.[129] This is false. The historical moment can tell us something about a particular liturgical change but very often the reason God introduces liturgical change is not tied to that specific moment but to the whole of time, i.e. God moves the church to introduce that liturgical change which is rooted in a transcendent meaning. As long as Immanentism rules within the historical intellectual community, this Hegelian understanding will prevail.

Moreover, there is something even graver afoot in the current liturgical situation. Since liturgy equals self-expression and self validation, what is left is a kind of Spinozan or Hegelian understanding of the liturgy. Spinoza and Hegel posited that there was only one substance, i.e. God, and we are all part of this one substance. For Spinoza, this one substance was static and unchanging but for Hegel it was dynamic and constantly changing. Yet the differences between Spinoza and Hegel do not change the fact that the

---

[128]Here we are putting aside the fact that there were serious and multitudinous changes made even to the old ritual prior to the 1960s.

[129]Of course, the content of that change being subject to the principle of immanence requires that the past liturgical actions found in missals and other liturgical books are subject to modern historical categories. This follows from the fact that since the interpreter must interpret things based upon the judgment of self, he will judge based upon his own historical experience in context.

transcendent, i.e. the consideration of God, is reduced to the immanent. If we are part of God, what we want to know about God, we simply do by reflecting upon ourselves. Psychologically, man has a natural inclination to recognize that he is in fact not God. Once the religion is reduced to an immanentist's consideration, which embodies this Hegelian and Spinozan understanding, and the psychological inclination of man is figured into the mix, the final product is a religion without God. This is said more with the practical than a theoretical view. Here the practical atheism of immanentism rears its ugly head. Even if there is a lot of talk about God, God is *practically* ignored. Applying this reasoning to the liturgy, immanentism begets a liturgy without God. Even if God is mentioned and appealed to throughout the liturgy, He is, again, *practically* ignored. Again, altar orientation manifests this very thinking, along with Communion in the hand (which ignores the gravity of handling God), replacing the tabernacle with the "preside's" chair, and similar actions.

Once God is out of the picture and the liturgy becomes about man, then focus is given to the role of the laity. Since religion is, for the Immanentist, about self-expression, self actualization and self validation, the liturgy must accommodate the laity's self-expression, self actualization and self validation. Once the liturgical movement in the 1910s and 1920s was taken over by the Immanentists/modernists[130] there was the introduction of the dialogue Mass.[131] The dialogue mass made it possible for the people to express themselves and to be part of the liturgy.[132] Consideration is not given to other fundamental principles governing the liturgy but only to people's self-expression. Other magnificent parts of the liturgy are leveled, such as the hierarchical representation of the Church by the priest being answered by the servers who represent the laity; the beauty and symmetry of the priests being answered by the servers; the silence of the laity as an expression of the modesty and humility in the presence of the heavenly court, which is designated by the Communion rail and the presence of the tabernacle which

---

[130]For discussion on how the liturgical movement shifted from being something acceptable to something disordered, see Didier Bonneterre, *The Liturigcal Movment: Guéranger to Beauduin to Bugini.*

[131]If one understands the historical genesis of the dialogue Mass, one realizes that the dialogue Mass has the same pedigree as "altar girls". It was a liturgical abuse which was originally forbidden by Rome, it became widespread, it was later approved and then finally promoted by the Roman authorities.

[132]Bonneterre, *The Liturigcal Movment: Guéranger to Beauduin to Bugini*, p. 41.

contains God.[133]

We could go on showing how the principle of immanence has been applied in virtually every area of theology. However that would constitute something far more extensive than a chapter in a book.

E. Solutions to the Problem of Immanence

Since the very problem of immanentism is rooted in the *cogito* (i.e. making self the principle of judgment of all things), the solution consists in its contrary. By this we mean that instead of making self the principle of judgment, objective reality must be our principal of judgment. Cornelio Fabro observed:

> Anyone adopting the Parmenidean stand that being is the foundation of thought is thereby positively setting out on a road that will eventually lead to the Absolute, provided he does not get bogged down under way or take a wrong turn as a result of some methodological blunder.[134]

What Fabro is essentially saying is that as long as we make reality the foundation of our knowledge we can eventually attain to knowledge of God, either by the natural light of reason or by Revelation. Therefore the first principle which must be adopted is the Parmenidean principle which states that being or reality is the foundation for thought and the truth. This means, at the most fundamental level, that our obligation intellectually is to conform ourselves to reality, and in the context of the Catholic Church this means the reality of what the Church has "always, everywhere and in all cases taught". This Vincentian Canon (always, everywhere and in all cases) only has significance when we have an absolute adherence to reality, i.e. theologically it only has significance when it is joined to the Parmenidean principle. This must be recognized and adhered to regardless of the personal cost. Then and only then can we be true traditional Catholics and then and only then can the Church overcome its immanentist problems.

On a practical level, the Church has encouraged absolute adherence to reality by virtue of the fact that it has encouraged a system of theological

---

[133] Once the people are seen as in integral part of the Mass and are allowed to express themselves in the liturgy, the Communion rail must be brought down since the people are now to be taken into the sacred action which is proper to the sanctuary and therefore should be included in the sanctuary. This is why the roles of the laity affect church architecture.

[134] Fabro, *God in exile*, p. 26.

and philosophical thought which embodies it, viz. Thomism. In papal and other ecclesiastical documents, Thomism has very frequently been promoted.[135] In fact, we may say that Thomism is the solution to modernism based on the fact that the starting point of the Cartesian *cogito* and Thomistic theology and philosophy are diametrically opposed. The Cartesian *cogito* begins in self; Thomistic theology and philosophy begin in reality.

We must avoid giving notional assent to the tradition and give real assent to the tradition, its ascetical and spiritual practices and its requirements in the moral sphere. In other words, we have to prevent ourselves from merely talking like traditionalists but must always act like them. This is going to cause a lot of pain, especially to modern man who is accustomed to an easy and comfortable life.

The Magisterium must begin policing the doctrinal integrity of the members of the Church, but this doctrinal integrity can only be judged in light of the tradition, which requires it to readopt the teachings of the Church from prior to the second Vatican Council. Policing must be done in a fatherly manner in which those in charge of the Church seek the salvation of the souls of those under their pastoral care, much like a father seeks the spiritual welfare of his children. This requires correcting, admonishing, and not tolerating error. In effect, the Magisterium must recoup its moral authority in relation to the judgment of doctrinal matters. This itself is directly contrary to the principle of immanence, which leaves the judgment of doctrinal matters to self.

Sincere humility is absolutely required. Humility is a virtue by which we do not judge ourselves greater than we are and we are willing to live in accordance with the truth. We as traditionalists must admit our defects humbly and come to knowledge, not only of the tradition, but of ourselves. We must recognize that we are not the center of the Church nor the center of the universe but that Christ is. It is Christ who will save the Church, not us. We must admit that we are part of the problem in the world because of our sin and our lack of living perfectly according to the tradition. And we must stop counting ourselves as the sole solution. To state that we are the solution is to be Immanentists. Rather we must state that God and his teaching are the solution, which is manifest in nothing other than the tradition.

On the side of those running the Church, there has to be humility and detachment in relationship to the last 40 years. There must be an admission that the current state of the Church does not adhere to the precepts of

---

[135] See, among others, Leo XIII, *Aeterni Patris*; CIC/17, can. 589, §1; CIC/83, can. 252, §3; Pius V's bull *Mirabilis* which is the declaration of St. Thomas as a doctor of the Church; the evident use of St. Thomas' writings at the Council of Trent; Pius X's *Pascendi*, para 45. The phrase *Ite ad Thomam* (Go to Thomas) is another way of saying: *Ite ad Traditionem* (Go to the Tradition).

Catholicism and authentic Christian life. Much like alcoholics, many who govern the Church cannot bring themselves to admit that something is wrong. This itself is a manifestation of immanentism insofar as they deny reality in order to maintain what is pleasing to self. But like alcoholics, the members of the Church cannot be reformed and its discipline will not be corrected until there is an admission of the problem. This requires humility, and authentic spirit of self mortification and self-denial. At root this means that there must be a twofold conversion among the members of the church: (1) there must be an intellectual submission to reality, both as to what is revealed and to the actual situation in the Church and (2) there must be a moral conversion in which the self gratification, seeking of spiritual consolations, etc., of immanentism is put aside and spiritually we become selfless and seek God alone.

These prior two conversions, the one intellectual, the other moral, make it possible for charity te reign once again. Since one cannot have charity without right faith, then without this twofold conversion (the one in assuring faith, the other removing impediments to the operations of charity), we will never have charity in the Church. On the other hand, charity is a supernatural virtue, which means that as we act more according to charity, charity will begin to rise in our souls. Charity will direct this towards the tradition, for it is through the tradition that the desires of charity to know more about God find their fulfillment.

Chapter 4: Modern Man's Superiority Complex
Is Modern Man Superior to His Predecessors?

Christopher Dawson, in his well known work, *Progress and Religion* encapsulates the modern notion that newer is always better in the following words: "The Doctrine of Progress in the full sense must involve the belief that every day and in every way the world grows better and better."[136] Yet, not only is the world getting better, but man himself is getting better. There is a not so subtle superiority complex in modern man when he considers himself in relation to his predecessors. After all, modern man has computers, DVDs, hi-tech automobiles, jet aircraft and the achievement of putting men on the moon, among other things. There is a certain smugness in the average modern man who thinks to himself how much better he is than those earlier in history who knew nothing of digital movies, atomical physics and evolution.

This superiority complex has a serious side to it. The idea that modern man is somehow better is a psychological motive force behind embracing the principle of immanence, which makes the individual or self the principle of judgment of all things. As a result, some modern intellectuals have rejected realistic metaphysics and philosophy. After all, if modern man is as superior as we say, he ought to think of himself and not the dry arguments of his unknowing, and perhaps even less intelligent, predecessors.

For these reasons, this chapter will focus on the following claims. The first is that modern man is superior to his ancestors in the order of knowledge. Second, that modern man is superior to his predecessors in the moral order. Third, modern man is superior to his predecessors in the sociological/political order. Lastly, because of modern man's superiority together with the intellectual foundation for that superiority, modern man is not able to accept the scholastic arguments in areas of philosophy and natural theology. While these claims will be considered, it must be conceded that not all men today consider modern man as superior. However, those more "up-to-date" individuals look upon the objectors as naive, unintelligent or ignorant.

A. The Intellectual Genesis of the Complex

We must ask ourselves how we got to a point in history where many have contracted the idea, at least vaguely in the day to day living of their lives, that newer is always better. Philosophically, this idea gets off theground with G.W.F. Hegel. The well-known Hegelian dialectic consists in three stages. The first is what came to be known as the thesis, in which a particular state of

---

[136]Dawson, *Progress and Religion*, p. 4.

affairs was in place. Then, the negation of that state of affairs by the antithesis comes to pass and finally the resolution of the thesis into the antitheses occurs by means of a synthesis. Process or change in history and in things according to the Hegelian mind was inevitable. In his text *Introduction to the Philosophy of History*, Hegel lays out the ramification of his theory of this dynamic principle of development. He says: "Abstractly considered, historical change has long been understood in general as involving a progress to something better, something more perfect."[137] In Hegel's mind, the world is in a constant state of flux but this flux is not directionless. What Hegel calls the "Spirit" moves the dialectic in history toward a more perfect state.

But Hegel does not stop there regarding the various aspects of this change. He observes:

> In this regard, doubt has been raised as to whether human beings have become better at all through the progress of history and civilization, whether their morality has improved: i.e., insofar as morality is seen to be based only on subjective intention and insight, on whatever the acting individual sees as right or wrong, good or evil – not on a principle concerning what is right and good, bad and evil in and for itself (or on the basis of a religion regarded as being true). We can spare ourselves the trouble of illustrating the bare formalism and error of such a view, and of establishing the true principles of morality (or rather, of ethics) against this false morality. For world history moves on a higher level than that on which morality properly exists. (We shall take morality to refer to private sentiment, the conscience of individuals, their own personal wills and modes of action. These have their own independent value, responsibility, reward or punishment.)[138]

One can hear Nietzsche in the background with his *ubermensch* or superman who is beyond good and evil. Yet, the thing of importance for our discussion is the inversion of morality. Morality is no longer concerned with establishing objective unchanging principles since everything is changing. Rather, the morally upright person is the one who follows his own private sentiment. In these passages we begin to see the intellectual foundation for modern man's superiority complex. Modern man is proud, in the sense of estimating himself to be better than prior generations, because he takes himself and his private sentiment as the principle of judgment of what is right and wrong. Prior generations did not have this insight. The good person is not the one who

---

[137] Hegel, *Introduction to the Philosophy of History*, p. 57.

[138] Ibid., p. 70.

conforms himself to an objective moral standard based upon the nature of man and the natural law, but the person who follows private sentiment.

If change is inevitable, what of virtue which makes a man more constant? Hegel says:

> Habit (like the watch wound up and going by itself) is what brings natural death. Habit is activity without opposition: only formal duration is left to it, in which the fullness and depth of one's purpose no longer needs to be given voice – one leads an external sensory existence, so to speak, no longer immersed in the object. In this way, individuals as well as peoples die a natural death. And although a people may go on existing, it is an existence without life or interest, without need of its institutions because the need has been satisfied - a political nullity and boredom. For a truly universal interest to arise, the Spirit of a people must come to the point of wanting something new. But where could this new thing or purpose come from? It would be as if the people had a higher, more universal ideal of itself, going beyond its present principle – but in this there would be a new and more determinate principle, a new Spirit.[139]

If habit leads to natural death, then so does virtue, since virtue is a good habit. For Hegel, those stuck in habits are no longer immersed in the object. By this it would seem that Hegel is saying that one cannot live, one cannot experience the object (i.e. one dies), if one always relates to something in the same way all of the time. But since change is for the better, to be stuck in habits is to be outmoded, or in modern parlance, to be passe. Those who change with the times are simply better or, we may say, more enlightened people who experience life more.

What assurance does Hegel give to those who do not share his optimistic view of modern man or the future? He says:

> This restless succession of individuals and peoples that are here for a time and then disappear suggests one general thought, one category above all, that of universally prevalent *change*. And what leads us to apprehend this change in its negative aspect is the sight of the ruins of some vanished splendor.[140]

Hegel goes on to say that this death or change of things is the emergence of new life. In other words, just wait and things will get better. So those who

---

[139] Ibid., p. 78.

[140] Ibid., p. 76.

think things are bad must simply be patient, let the changes in modern life take hold, and then things will be better.

At roughly the same time but a bit before Hegel, lived a man named Marie Jean Antoine Caritat, also known as the Marquis de Condorcet or Condorcet for short. In a text entitled *The Future Progress of the Human Mind*,[141] Condorcet goes a little further than Hegel in applying this progress to man by saying that man is perfectible. Now even the Christian would admit that man is perfectible but not without God's grace and help. However, materialism was (and is) dominating the natural sciences and so, if man is going to be perfected, he must be perfected by natural causes.[142] For Condorcet, the progress in relation to man was also more than Hegel had envisioned: "in the end, the human species must become better, either by new discoveries in the sciences and the arts, and by a necessary consequence, in the means of particular well being and common prosperity, or by progress in the principles of conduct and in the moral experience"[143] and "..the truths whose discovery has cost the most effort, which at first could be grasped only by men capable of profound thought, are soon developed and proved by methods no longer beyond the reach of ordinary intelligence."[144] Condorcet thought that man would be perfectible because he would make new discoveries which would make it possible for him to be perfected, not just morally, but intellectually as well. What is more, the person of average intelligence would eventually learn those things known only to those capable of profound thought. The modern man appears to believe that since he is aware of modern scientific theories, he is somehow more knowledgeable than his predecessors.

Condorcet goes on to note the sociological changes that would occur

---

[141] In French it is known as *Esquisse d'un tableau historique des progrès de l'esprit humain.*

[142] Later with Darwin, et al., the perfectibility of man would be rooted in material and natural efficient causes only.

[143] Condorcet, *Esquisse d'un tableau historique des progrès de l'esprit humain; suivi de Réflexions sur l'esclavage des ègres*, 1 vol. in-8E, pp. v-viii, dixième époque: "Enfin, l'espèce humaine doit-elle s'améliorer, soit par de nouvelles découvertes dans les sciences et dans les arts, et par une conséquence nécessaire, dans les moyens de bien-être particulier et de prospérité commune; soit par des progrès dans les principes de conduite et dans la morale pratique."

[144] Ibid.: "les vérités dont la découverte a coûté le plus d'efforts, qui d'abord n'ont pu être entendues que par des hommes capables de méditations profondes, sont bientôt après développées et prouvées par des méthodes qui ne sont plus au-dessus d'une intelligence commune."

from these discoveries and from man's process of being perfected:

> Among the progress of the human mind that is most important for human happiness, we must count the entire destruction of the prejudices that have established inequality between the sexes, harmful even to the sex it favors. One would look in vain for reasons to justify it,by differences in physical constitution, by those one might try to discover in the strength of their intelligence, moral sensibility. This inequality has no other source but the abuse of power, and men have tried in vain to excuse it by sophisms.[145]

One of the signs of the civilization that has reached a certain level of advancement, i.e. once man himself has advanced to a certain stage, inequality among the sexes will be wiped out. Those in the modern context would agree that we are more advanced than our predecessors because we recognize the radical equality of men and women.[146]

Before we pass to Auguste Comte, there is a French individual in this area of discussion that is worthy of note. Anne-Robert Jacques Turgot, in his second discourse in the work entitled *Successive Progresses of the Human Spirit,*[147] argued that human societies pass through cycles of barbarism and civilization. Barbarism is accompanied by superstition whereas civilization is accompanied by the fruits of reason. Human restlessness, a taste for liberty and a critical spirit elevate societies into civilization, but then these drives become institutionalized and conservative and eventually the very impediments of further progress. Reason gives way to superstition, and society falls back into barbarism. The point here, at least for our modern man, is that if he is to be civilized, he must be a liberal. Conservatism is associated with barbarism, superstition and lack of progress.

While prior authors had argued that man would continue to progress

---

[145]Ibid.: Parmi les progrès de l'esprit humain les plus importants pour le bonheur général, nous devons compter l'entière destruction des préjugés, qui ont établi entre les deux sexes une inégalité de droits funeste à celui même qu'elle favorise. On chercherait en vain des motifs de la justifier par les différences de leur organisation physique, par celle qu'on voudrait trouver dans la force de leur intelligence, dans leur sensibilité morale. Cette inégalité n'a eu d'autre origine que l'abus de la force, et c'est vainement qu'on a essayé depuis de l'excuser par des sophismes.

[146]One is left with the ironic fact that Condorcet committed suicide when he was arrested during the French revolution (See Fredrick Copleston, *A History of Philosophy*, vol. IX, p. 19). Apparently things were not getting better, at least for him.

[147]It appeared in French in 1750 under the title of *Progrès successifs de l'ésprit humain.*

intellectually, it is Comte who gives a more explicit direction to that development. He says:

> This law consists in the fact that each of our principal conceptions, each branch of our knowledge, passes in succession through three different theoretical states; the theological or fictitious state, the metaphysical or abstract state, and the scientific or positive state. In other words, the human mind – by its very nature – makes use successively in each of its researches of three methods of philosophizing, whose characters are essentially different and even radically opposed to each other.[148]

Comte gives a kind of intellectual finalization to the Cartesian desire for certitude in knowledge.[149] While Descartes sought to give philosophy the same certitude as the empirical sciences, Comte simply dismisses the theological and metaphysical sciences all together. Only empirical sciences provide certitude and reflect mature thought. Comte continues:

> Finally, in the positive state, the human mind, recognizing the impossibility of obtaining absolute truth, gives up the search after the origin and hidden causes of phenomena. It endeavours now only to discover, by a well-combined use of reasoning and observation, the actual laws of phenomena – that is to say, their invariable relations of succession and likeness.

In relation to the discussion of the modern man, he will be scientific and will not allow theological and metaphysical (or even philosophical) opinions to enter into his discussion of truth. Our generalized modern man is thoroughly committed to the empirical sciences as the only real means of improving the human condition and of providing clear answers to life's questions. On the societal level, empirical sciences would be applied to everything, including psychology and sociology.

Given the aforesaid, even though it is not by any means a complete account of the philosophical genesis of the modern superiority complex, we can see why Maurice Blondel makes the following observation:

> If the outworn forms of a supposedly philosophical apologetic no longer make any impression on the mind of an unbeliever, and if the general movement of modern thought turns more and more against

---

[148]Comte, *Introduction to Positive Philosophy*, p. 1.

[149]See Descartes, *Discourse of Method*, passim.

it, this is not, as we have seen, without good reason.[150]

Modern man cannot accept the old philosophical arguments in favor of a natural knowledge of God or the faith. These words sound similar to Schleiermacher's rejection of metaphysics as part of religion.[151] The reason is that the arguments do not appeal either to an immanentist whose principle of judgment is himself or to someone who only trusts the empirical sciences. Blondel delineates the immanentist mind even further, as we saw above:

> In a phrase which must be explained but which indicates at once the seriousness of the conflict, modern thought, with a jealous susceptibility, considers the notion of *immanence* as the very condition of philosophizing; that is to say if among current ideas there is one which it regards making a definite advance, it is the idea, which is at bottom perfectly true, that nothing can enter into man's mind which does not come out of him and correspond in some way to a need for development and that there is nothing in the nature of historical or traditional teaching or obligation imposed from without that counts for him, no truth and no precept which is acceptable, unless it is in some sort autonomous and autochthonous.[152]

Blondel, accepting this principle himself insofar as he states that it is "perfectly true," asserts that immanentism makes self the principle of judgment of the very condition of philosophizing. He goes on to note that even our idea of the transcendent truths and beings is immanent insofar as it is our own.[153] Even the discussion about God for the modern man only has meaning insofar as he experiences Him or some supernatural thing, i.e. even the discussion about God is in immanentist terms. Yet because our modern man puts his real trust in the empirical sciences, either he compartmentalizes the life of faith from the life of science or he simply leads a life of a practical atheist or agnostic. On the other hand, the "modern" man holds to Comte's assertion that theological assertions are fictitious and in the end reflect a lack of maturity in thought.

---

[150]Blondel, *The Letter on Apologetics*, p. 150.

[151]Schleiermacher, *On Religion*, second speech, passim.

[152]Blondel, op. cit, p. 151f.

[153]See ibid., p. 156. Some authors argue that Blondel did not commit himself entirely to the principle of immanence. See translators note on page 152 of Blondel, op. cit. and Peter J. Bernardi, "Maurice Blondel and the Renewal of the Nature-Grace Relationship", p. 811.

Our modern man, then, can be described as following: he is immanentized which means he is focused on himself and makes himself the principle of judgment of reality and his experiences. He follows private sentiment, which makes sense since he is an immanentist. He lacks habit or virtue since he is not stuck in a rut, so to speak, and this allows him to live life to the fullest by being "immersed in the object." He may see the ruins of past glory but does not concern himself with it and waits for things to get better. He is more perfect than his predecessors and he is more knowledgeable about things known to those of profound thought. He is a feminist and a liberal and a believer in the empirical sciences.

B. Is Modern Man Truly Superior?

For the sake of coherence, a two-fold approach to modern man's superiority complex will be taken. The first is to examine the interior arguments of the authors in favor of man's progress. The second is to take a look at the reality of modern man to see if, in fact, he is superior to his ancestors (a) in the order of knowledge, (b) in morals, (c) socially and politically and (d) in the order of philosophical and religious understanding.

When considering the various arguments in favor of modern man's superiority, a number of problems come to mind but we will focus only on a few. The first is the premise upon which the entire discourse is based, viz. that (a) all things are changing (b) for the better. It is not true that all things are changing. While it does appear to be true that all material things change accidentally, it is not true that they are changing in their natures. The nature of man has not changed since man appeared on this planet. If one were to assert that the human species is not the same now as it was when man first appeared, then one would be forced into saying something very different. For instance, if one were to assert that modern man had evolved to something different in his nature, he would no longer be man in the same sense. If the essence of man changes, he is no longer a man and to call two things with different natures the same species is at best equivocation and at worst contradictory. This is the weakness of evolution in relation to the changing of species. For instance, to say that man evolved out of an ape is a non-sensical statement from a grammatical and epistemological point of view. One cannot say that "*man evolved* out of an ape" because man did not exist yet to evolve. If one asserts that apes evolved into human beings then one has the same problem. The ape does not become man because once the essential characteristics of the ape change, it is no longer an ape. Rather, one would have to assert that the ape existed until a certain point at which time the ape would cease to exist and then man appeared. The nature or essence of man has not changed. Therefore, it is not true that everything is changing. Nor is it the case that everything is changing for the better and we will discuss that in relation to man below.

The next thing that does not change are the laws of nature. In fact, the entire empirical scientific endeavor is based precisely on the fact that one can predict the outcome of an experiment based on the laws that govern the experiment. In the empirical sciences, unless an experiment can be reproduced under the same conditions and achieve the same result because of the unchanging laws of nature, then it is not permissible to assert the outcome of one's experiment as proving with certitude one's theory or hypothesis. We are able to put a man on the moon because the laws of gravity and thermodynamics are constant and never change. Therefore, it is more accurate to assert that some things change and some things do not and only those things change which by their nature are capable of being changed while those which cannot change do not.

Hegel's assertion that habit brings death is hardly the case. While it is true that bad habits can bring death to a person or even to a culture and civilization, good habits are the very life and foundation of a culture or civilization. For example, the moral virtue of justice is the foundation for the existence of any society. To see the truth of this, imagine a society where the habit of justice was lacking. People would be stealing, killing, hurting each other, etc. Commerce would be impossible because people would be constantly committing theft, fraud and deceit. These are just a few examples to demonstrate that no society could last very long if people were not habitually just to each other. In fact, the more a society is imbued with the habit of justice, the more peaceful it is.

Hegel also asserts that when one falls into a habit one cannot be immersed in the object. Nothing could be further from the truth. Because human beings require repeated exposure to things to learn about them in depth, habit is the very basis of learning. It is only after dealing with an object in the same way over the course of time that a person begins to understand how the object functions and it is the foundation for the certitude of what a person knows about the object. If someone never had the same experience with an object, he would not know if his past experience is the way the thing normally is. How would one ever come to know that physical laws are, in fact, laws which apply always and everywhere if our approach to things constantly changed? It must be conceded that from time to time it does help to take a different approach and a fresh look at something, but this can only be beneficial when one has developed proper habits in relation to a thing so that one has some foundational knowledge of the thing.

Next, in examining Comte's assertion that (1) there are laws of successives states of the human mind and of phenomena and (2) his assertion that one gives up on coming to knowledge of the absolute truth, we see that they are inherently contradictory. For a law is precisely something which applies everywhere in all cases; in other words, it is absolute. If one can discover the truth about it, one would have knowledge of a truth which is absolute. Comte has an even greater problem. There is no way to empirically verify his assertion that all human minds go through the three stages. Indeed, such a statement is not an empirical statement but an abstraction or induction from a few instances or "perceived" states of affairs. Therefore, are we to assume that his abstraction is merely an extension of the fictitious or theological state of Comte's mind?

To stop looking for absolute truth is irrational. First, to say that there is no absolute truth is an absolute statement. Hence, it is contradictory and irrational. The same criticism applies to those who say that all truth is relative. It is contradictory because one is asserting an absolute (all truth) of a relative subject (is relative). To proceed in discourse denying the principle of non-contradiction is irrational.

As to the assertion of Blondel's that "the outworn forms of a supposedly philosophical apologetic no longer make any impression on the mind of an unbeliever" and "the general movement of modern thought turns more and more against it, this is not, as we have seen, without good reason" needs clarification. To the immanentists and to the person who has adopted modern philosphical thought, this line will ring true since modern philsophical thought has epistemologically cut itself off from reality,[154] which is the basis of the scholastic philosophical apologetic or argumentation. In other words, when the principle of judgment is self and not reality, the scholastic arguments will have no appeal since they are based in reality. However, it is not true that these apologetics or arguments have no appeal to the unbeliever: there are examples of men who have converted as a result of these philosophical arguments, even after the time of Blondel. It is not that *modern* man cannot accept the scholastic arguments as it is that *modernist* man cannot accept them. Those men who live in the modern world but who do not accept the philosophical points of departure of modern philosophy are capable of accepting the scholastic arguments as true.

Now we come to the question of whether modern man is in fact superior to his predecessors. The first area we want to look at is whether modern man is superior to his predecessors in the order of knowledge. Condorcet asserted that what could be grasped only by men capable of profound thought would not be beyond the reach of ordinary intelligence. In one sense this is true, insofar as many of the scientific discoveries which required a depth of knowledge and intelligence beyond the ordinary man are capable of being known to those without the same degree of intelligence and depth of thought, e.g. scientists who discovered various radio waves and designed devices to transmit by means of radio waves were on the cutting

---

[154]See Etienne Gilson, *Thomist Realism and the Critique of Knowledge.*

edge of scientific knowledge of their day. Today many of us are aware of radio waves and how one can transmit information, voices, etc. over them. However, we must recognize that while many of us might be knowledgeable about radio waves and the ability to transmit them, how many of us know the actual mechanism in nature which makes this possible? How many of us understand how a radio actually works as to the details as well as the physics behind its means of reception and transmission? Not many. Most of the technology and scientific theories grasped by the common man are done in a superficial fashion, understanding only the basics of the theory. The gap between those in the various sciences and the common man without formal scientific training is widening. We might be aware of DNA but how many of us understand chemistry well enough to discuss the molecular makeup and chemical forming of DNA in a cell? Not many.

There are also certain things which the man of average intelligence simply does not have the time or the intellectual wherewithal to be able to understand.[155] For example, some might be aware that God's existence can be demonstrated through the natural light of reason without an appeal to Revelation,[156] but how many understand the philosophical principles which make grasping the truth of the argument possible? We might be aware of the fact that Einstein came up with the theory of relativity which gave us the ability to know that time is not always constant due to the effect that motion has on the passage of time, but how many of us can even give a definition of time? The point is that there simply are certain things which go beyond the person of average intelligence because of the degree of intelligence necessary to grasp them. Only in a radical egalitarian society would this be denied because radical egalitarianism fails to take into account that people have various degrees of intelligence and abilities. While it might be appetitively appealing, radical egalitarianism is not rooted in reality.

Another aspect of the knowledge of the average person today manifests that there is a growing ignorance in the average person on the street. For instance, the person of average intelligence a hundred and fifty years ago knew how to saddle and ride a horse; how many people today know how to do that? One of the side effects of technology is that it frees up the average person on the street from having to know how to do certain things to get the desired results. Our making use of a technological gadget as a medium between us and the thing separates us from a more concrete knowledge of the thing. For example, someone who knows how to turn on a sewing machine which is computer controlled and can make beautiful and intricate designs is more than likely not going to know how to make those designs if he has sew

---

[155]St. Thomas Aquinas, ST, I, q. 1, a. 1 and SCG, b. I, c. 4.

[156]For example, see ST I, q. 2. 3 and Vatican I, *Filius Dei*.

them by hand. In fact, one of the complaints in the various trade industries is that people are becoming less capable of working with their hands or developing a trade due to a lack of practical knowledge. A hundred and fifty years ago, the average person had to work with his hands day in and day out to do the simple chores around the house; when he was hired on to learn a trade, he had a basis for learning the trade because of his experience with working with various things. The average male in this country is raised spending a vast majority of his time in front of a television, computer or in recreation. As a result, he does not have the knowledge that comes from working with materials that someone a hundred and fifty years ago would have. Anecdotally, the author of this work was told the story of a young man who was hired on at a construction job but did not know how to use a shovel. The fact of the matter is that technology does free us up and makes it possibleto know certain areas of knowledge but, at the same time, it can cause a decline in knowledge in other areas, since the person has no necessity to work on knowledge in those areas because the technology takes care of him. What is happening in our culture is that extremes of knowledge are being known more and more by fewer and fewer people. Nor does it seem to be the case that the average modern man understands human nature any better than his counterpart a hundred years ago. While we might know more about the things that pertain to bodily health and things of that sort, modern man seems to be bent on the philosophical ignorance of his own nature. While some still study these things, they are fewer and fewer, or so it seems, as time goes on. Fewer and fewer people seem to have a rightly ordered and adequate grasp of the philosophical underpinnings of the modern empirical method and its limitations. At least in the past, men had a grasp of the fact that man was essentially different from all of the other animals and therefore had to be treated differently.

Moreover, our modern arrogance regarding our knowledge seems to have made us forget that we would not be where we are today both in the order of technology and in the order of empirical knowledge (or even philosophical and theological knowledge, for that matter) if it were not for our predecessors. It was their work, discoveries and intellectual achievements which made possible our modern society with all its technology and wonders. We tend to forget that the method of observation in the empirical sciences in not a modern invention. It began with Aristotle over 2300 years ago. This is why Hegel's observation that we ought not be worrying about the ruins of the past is not at all comforting. The "ruins" to which he refers are precisely the good things of the past that are denied those who follow them in the present and in the future. The growth in knowledge is something which requires that one person stand on the shoulders of his predecessor, meaning he is dependent on his predecessor for what he has provided him. Given all of the aforesaid, modern man appears to be digressing more and more into a shallow ignorance since technology makes it possible for him to do so and still survive.

What of the claim that modern man is morally better than his predecessors? It is hard to see how this assertion can stand. The twentieth century, by all accounts, is considered one of the most bloody, if not the bloodiest, century in history. That century saw the rise of mass murderers, such Stalin and Hitler. There is no evidence that modern man is more just, more temperate, more prudent or more courageous than his predecessors. In fact, the opposite seems to be the case.

One of the internal weaknesses in the above arguments has to do with Turgot's idea that conservative societies are barbaric and liberal ones are civilized. There is no real foundation for making such an assertion. Our society is a contradiction to this very assertion. It is the opinion of this author that we live in a very liberal society and yet it appears that we are no more civilized than any other culture. For example, the United States has one of the highest murder rates of the world.[157] For those who are pro-life, this is one of the most barbaric countries in history; upon that analysis, one can say that considering how many countries have abortion, it is one of the most barbaric centuries in history. The French Revolution occurred during one of the most liberal periods in France, and yet it was one of the bloodiest period of its history.[158] Advancements in technology and in certain aspects of empirical knowledgedo not necessarily make modern man more moral. These things can actually be the means by which he is more treacherous, murderous and unjust.

What of modern man's sociological developments? Here again, there is no real indication that modern man is any more sociologically developed than his predecessors. The development of Nazism and Communism are indications that modern man does not understand how man functions. Given the general crime rate in the United States, it is hard to see how modern man can have any claim to a superiority over his predecessors. It is for these reasons that it is hard to see the truth of the statement from *Gaudium et Spes*: "Modern man is on the road to a more thorough development of his own personality, and to a growing discovery and vindication of his own rights"[159] or even the words from the same document: "The circumstances of the life of modern man have been so profoundly changed in their social and cultural aspects, that we can speak of a new age of human history. New ways are open,

---

[157] A 1991 Senate Judiciary Committee report stated that "In 1990, the United States led the world with its murder, rape and robbery rates."

[158] See Jones, *Libido Dominandi - Sexual Liberation and Political Control*, part I, passim.

[159] Vatican II, *Gaudium et Spes* [Translation of Latin Original by the Holy See], para. 41.

therefore, for the perfection and the further extension of culture."[160] What appears to have failed to be understood is the doctrine of original sin. Modern man is just as plagued by original sin as his predecessors and so it is hard to see how we have entered into a new age. Moreover, modern man appears to be more sinful and less contrite than in the past which is proof that technology does not necessarily take away sin and perfect the person morally but can be the opportunity for greater means to commit sin.

As far as the feminism of today, it is hard to see how it has improved the general lot of women. Now that most women work, they *must* work. Since there is a glut of workers on the market because of the presence of women in the workplace, the average wage can be much lower than that which would be required if only the husbands worked. Here it is a simple case of supply and demand. Nor is it all clear that the treatment of women as a group of persons has improved. Women are raped, taken advantage of, used as objects of sexual manipulation and exploitation in an ever bourgeoning pornography industry. The "free choice" movement, while asserting that women should have the right to work, generally looks down on women if they "choose" to stay at home. Ironically, the feminist movement has become a banner for bigotry against women who would prefer to stay home and raise their children. Women have fewer privileges than they did in the past; they were treated with greater reverence in the past. Granted physical and other forms of abuse occurred in the past, but there is no indication that this has waned. In fact, the feminist mentality has created such an atmosphere that it has become permissible or at least ignored when women batter their husbands.[161] It is hard to see how women are any happier.

Ironically, at the advent of modern man's breakthrough to a more "enlightened" understanding of men and women, modern studies are showing more and more that men and women are simply wired differently.[162] What was known by virtue of common sense a hundred years ago seems to have to be discovered today through a formal study. Women have different emotional lives and needs than men. Women have a different physiological make-up and needs than men. It is a bit foolish to expect women who are chemically and biological different from men to act in the same way as men. It is analogous to expecting a car and plane to behave the same way even though they are mechanically different. Radical egalitarianism refuses to take into

---

[160] Ibid., para. 54.

[161] See article by Karen S. Peterson entitled "Studies Shatter Myth about Abuse".

[162] Recent brain studies provide ample proof that men and women are designed differently. Any general search on the internet will provide ample examples.

consideration the differences between men and women. As a result, radical egalitarianism is not capable of accentuating the perfections of feminine nature so that women can contribute more significantly to the welfare of society.

The last area in which we can consider whether modern man is superior to his predecessors is in the area of philosophy and theology. As to philosophy, it is clear that less and less philosophical advancement appears to be taking place. Few people study the various philosophers. Because of man's diminishing philosophical knowledge, man understands himself less. This is manifest in the basic philosophical errors that manifest themselves in reasoning regarding evolution. In fact, one may say that basic philosophical errors are the very foundation, as has been seen in this chapter, for modern man's superiority complex. His self judgment is not moderated by the humility that comes from studying the great philosophers, which gives one an intellectual grasp of modern man.

Regarding matters of religion, one thing is clear, most of the youth of today and even most adults are essentially religiously illiterate. Most Americans have some denominational background and yet a vast majority of people today do not even know the basic tenets of the particular religion to which they belong. Since the moral code of a society is often based upon the predominant religion and since most Americans do not know the basic tenets of their religion, perhaps this is one of the reasons behind the gradual decay in the moral life of America. There also does not seem to be a general deepening in religiosity in the average man today; if anything, modern man is becoming more and more irreligious, both in the order of knowledge and in the order of practice.

Within the Catholic Church itself, we also see modern man has a serious difficulty with doctrinal and moral authority. Since the principle of modern man is immanentism (self), he makes himself the standard of judgment rather than the authority of the Church. This does not mean that he always rejects what the Magisterium or Church says. Rather, he accepts or rejects a teaching, not because of the authority of the Church as such but only insofar as it fits his immanentist judgment.

Given all of the aforesaid, we can begin to see why, during the Second Vatican Council and afterwards, there was an ignoring of prior Magisterial documents. First, because in the modernist scheme things are always changing, the decrees and acts of the Magisterium prior to the Vatican II are outmoded and only have a meaning insofar as they congrue with the experience of modern man. Second, according to Blondel, religious matters have significance only when they come from us; this is behind his use of the terms *autonomous* and *autochthonous*. Therefore, tradition is blocked at its source since tradition does not come from us but is received from us. Yet, this thinking does establish an alternate tradition. Since religious matters come from us, we do not accept what came from others, but we do pass to others what comes from us. In other words, this thinking about religious matters is inherently contradictory. If the teaching is that religious matters must come from ourselves, it would begin and end with a single generation since the subsequent generation could not accept the teaching that religious matters come from ourselves since that would require us to accept that teaching from someone else. However, in the context of the Church, this contradiction never came to the fore of the minds of either those who propagated it or those who received it. What was received in the end was a rejection of all doctrinal and moral authority because it fits fallen man who judges what he is going to do based on self.

We also see that the idea that modern circumstances (we can say therefore modern man) was somehow different was one of the rationales behind changing the liturgical rites of the Church.[163] But it is clear as, a general rule, that modern man is not better than his predecessors, nor is he any better morally or spiritually. Therefore, it is hard to see how using the rationale that modern man or modern times need a changed liturgy will be cogent. In considering the last century and given the constant flux in the lives of people today on every level, it would have been better if the Church had kept the liturgical rites fixed so as to provide psychological and theological stability to modern man. In a certain sense, the Church lost a golden opportunity: if it had not tried to adapt itself to the times, it could have provided an unchanging beacon in a world that was changing, i.e. moving toward moral, sociological and psychological collapse under the weight of sin.

Conclusion

The assertion that man is perfectible (without God's grace) and that he is getting better all of the time is simply unsupported both intellectually and in the concrete reality of modern man. If anything, culture and civilization seem to be collapsing. Modern man has no foundation intellectually or justification in reality for his superiority complex. His lack of humility is glaring in relation to his predecessors who, by means of secular and religious tradition, passed on good things and knowledge of the past making it possible for modern man to even have the lifestyle that he enjoys. If modern man is to recoup his humility, he must re-embrace his religious, intellectual, moral and spiritual patrimony.

---

[163] See Vatican II, *Sacrosanctum Concilium*, paras. 4, 88 and 107.

Chapter 5: Philosophy of Man and Pastoral Theology[164]

There is often a great discrepancy in pastoral activity between one diocese and another, between one parish and another, and between one priest and another. Some of this is due to the differences of circumstances and some of it is due to the way different people's view man, i.e. how they view man's nature. It is to this topic that we should direct a few comments, viz. the role of one's view of man, one's philosophy of human nature and one's pastoral action.

Before man performs any action, he must always make a judgment about which means or actions are the best, most suitable or desirable, etc. Since action proceeds from judgment and since judgment is always based on some principle, i.e. some idea about the action itself and that upon which the action comes to bear, then pastoral action, insofar as it is action, is based upon some principle. Pastoral theology is the practical science in which we apply certain theological principles to our action. In fact, many of the problems in the Church today are the result of the divorce between the theological and the pastoral, e.g. how often do priests not fraternally correct someone under their pastoral care because they do not want to hurt the person's feelings. In effect, the person's feelings become the principle of pastoral action, which is dangerous indeed. It seems that most priests suffer from this a bit. Rather than basing their fraternal correction on objective Catholic theology or principle, their pastoral approach to the faithful is often governed by their personal weaknesses or inordinate concerns for people's feelings.

It seems to me that since the work of a priest is to help people save their souls, then his pastoral action, i.e. what he does for the faithful, must be based upon two essential principles, viz. authentic/orthodox Catholic theology as taught by the Magisterium of the Church and the nature of man. Obviously, since the job of the priest is to help people save their souls, then they must accept and use the teaching of the Church which is the means of salvation established by Our Lord. Therefore, no authentic pastoral action, sometimes called *orthopraxis*, can be divorced from the official teachings of the Church. This is why in the past in moral manuals, pastoral theology essentially comprised the administration of the sacraments. However, while essence of the priest is to offer sacrifice for the sake of his people and therefore the most pastoral thing he can do in general is to offer Mass, nevertheless there is more to saving people's souls than offering Mass. Indeed, it is the most important, but we also know that part of saving peoples' souls is hearing their confessions, baptizing them, instructing them, good

---

[164]Conference given for a Lincoln Deanery Meeting on 11/29/2000.

preaching, etc. The threefold munus of a priest to teach, sanctify and govern naturally flows from the essence of the priesthood. Often the first thing that must be done is preaching in order that people will obtain the salving knowledge entrusted to the Church. But pastoral theology includes more than that. Part of pastoral theology is counseling people in the concrete about what to do and what not to do, how to overcome their sin, their difficulties arising from sin and how to become perfect so that they can fulfill Christ's command to "be perfect as your heavenly Father is perfect." As the document *Veritatis splendor* rightly pointed out, our salvation, what is good and the knowledge of goodness does not come from ourselves; we must be perfected and come to knowledge of the good by the instruction of God; God tells us what is good and since the Church is the *Vox Dei*, i.e. the Voice of God, we learn what is good, what is necessary to be perfect from the Church. Hence, if a priest is to help his people to be holy, to be perfect, to do what is right, that priest must counsel according to orthodox theology and it must be his primary set of principles.

However, since it is man who is being counseled,we must have an accurate knowledge of the nature of man. For if we have false understandings about man's nature, it can lead to a great deal of confusion and pastoral ineptness. We should take some time to discuss some erroneous views of the nature of man and how they have affected pastoral action and how we must learn about the nature of man, the Church and from those who the Church recommends. As we know that the Church has repeatedly exhorted us "ite ad Thomam,"i.e. go to Thomas, it appears that the safest philosophy to adopt for the sake of our pastoral action is Thomism.

There are, it seems to me, a few philosophical outlooks regarding man that are particularly dangerous. The first is the philosophy of materialism which holds that there is nothing beyond the material and, if there is, we cannot know it. This philosophy has led to a denial of the primacy of pursuing the things of the soul since for them there is no immaterial soul. Everything is at the service of the body rather than the body being for the sake of the soul. This philosophy has also denied that man has a supernatural end to which he is ordained by God. The result of this philosophy is that since nothing is beyond man to which he is called, the highest science becomes the philosophy of man himself and within that psychology. Hence, in the last forty years, there has been many who have drained their pastoral theology of theology itself and replaced it with psychology. While one must have mental health in order to advance spiritually, nevertheless, psychology cannot be substituted for pastoral theology for two reasons. The first is that most priests are not adequately trained in psychology, but the second, more important reason is that psychology does not principally take into account the final end of man. As a science, it is not directed, nor can it direct man to something beyond himself as the primary scope of the science, since the science is concerned with man himself.

Connected to this is the view that spiritualityconsists in emotions. This came from Friedrich Schleiermacher who said that piety was an emotion rather than a filial love of God and love of neighbor because he is in God's image. Piety became immanentized, i.e. it become fixated on ourselves rather than on God and this is the product of a materialistic approach to man. Hence, many priests in their pastoral actions are more concerned about people's emotions and appetites than they are about God. Obviously, people must be taken where they are at and led to the truth and that means that we have to take into account their emotional state but their emotional state, i.e. eliciting certain emotions, is not the end of our pastoral work. In fact, St. John of the Cross has rightly pointed out that any advancement in the spiritual life consists in basing our spiritual life in God and not in ourselves, our attachment to things, or the consolations they bring. Pastoral practice has often degenerated into placating people's emotions rather than helping the person to overcome their dependency on their emotional life as governing the spiritual life to an authentic self-denial by which we are able to love God perfectly. Pastoral theology must be about concretely helping people to attain their supernatural end to which they are ordained. St. Thomas tells us and we all know this from our own experience that we naturally desire perfect beatitude and we also know that all of the faculties of man are ordered to God as their end. So our pastoral action cannot degenerate into a psychology but it must be based on an understanding that man is ordained by God, to something outside of man himself, in order to be happy.

Another dangerous philosophy of man is rationalism. Rationalism essentially states that we do not derive a true intellectual understanding of things by means of the senses; rather all our knowledge is innate, i.e. within ourselves. This too has led to a type of immanentism in which people get locked up in themselves. How many of us have heard about catechetical programs in which nothing is taught to the child but the presumption is that the child has everything in himself already. He just needs to express himself and that will be his theology. Rationalism forgets that man is a *tabla rasa*, i.e. that when the child was born, he did not have any explicit knowledge and that he needs to learn by looking outside of himself. Catechetical programs which have a rationalist view of man, and some priests in their pastoral action, just tell people to "follow their conscience" or "do what you feel" rather than taking the opportunity to teach the child or person what they need to know. Since we learn by means of the senses and since we do not have everything in ourselves, this means that priests must enact catechetical programs which provide a clear, coherent and orthodox presentation of the faith to the child or adult to the degree that they can understand it. Obviously, everything that is received is received according to the mode of the receiver and so we must take people where they are at and lead them to the truth to the degree that they can understand it. Now since most of a truths of faith can be grasped, at least, minimally with very little intelligence, there is no excuse for a priest not to teach his faithful in catechetics and preaching.

If one takes rationalism and materialism together and apply them to the moral code, which has been done in the last 100 years, it produces a very dangerous error. Materialism, since there is nothing beyond the material, leads man to think that he has no responsibility to God or freewill since freewill is immaterial. Since man is only material then he is merely the product of physical laws. Rationalism, on the other hand, proffers a negative attitude toward the body. The body is merely there, like a tool or instrument, which one can manipulate as one sees fit. The irresponsibility begotten by materialism and the erroneous understanding of our body by rationalism has produced the contraceptive mentality, which we all know is a very grave pastoral problem. Contraception, despite the fact that many say it is "responsible" since one is taking one's reproduction into one's own hands, is not responsible at all. In fact, the very nature of contraception is to provide an avenue in which one can engage in the conjugal act without taking the natural consequences of the action which is nothing other than being irresponsible. This rationalistic mentality regarding the body also leads people to say things like "I am a woman in a man's body," since what one is, is not connected to the body. This has eroded people's understanding of the natural law, which we shall speak of shortly. But pastors who fall prey to rationalism and materialism will find it very difficult to preach against contraception, which is why pastors must base their apostolate on an authentic view of man.

Now, often people do not hold these philosophies explicitly. Most priests would not consider themselves rationalists or materialists, but one does not have to hold something explicitly for it to be an operative principle psychologically. Because of our depraved culture and because many priests were not given a solid intellectual formation, they are very susceptible to listen to agencies like the media and polls. Since the culture we have now is the product of 500 years of bad philosophy, unless one can break psychologically with the culture and come to an explicit knowledge of the philosophies which produced our culture, it is very hard not to succumb to the easy answers given by the culture to difficult questions. Those easy answers, of course, are the product of bad philosophy. Therefore,priests must be particularlysensitive to the principles upon which they judge what they do pastorally. They should examine what their principles are to make sure that they are in accordance with Church teaching and a proper view of man's nature. The Church is often called the "expert on humanity" and this is because the Church draws not just on good philosophy but upon Scripture and Tradition which embody the teachings of God Himself.

The next dangerous philosophy that affects priests view of man and, consequently, their pastoral action is naturalism. Naturalism is an error which states that man is naturally good and that the evil he does is the result of exterior influences so that if man is left to himself he will naturally due what is right. Now it is true that man is by nature good but man's nature is a wounded nature. Even the philosophers have noticed that there is something wrong with man. They have noted that sometimes man knows what is right but does what is wrong; they know that man's perfection consists in virtue and yet man has a tendency to vice. Moreover, the Church's doctrine of Original Sin can never be removed from authentic pastoral considerations. For man's nature labors under the effects of Original Sin, viz. darkness of the intellect (which the rationalists would deny), disordered appetites (which the materialists would deny since man should just follow his appetites) and a proclivity to evil (which the naturalists would deny). Man's condition is serious since he is debilitated in doing the good. He finds it hard to know what is good which is why pastors must convey the teaching of Church in their pastoral activity, which is why one of munera of the priest is to preach. He must govern his people in his pastoral action because they have a proclivity to evil which means they have a tendency to disorder and so God gave the munus of governance to the priest. Finally, since we have disordered appetites, they are the first thing which must overcome in the process of becoming holy and so the pastor must administer the sacraments, provide devotions, encourage prayer, etc. so that people can overcome their disordered passions and become holy. A priest is the remedy for the effects of Original Sin, but unless one has a grasp of Original Sin, the Church's other teachings and the nature of man, he will never fulfill his three fold munus, i.e. his three fold pastoral responsibility, to teach, sanctify and govern. The loss of the sense of the doctrine of Original Sin and a loss of a grasp of man and his nature has led to priests engaging in pastoral action which is not in congruity with their priesthood.

The last erroneous philosophy is historicism, primarily found in Hegel. Hegel essentially thought that things were in a constant state of flux and could not help be in a state of flux. Therefore, things are never the same but always changing. This has resulted in people thinking that what someone says or teaches is always the product of their historical circumstances. Of course, we know this is not the case. We know through realism that essences never change and this means that man never changes. Now since Christ said that His teaching will not pass away and since He warned about teaching things contrary to His teaching, then the teachings of the Church will never change. Since pastoral action is based upon the teachings of the Church and essence of man, both which never change, then the essence of pastoral action never changes. Every generation is capable of receiving the teachings of the Church and living according to the teachings. While the circumstances change and so we must, again look where people are at, our ultimate goal in every generation is the same: to save the souls of those of that generation.

Since man's essence does not change, then the vices, virtues and perfections never change. The only thing that can change is the external influences on man. An authentic pastoral theology does not seek to constantly change everything. Rather, it only changes what is necessary to bring it in more perfect conformity with the teachings of the Church and the nature of man.

Part of the historicism has been a systematic rejection of our spiritual and pastoral patrimony produced by the popes and saints through the ages. Just as the Church tells us to go the patristics to learn about Scripture, so too must we recover the pastoral teachings of the saints. The work of the saints was drawn from Catholic doctrine and applied with full knowledge of man's nature and his condition. We must recover our pastoral sensibilities by learning anew from the saints and accepting that teaching and example in pastoral action as our personal priestly patrimony and heritage.

Finally, we all know that grace builds on naturewhich means if we are goingto increase in grace and seek to increase the grace of those under our pastoral care, we must know what man's nature is. Obviously, if we have a false understanding of man's nature, it will debilitate our advancement toward sanctification. We must therefore learn about man's nature and the order that God has placed within it called the natural law. There are three ways of knowing man's nature; viz. 1) revelation; 2) the nature law and 3) our own experience of ourselves and others. The teaching about man is incorporated in the teachings of the Church and so we will not say too much more about that aspect of our knowledge. Since our own experience of ourselves and others develops prudence in us and how we judge our experiences of ourselves and others is largely contingent upon our philosophical presuppositions, I will stick to making some basic comments about the natural law and its relation to pastoral action.

The Church has made it very clear, as it does in *Veritatis Splendor*, that the She takes the Thomistic teaching of the natural law as its own. This means that since we must follow the natural law in order to be saved, how we view man's nature will determine what we think we should and should not do which in turn affects our pastoral approach. St. Thomas tells us that man is ordered in himself and in his faculties towards specific goods and that ultimately man is ordered toward God. Now this being the case, our pastoral action, being based on man's nature, is really about getting people to that Good to which they are ordered, viz. God.

The question, then, will be, how are we to teach the people the natural law and how are we to employ it in our pastoral work. St. Thomas says that the end of the moral life is virtue and he also says that the natural law commands the virtues, i.e. it is God's intention that we seek after and perfect ourselves by means of the virtues. This is, concretely, one of the ways that pastoral work is to be done, viz. by teaching people the virtues. Our goal is sanctified perfection and that consists in the obtainment of a high level of sanctifying grace as well as the perfection of the virtues. Hence, pastors much preach, teach and encourage people to pursue a life of virtue. We know that the highest of the virtues, i.e. the theological virtues, is charity, which consists in the love of God and the love of neighbor for the sake of God. Charity has God as its beginning and end and so virtues which help us to seek the true good help us to approach our end which is God Himself. Pastoral theology must take into account virtue and it cannot be satisfied with leaving people in their ignorance because ignorance impedes our advance in virtue. Priests are not doing people a favor by leaving them in ignorance about what they should and should not do; in a sense, this type of pastoral behavior is inimical to the very notion of the priesthood which has as one of its munera to teach.

Lastly, we must say a bit about culture and custom. If one understands the history of the Catholic Church in the United States well enough, one of the ways that Catholicism advanced and survived in this country is because Catholics created pockets within the country where there was a Catholic culture. This culture, like all culture, is based upon a set of customs which govern the daily relationships people had. In the last forty years, Catholic Culture, not just in this country, but in virtually every country in the world, collapsed. It collapsed because man had changed his view of himself and this resulted in his changing his customs. A custom is a habitual way of doing something which is usually a public habit, i.e. a repeated way of doing something in society. The role of custom is first and foremost the promotion and the protection of virtue. In older cultures, for instance, courting practices where heavily regulated by the customs of the country. For instance, in the movie, the Quiet Man, an American comes to Ireland and finds a woman he wants to marry but because he comes from a country which lacks those customs, he is unable to see that the courtship ritual of Ireland was designed to protect and promote chastity, modesty and a reverence between people of the opposite sex. When man's view of himself changed, the customs based upon his view of himself collapsed. In the Catholic sphere, our custom use to be based upon Church teaching and the nature of man. Both of these principles have been under severe attack and this has resulted in a collapse of Catholic culture.

Pastoral activity is much easier within a Catholic culture because people are already doing, according to custom, the very thing the priest must encourage, i.e. pursuit of holiness and the living according the natural law through virtue. Since the custom has collapsed, it has made it very difficult for people to lead an authentic Catholic life. Priests, one a pastoral level, must be aware of this. Since the job of a priest is to help people save their souls, then a priest must work to the establishment and the maintenance of a Catholic culture and Catholic customs which make the priest's work easier and the faithful's task of saving their souls easier. Custom provides an exterior motivation for leading a life of virtue and since that has collapsed, leading a

Catholic life is harder because this exterior motivation is wanting. We must do what we can to promote activities which seek to give Catholics a sense of identity and this comes through establishing Catholic custom and culture.

Part III: Tradition and the Liturgy

Chapter 6: What Constitutes a Rite

Historically, there has always been some question about the exact requirements necessary to conclude that one rite of Mass is a different rite than another. The Church makes the distinction between a canonical rite and a liturgical rite. A canonical rite (not right) refers to what is called a "Church *sui iuris*" and indicates a specific part of the Church which celebrates, normally speaking, a specific rite. A liturgical rite, rather than being part of the Church as such, specifically refers to how a particular ritual is performed:

> "rite (Lat. *ritus* – religious observance). In ecclesiastical usage it is the total amount of ceremonies (bows, benedictions, signs of the cross, imposition of hands, anointments, etc.) and formulas (prayers, hymns, antiphons, versus, etc.), of which the liturgical acts are composed."[1]

For example, the Latin Church (canonical rite) was distinguished from the Byzantine Church (canonical rite) by virtue of the fact that the two sister Churches[2] offered the Mass according to different rituals (liturgical rite). It is possible to have several different rites still fall into one canonical Church and not constitute a canonical rite of its own[3] when the rites are derived from the same historical source, such as a particular Apostle, while different in some element generally considered to differentiate one rite from another.

Gihr observes that:

> the Eucharistic sacrificial action (*actio sacrifica*) consists in the double consecration, by which the Body and Blood of Christ, under the appearances of bread and wine, are placed in the state of sacrifice and

---

[1] Parente, *Dictionary of Dogmatic Theology*, p. 244.

[2] Here we are forced to observe the change that has occurred in relation to the term "sister Churches". Before the influx of Protestant thinking into the Church and the second Vatican Council, the term "sister Church" referred to a Church *sui iuris* that was, in fact, inside the Catholic Church itself by virtue of the unity of the sister Church to the Church of Rome, i.e. the pope. The reason why those outside the visible unity with the Roman Church were not considered sister Churches is because there is only one Church and that Church was considered to be identical with the Roman Catholic Church. Since the influx of Protestant thinking which held that there were various Churches which partook in the one Church of Christ by varying degrees, the terminology within the Church itself shifted as modernists who adopted the new ecclesiology gained ascendancy.

[3] For example, the Carmelite rite of the Holy Sepulcher as considered one of the Latin rites, canonically speaking.

are, therefore, sacrificed. – All the prayers, ceremonies and actions that partly proceed and partly follow the consecration in the celebration of the Mass are, consequently, not essential to the Eucharistic Sacrifice. – The oblation-prayers at the Offertory and after the Elevation, the fraction of the consecrated Host and the co-mingling of a particle of it with the Sacred Blood, or important and profoundly significant constituent parts of the ancient, venerable rite prescribed for the Sacrifice by the Church, but in no wise are they the integral or essential portions of the sacrificial action instituted by Christ. That the Communion of the faithful who are present is not necessary for the Sacrifice, is admitted by all Catholics. – But the case is quite different with regard to the Communion of the officiating priest. The officiating priest must necessarily communicate at the celebration of the Eucharistic Sacrifice, not merely by reason of a command of the Church, but in virtue of a divine ordinance from Christ Himself. The Communion of the celebrant, therefore, is so necessary, because although it does not appertain to the essence, it is, however, indispensable to the external completeness of the Eucharistic sacrifice; for by this Communion the Sacrifice obtains its end as a food-offering and, consequently, by it the Sacrifice is in a certain sense perfected and consummated. The celebrating priest must partake of the same sacrificial matter which he has just consecrated, in order that the unity of the visible Sacrifice may in its essence and integrity be perfectly secure.[4]

From Gihr's observation, we must make a distinction. As was discussed by this author in a prior article,[5] there is a distinction between the intrinsic sacrifice and the extrinsic or ritual sacrifice. The intrinsic sacrifice pertains to the actual Eucharistic or sacramental sacrifice in which Christ becomes present which is distinct from the ritual sacrifice which includes all the various elements of the liturgy aside from those things which pertain to the actual Eucharistic or sacramental sacrifice.

Yet, a close reading of Gihr yields certain aspects that are proper to or essential for a sacrifice. The first is the offertory in which the *oblata* (those things which are to be sacrificed, i.e. the bread and wine) are offered to God in which they are set aside by a specific liturgical action, ordained specifically to the worship of God. Once the offertory is accomplished, the *oblata* are only to be used within the confines of the Eucharistic sacrifice since they have been

---

[4]Gihr, *The Holy Sacrifice of the Mass*, p. 199f.

[5]See *The Latin Mass: A Journal of Catholic Culture,* vol. 12, no. 3 (2003): p. 20-31 under the title of "The Merit of a Mass".

dedicated to God through the specific action.

The second element in each sacrifice is the slaying of the victim. In the Old Testament, the various animals were sacrificed upon the altar by putting them to death. The third element is the consummation insofar as God in the Old Testament ordered that which is sacrificed to be consumed.[6] We also see Christ doing the same thing on Maundy Thursday when He told the Apostles to take and eat the bread and wine which had been changed into His Body and Blood. In fact, on Maundy Thursday these three elements are clearly present insofar as our Lord offered the bread and wine to God (the Father), broke the bread and told them to eat (consummation) His Body and Blood (slaying of the victim by the splitting sacramentally of His Blood from His Body – Consecration).

We can see therefore that there are actually two levels of sacrifice taking place at every Mass. The first is the Eucharistic sacrifice or the intrinsic sacrifice in which the bread and wine are changed into the Body and Blood of our Lord, which we will talk more about later.[7] The second is the ritual sacrifice which includes the ritual offertory, the Consecration and the Communion of the priest. In the history of the Church, there were various formulas of the offertory and the Communion of the priest. The Consecration was also according to set formulas which varied only slightly.

From this, we can therefore conclude that a rite is constituted by the structure or nature of the prayers and liturgical actions constituting the offertory, the Consecration and the Communion of the priest. Therefore, one rite may be distinguished from another by the comparisons of the differences of the offertory prayers and actions, the Consecration and the rite of Holy Communion of the priest. If one of these three elements differs significantly,

---

[6]Among others, see Exodus 12:8, 11; Exodus 29:33 and Lev. 7:15. The requirement of these three to constitute a proper sacrifice can be seen by the negation of one of these three. For example, a ritual without a proper offertory is a meal because one slays something and eats it but it is not dedicated to God. Without a slaying of the victim, there is no sacrifice because nothing is lost. Without the consummation, what is sacrificed is not guaranteed to be offered only to God or used only in His worship.

[7]The sacrifice offered by Christ on Calvary had its three element's: offertory - when in the agony of the garden He said to God the Father "not My will but Thine be done" and also when He said upon the Cross to God the Father: "into your hands I commend my spirit". The sacrifice proper or slaying of victim occurs when He dies upon the Cross. The consummation He himself announces when He says, "it is consummated".

it is a different rite.[8]

We are now in a position to ask the question: is the *Novus Ordo Missae* initially promulgated in 1969 the same as the Roman rite which went before it? This is not a question which has only come up since the promulgation of *Summorum Pontificum*. To begin answering the question let us take a look at Msgr. Gamber's book *the Reform of the Roman Liturgy*:

> *Ritus* can be defined as mandatory forms of the liturgical cult that, in the final analysis, originated with Christ, and then, based on shared traditions, developed independently, and were later officially sanctioned by the Church hierarchy.[9]

This definition is not an essential definition but a descriptive definition. What is of import is the part of the sentence where he says that they "developed

---

[8]In the old *Catholic Encyclopedia* under rite we read: DIFFERENCE OF RITE: The Catholic Church has never maintained a principle of uniformity in rite. Just as there are different local laws in various parts of the Church, whereas certain fundamental laws are obeyed by all, so Catholics in different places have, their own local or national rites; they say prayers and perform ceremonies that have evolved to suit people of the various countries, and are only different expressions of the same fundamental truths. The essential elements of the functions are obviously the same everywhere, and are observed by all Catholic rites in obedience to the command of Christ and the Apostles, thus in every rite is administered with water and the invocation of the Holy Trinity; the Holy Eucharist is celebrated with bread and wine over which the words of institution are said; penance involves the confession of sins. In the amplification of these essential elements in the accompanying prayers and practical or ceremonies, various customs have produced the changes which make the different rites. If any rite did not contain one of the essential notes of the service it would be invalid in that point, if its prayers or ceremonies expressed false doctrine it would he heretical. Such rites would not be tolerated in the Catholic Church. But, supposing uniformity in essentials and in faith, the authority of the Church has never insisted on uniformity of rule; Rome has never resented the fact that other people have their own expressions of the same truths. The Roman Rite is the most, venerable, the most archaic, and immeasurably the most important of all, but our fellow Catholics in the East have the same right to their traditional liturgies as we have to ours. Nor can we doubt that other rites too have many beautiful prayers and ceremonies which add to the richness of Catholic liturgical inheritance. To lose these would be a misfortune second only to the loss of the Roman Rite. Leo XIII in his Encyclical, "Præclara" (20 June, 1894), expressed the traditional attitude of the papacy when he wrote of his reverence for the venerable able rites of the Eastern Churches and assured the schismatics, whom be invited to reunion, that there was no jealousy of these things at Rome; that for all Eastern customs "we shall provide without narrowness."

[9]Gamber, *The Reform of the Roman Liturgy*, p. 27.

independently". What Gamber is pointing out is that the rites are distinguished by virtue of the fact that they underwent an independent development historically. In this respect, it cannot be not denied that the new rite of Mass historically underwent an independent development, or we may say, it did not undergo an organic development in relationship to the old rite.

Gamber goes on to note that:

> to change any of its essential elements is synonymous with the destruction of the rite in its entirety. This is what happened during the Reformation when Martin Luther did away with the canon of the Mass and made the words of consecration and institution part of the distribution of Communion.[10]

The essential elements of the liturgy which we saw above are the offertory, the Canon and the rite of Communion. It may be arguable that the rite of Communion in the old rite and the new rite are substantially different and therefore that itself suffices to constitute a different rite. However, the most notable differences are in the respective offertories. In fact, the offertories are so divergent that it appears impossible to assert they are the same rite. While it is true that the first Eucharistic Canon is in substance the same as the Canon of the old rite despite the fact that many of the gestures were removed, the other Eucharistic canons can in no way be said to be of the same rite as the Canon of the old rite of Mass.

What of the assertion that certain elements of the old rite are in the new rite? Gamber addresses this as well when he says: "as we have already shown, the assertion, which continues to be made, that the inclusion of some parts of the traditional Missal into the new one means a continuation of the Roman rite, is unsupportable."[11] Essentially what Gamber is noting is that the new rite of Mass is not, in fact, organically developed from the old rite, despite the fact that there are certain elements which they share in common. His reason for this was that:

> obviously, the reformers wanted a completely new liturgy, a liturgy that differed from the traditional one in spirit as well as in form; and in no way a liturgy that represented what the Council Fathers had envisioned, i.e., a liturgy that would meet the pastoral needs of the faithful.

> Liturgy and faith are interdependent. That is why a new rite was created, a rite that in many ways reflects the bias of the new

---

[10]Ibid., p. 31.

[11]Ibid., p. 34.

(modernist) theology.

... At the same time, the priests and the faithful are to hold that the new liturgy created after the Second Vatican Council is identical in essence with the liturgy that has been in use in the Catholic Church up to this point, and that the only changes introduced involved reviving some earlier liturgical forms and removing a few duplications, but above all getting rid of elements of no particular interest.[12]

These words are pretty strong, especially considering the fact that they come from one of the most influential liturgists in the last 50 years. The divergence of the rites is significant enough to constitute the fact that they are not in fact two forms of the same rite but rather two distinct rites since their essential elements differ and their historical developments do not coincide.

When we therefore consider the use of the term *form* by the Holy Father in *Summorum Pontificum*[13], if we take into consideration the traditional understanding of what constitutes a rite, we are left with the fact that they can be asserted to be in the same canonical rite but not in the same liturgical rite. If they were in fact simply two forms of the same rite, liturgically speaking, why is there such strident opposition on the part of many who offer the new rite in relationship to the old rite and those who offer the old rite in relationship to the new rite? This is a sign that even the faithful recognizes that there is something different between the two rites and this is also why the bishops, as well as the Holy Father himself, treat them differently. We are also struck by the fact that many venerable and noted theologians use terminology which indicates a distinction of rites in relationship to the old and new rite.

It is hard, therefore, to see how this distinction of extraordinary and ordinary form will stand the test of serious theological scrutiny over time, especially as the old rite gains ascendancy. We must also ask, if the differences in the elements of the old and new rites do not constitute different rites, upon what basis can one say that the Carmelite rite or any of the other rites are not just different forms?

---

[12]Ibid., p. 100.

[13]For example, see Pope Benedict XVI, *Summorum Pontificum*, Art. 1.

Chapter 7: The Value of a Mass[14]

Among the traditional faithful there appears to be a kind of intuitive sense that the old rite of Mass is more efficacious than the new rite. Many believe that they derive more spiritually gain from the old rite of Mass than from the new. However, to give a more precise expression to the intuitive sense of which is more efficacious, the new or the old rite, it is necessary to make several distinctions. Since the purpose of this chapter is very specific, i.e. to ascertain which ritual is more meritorious or efficacious, certain issues regarding the value or efficacy of the Mass will be avoided.[15]

Yet, to answer the question of whether the old rite of Mass is more efficacious than the new is of paramount importance. It is the point of departure between priests of the respective rites, since each holds that he is saying the Mass that is best for the faithful.[16] Nevertheless, the question is a key one since, in the end, whichever ritual is more meritorious ought to be the one that the Roman authorities encourage. Since one of the primary obligations of those in authority in the Church is the glory of God through the salvation of souls, they have the obligation to encourage and, in some cases, require the ritual of the Mass which is most efficacious.

I. Distinctions of Value

The distinctions within the different kinds of value of the Mass are first founded on a distinction between intrinsic and extrinsic value. *The Catholic Encyclopedia* says:

We must also sharply distinguish between the intrinsic and the

---

[14]This chapter first appeared as an article in *The Latin Mass: A Journal of Catholic Culture,* vol. 12, no. 3 (2003): p. 20-31 under the title of "The Merit of a Mass". Subsequent to its publication, there were criticisms that the article did not observe the theolgical distincton between vlaue and merit, where value is the objective worth of the nature of the action performed and merit is defined as the reward due to a person (subjective) due to their conditions and the value of the action performed. While in English, the word "merit" can also be used for "value", in order to avoid confusion and criticsm, this article has been edited to observe the stricter theological language based upon the distinction in language.

[15]For example, when a priest offers the Holy Sacrifice of the Mass for five people, does each person receive the full benefit of the Mass or is the value of the Mass divided into five equal fruits given to the five people?

[16]Here we are not speaking of those priests who are incapable of offering a more efficacious ritual due to matters of obedience and/or circumstances.

extrinsic value of the Mass (*valor intrinsecus, extrinsecus*). As for its intrinsic value, it seems beyond doubt that, in view of the infinite worth of Christ as the Victim and High Priest in one Person, the sacrifice must be regarded as of infinite value, just as the sacrifice of the Last Supper and that of the Cross. But when we turn to the Mass as a sacrifice of impetration and expiation, the case is different. While we must always regard its intrinsic value as infinite, since it is the sacrifice of the God-Man Himself, its extrinsic value must necessarily be finite in consequence of the limitations of man. The scope of the so-called "fruits of the Mass" is limited.[17]

In discussing the value of the Mass, one must make a distinction between intrinsic and the extrinsic value. The intrinsic value of any valid Mass is infinite since It is Christ, Who is infinite, Who is offered. Hence, in this respect every Mass has an infinite value.[18] The new rite of Mass is just as efficacious as the old rite of Mass in this respect since they are both the same sacrifice of Christ.[19] The Mass, because it is the offering of God the Son to God the Father, gives infinite glory to God.[20]

However, the extrinsic value of the Mass is finite.[21] This is so because man, a finite creature, is incapable of receiving infinite effects. In this respect, the value of the Mass is "intensive limited",[22] which means that the fruit of the Mass is limited in its measure. Normally, the liturgical writers state that, as to its impetratory and expiatory value, the Mass is finite,[23] "since the operations of propitiation and impetration refer to human beings, who as creatures can

---

[17]OCE, vol. 10, p. 17.

[18]See also, Ludwig Ott, *Fundamentals of Catholic Dogma*, p. 414 and St. Alphonsus Ligouri, *Theologia Moralis*, lib. VI, tract. 3, c. 3, d. 1.

[19]One of the fundamental presuppositions of this article is that the pope enjoys infallibility in the promulgation of the official Latin texts of liturgy. In other words, it is presupposed that the new rite of Mass is valid.

[20]OCE, vol. 10, p. 17.

[21]See also Ott, *Fundamentals of Catholic Dogma*, p. 414.

[22]Gihr, *The Holy Sacrifice of the Mass; Dogmatically, Liturgically and Ascetically Explained*, p. 141.

[23]See OCE, vol. 10, p. 17; Ott, *Fundamentals of Catholic Dogma*, p. 414 and St. Alphonsus Ligouri, *Theologia Moralis*, lib. VI, tract. 3, c. 3, d. 1.

receive a finite act only."[24] When one considers the actual sacrifice of the Mass, which is the sacrifice of Calvary, it is infinite, but as to its effects, other than the infinite effect of giving God glory, it is finite.

In addition to man's finitude, the liturgical writers give other reasons for the limitation of the extrinsic value of the Mass. While the Mass is infinite as to What is sacrificed, nevertheless we derive only finite fruits from the Mass. The writers say that the extrinsic merit of the Mass is based essentially upon six things. These six things are intermediaries between the infinite efficaciousness of the Mass and those who receive the actual effects from the Mass.

A. The Church

The first principle of value by which the infinite merits of Christ come to man in a finite way is the Holy Roman Catholic Church herself. Since the Holy Sacrifice of the Mass is an act of the Church (by means of the priest), then the merit of the Mass is founded upon the holiness of the Church.[25] This notion is connected to the fact that one cannot value a thing without being holy, i.e. without being pleasing to God by being in the state of grace.[26] While this point applies principally to human beings in this life, it can be said analogically of the Church insofar as she is holy. Since the Holy Sacrifice of the Mass is an act of the Church, the moral status of the priest does not increase or decrease the value of the Mass in this respect.[27] Nicholas Gihr observes that it is because of the essential mark of holiness that the prayers and gestures of the Mass that the Church offers by means of the hands of the priest are always viewed favorably by God.[28] The faithful can always take comfort in knowing that even if the priest and other faithful at a particular Mass are not holy, they can still derive fruit from the Mass based upon the holiness of the Church.

At the same time, Gihr goes on to observe: "But since the holiness of the Church consists in the sanctity of her members, it is not always and invariably the same, but greater at one period than another; therefore, the Sacrifice of the Church is also at one time in a greater at another in a lesser

---

[24] Ott., loc. cit.

[25] Gihr, *The Holy Sacrifice of the Mass*, p. 141. See also ST II, q. 82, a. 6.

[26] The foundation for merit of a human agency will be discussed below in relation to the priest and faithful.

[27] ST III, q. 82, a. 6.

[28] Gihr, *The Holy Sacrifice of the Mass*, p. 143.

degree pleasing to God and beneficial to man."[29] Writing in the *1913 Catholic Encyclopedia*, Msgr. Joseph Pohle seconds and expands upon this notion:

> We are thus compelled to concur in another view of De Lugo, namely that the greatness and extent of this ecclesiastical service is dependent on the greater or less holiness of the reigning pope, the bishops, and the clergy throughout the world, and that for this reason in times of ecclesiastical decay and laxity of morals (especially at the papal court and among the episcopate) the fruits of the Mass, resulting from the sacrificial activity of the Church, might under certain circumstances easily be very small.[30]

If the actual members of the Church are not very holy their lack of holiness has a direct impact on the efficacy of the Mass, since the Mass is offered always as a public prayer, even when it is offered privately. Given the current scandals in the Church among the clergy and bishops, we can begin to see why the faithful are suffering spiritually. The same can be said for mankind as a whole, since the fruits of the Mass can also be applied for those who are not Catholics. The moral and spiritual depravity of this moment in history has gravely affected this aspect of merit in the Church. This is why the pope and bishops have a grave responsibility for moral reform of the clergy and laity.

B. The Priest as Public Servant of the Church

The next principle of extrinsic merit is the priest insofar as he acts on behalf of the Church, i.e. as a public person and not as a private person.[31] Since the priest by virtue of his priesthood offers the Holy Sacrifice of the Mass, by his very priesthood he is able to merit something for whom he offers the Mass. The priest offers the Sacrifice as a minister (servant) of the Church and so by virtue of his status as a priest his work in the Mass can gain fruit for those for whom he prays. Again, in this sense, the sanctity of the priest does not affect the fruits coming from the Mass.

Given the aforesaid, it would seem that the particular office that the priest holds may have some effect on the fruits of the Mass. Here we have in mind the distinction between a bishop and a priest. It would appear that since the bishop has the fullness of priesthood,[32] the extrinsic merit flowing from his

---

[29] Ibid., p. 144.

[30] OCE, vol. 10, p. 19.

[31] See ST III, q. 82, a. 6.

[32] Second Vatican Council, *Christus Dominus*, para. 15.

episcopacy would be greater than that of a priest. (We are, of course, leaving aside the relative merit gained by their respective degrees of sanctity, for it is possible for a priest to be holier than a bishop and thereby merit more.) But insofar as the office is concerned, it would appear that a Mass offered by a bishop is more efficacious than one offered by a priest. This may also have to do with the fact, at least in the old rite, that the ritual of the Mass of a bishop is not the same as that of a priest. However, this is, again, outside the context of the very nature of the office.

It would also seem that, given this argument, the Mass offered by the Holy Father would likewise be more meritorious than the Mass offered by any other bishop. Yet even here we must make a distinction between the merit flowing from the office of the papacy and the value intrinsic to a specific kind of rite. In other words, it should not be presumed that the new rite of Mass is intrinsically more efficacious because the pope offers it. The actual intrinsic value of the ritual must be considered on its own, independently of the one who offers it.

Above, we saw that the Mass possesses a certain efficacy by virtue of the holiness of the Church, that is to say, the Mass derives fruit from the fact that it is offered on behalf of the Church. Msgr. Pohle makes an interesting observation in this connection:

> Next after Christ and in the second place comes the Church as a juridical person, who, according to the express teaching of the Council of Trent (Sess. XXII, cap. I), has received from the hands of her Divine Founder the institution of the Mass and also the commission to ordain constantly priests and to have celebrated by these the most venerable Sacrifice. When, however, as De Lugo rightly points out, an excommunicated or suspended priest celebrates in defiance of the prohibition of the Church, this ecclesiastical merit is always lost, since such a priest no longer acts in the name and with the commission of the Church. His sacrifice is nevertheless valid, since, by virtue of his priestly ordination, he celebrates in the name of Christ, even though in opposition to His wishes, and, as the self-sacrifice of Christ, even such a Mass remains essentially a spotless and untarnished sacrifice before God.[33]

This passage is extremely important for two reasons. First, the priest must be part of the juridic person of the Church and not suspended so that this ecclesiastical merit is maintained. Second, those who offer the Mass outside the Church or who are suspended displease Christ, since it is contrary to

---

[33] OCE, vol. 10, p. 18.

Christ's wishes, for the juridic Person who has been given the right to administer the sacraments is the Catholic Church alone. Effectively, this means that the right to administer and protect the sacraments was given by Christ to the apostles and their successors. To offer the Mass or employ any other element of sanctification outside the Church is contrary to the rights of the Church. The term juridic comes from the Latin word *ius*, which means right. While there is a great deal of clamor about how wonderful it is that Protestants, schismatics and heretics outside the Church possess these elements of sanctification, the reality is that it displeases God that they exist outside the Church. Since God has given the Church the rights over the sacraments, anytime they occur outside the jurisdiction of the Church, the rights of the Church are violated, since the Apostles and their successors have a right to protect and determine the administration of the sacraments. In effect, it is a violation of justice.

C. The Priest as Private Person

The liturgical writers make a distinction between the priest as a public servant (*minister* in Latin) and a private individual. The priest as a public person, by virtue of his priesthood, is able to merit. However, as a private individual, the priest is also able to merit.

> With Christ and His Church is associated in third place the celebrating priest, since he is the representative through whom the real and the mystical Christ offer up the sacrifice. If, therefore, the celebrant be a man of great personal devotion, holiness, and purity, there will accrue an additional fruit which will benefit not himself alone, but also those in whose favor he applies the Mass. The faithful are thus guided by sound instinct when they prefer to have Mass celebrated for their intentions by an upright and holy priest rather than by an unworthy one, since, in addition to the chief fruit of the Mass, they secure this special fruit which springs *ex opere operantis*, from the piety of the celebrant.[34]

When we consider the action of the Mass from the point of view of Christ who offers by means of the priest, by virtue of the Church as a juridic person and by virtue of the priesthood of the priest who offers, the fruits are derived *ex opere operato*.[35] It is by the very work performed that these fruits are derived

---

[34]OCE, vol. 10, p. 19. These same distinctions and observations are made in Gihr, *The Holy Sacrifice of the Mass*, p. 147 and Ott, *Fundamentals of Catholic Dogma*, p. 413f.

[35]See works cited in prior footnote as well as ST III, q. 79, a. 5.

from the Mass. However, since the priesthood and sanctity are ontologically distinct within the priest himself, it is possible for him to have these two kinds of merit, one which is *ex opere operato* and the other *ex opere operantis*.

This is why the holiness of the clergy has a direct impact on the life of the Church. If the priests are holy, the fruits derived from the Masses they offer are greater and the Church's faithful benefit more thereby. This is also why the faithful have a certain sense that it is better to have a holy priest rather than an unholy priest offer the Mass for their intentions. The fact is that the Mass said by a good priest is better and more efficacious than the Mass said by a bad priest.[36]

Yet, to understand fully the nature of the priest's merit, let us first consider the nature of merit in general. In his commentary on Peter Lombard's *Sentences*, St. Thomas Aquinas observes that one of the effects of grace is merit.[37] Yet how man is said to merit something from God must be understood correctly. For between God and man is an infinite distance which constitutes the greatest inequality. Yet justice is between equals.[38] Since God and creatures are completely unequal, God owes no mere creature anything in justice. Because there is an inequality, man cannot be just to God by absolute equality. Man, who is finite, is incapable of rendering something infinite to an infinite being. Rather, St. Thomas says, man can be just to God by a certain proportion. By this he means that man's merit with God exists only on the presupposition of the divine ordination so that man obtains from God, as a reward of his work, what God gave him the power to do.[39]

Now supernatural acts are goods exceeding a natural capacity. Therefore no created nature is sufficient as a principle of a meritorious act in relation to God unless some supernatural gift is added to man's nature, and this is called grace.[40] Since man moves by means of his free will, he can have a certain merit insofar as what is rendered to God is freely given. Therefore, merit in the eyes of God proceeds from free will and grace.[41] Merit means "to be worthy of something in return for something done" or "a right to a reward", and so grace makes the act supernatural or worthy of something

---

[36]ST III, q. 82, a. 6.

[37]II Sent., d. 26, q. 1, a. 5.

[38]ST I-II, q. 114, a. 1.

[39]Ibid.

[40]ST I-II, q. 114, a. 2.

[41]ST I-II, q. 114, a. 3 and Aumann, *Spiritual Theology*, p. 74.

from God. On the other hand, mortal sin kills sanctifying grace in the soul, and so no one in the state of mortal sin is able to merit, unless he be reconciled with God through grace. [42]

The conditions for performing a meritorious act are based upon several things. [43] On the side of the meritorious work itself, the work must be morally good. Obviously, an evil action does not deserve a supernatural merit or reward. The action must be free from external coercion and internal necessity, i.e., the person must do it freely. Next, the action must be supernatural, i.e. accompanied and motivated by actual grace and proceeding from a supernatural motive. On the side of the person meriting, in order that the action be meritorious, the person must be in the wayfaring state (here on earth). Once a person dies, he is unable to merit. [44] The person must also be in the state of sanctifying grace, as the aforesaid clearly shows. Lastly, merit is dependent on the free ordinance of God, for God determines those things which are meritorious.

Now the degree of our merit is based upon several things. [45] The first is the degree of sanctifying grace: the more sanctifying grace we have, the more meritorious are our actions. Therefore, the holier the person, the more he can merit for himself and others. The second is our degree of union with Our Lord. The closer we are to Him in prayer, for example, the more we can merit. The third is the purity of our intention or the perfection of the motive under which we act. If one seeks to merit the actual graces to overcome a spiritual imperfection from a motive of charity, i.e. he does so purely because he loves God, his action is more meritorious than that of a person who seeks the actual graces because he is tired of falling into a specific kind of sin. The fourth factor upon which the degree of merit is based is the fervor or intensity with which our actions are performed. Still another factor is the virtues with

---

[42] ST I-II, q. 114, a. 2.

[43] All of these can be found in Ott, *Fundamentals of Catholic Dogma*, p. 265ff.

[44] Obviously, the blessed in heaven and those in purgatory can offer prayers for us that will aid us. However, those in purgatory and in heaven cannot merit an increase of happiness in heaven through their works. Also, a distinction must be made between merit in the stricter theological sense, which means that a person is able to raise his reward in heaven, and merit in the broader sense, in which we can perform actions and derive fruits applicable to ourselves and others. The merit in regard to heaven is not transferable to someone else, but the fruits or merits of our works here on earth can be applied, by right intention, to the temporal and spiritual welfare of others.

[45] These four can be found in Adolphe Tanquerey, *The Spiritual Life*, nn. 237-243.

which the soul is adorned. From this we see that the virtuous man is more capable of performing actions in the right manner so that they will be more efficacious. This leads to the last thing upon which our actions are meritorious: the manner or the way in which the action is done. Obviously virtue will provide assistance here but here we are talking about the very way in which we perform the action. We see in our own experience that how a person performs an action often makes the action better, e.g. a mother who takes care of her child's needs but does so in a cold and unaffectionate manner is less pleasing to us than the woman who does so in a warm and affectionate manner.

Lastly, with regard to value, we may say that different kinds of actions have as their reward different graces as well as more graces. For example, the action of undergoing martyrdom is by its nature more meritorious than saying a Hail Mary. Yet relative merit must also be taken into consideration. It is possible for one person, because of the degree of his sanctity, to merit more from an action which is of lesser value than a person who performs a more meritorious action but is less holy. St. Louis Marie de Montfort observes, "Thus you share in the high quality of her intentions, which are so pure that she gave more glory to God by the smallest of her actions, say, twirling her distaff, or making a stitch, than did St. Laurence suffering his cruel martyrdom on the iron grid, and even more than all the saints together in all their most heroic deeds!"[46] However, relative merit does not change the nature of the action, and so different actions when considered on their own differ in the reward due to them.[47]

We can now return to the discussion of the priest's personal merit. If a priest is in the state of grace, he is able to merit additional fruit from the Mass. Moreover, the holier he is, the more he is able to merit. Now sanctified perfection consists in excellence in grace and the adornment of the soul with all of the virtues, and so the more virtue and grace the priest has, the more is he is able to merit.[48] On the other hand, if a priest is in the state of mortal sin, with respect to his personal merit he is useless to himself and the faithful who could be benefiting from his actions in the liturgy. How the priest offers the Mass also increases merit insofar as it is more meritorious if he offers the Mass reverently rather than irreverently.

---

[46] St. Louis Marie de Montfort, *True Devotion to the Blessed Virgin*, p. 115 (para. 222).

[47] This section on merit comes in substance from Ripperger, *Introduction to the Science of Mental Health*.

[48] The fact that virtue is necessary will be discussed in connection to the value of the ritual and the merit of the faithful.

D. The Faithful

What can be said of a priest as a private person can also be said of the faithful. Since the faithful cannot merit anything unless they are in the state of grace, they must ensure that they do not fall into mortal sin if they hope to derive fruits from the Mass by their own work. While the priest is the only one who is capable of confecting the Sacrifice, the people are able to join their prayers, sufferings and good works to the Mass during Mass and throughout the day to derive fruits from it. This also means that if the faithful have a higher degree of virtue and grace, they will be able to merit more from the Mass.

Regarding the faithful, Msgr. Pohle observes:

> Finally, in the fourth place, must be mentioned those who participate actively in the Sacrifice of the Mass, e.g., the servers, sacristan, organist, singers, and the whole congregation joining in the sacrifice. The priest, therefore, prays also in their name: Offerimus (i.e., we offer). That the effect resulting from this (metaphorical) sacrificial activity is entirely dependent on the worthiness and piety of those taking part therein and thus results exclusively *ex opere operantis* is evident without further demonstration. The more fervent the prayer, the richer the fruit. Most intimate is the active participation in the Sacrifice of those who receive Holy Communion during the Mass since in their case the special fruits of the Communion are added to those of the Mass. Should sacramental Communion be impossible, the Council of Trent (Sess. XXII. cap. vi) advises the faithful to make at least a "spiritual communion" (*spirituali effectu communicare*), which consists in the ardent desire to receive the Eucharist. In addition to the active, there are also passive participators in the Sacrifice of the Mass. These are the persons in whose favor it may be even without their knowledge and in opposition to their wishes the Holy Sacrifice is offered.[49]

The fact that the merit of the faithful, whether active or passive participants, is derived *ex opere operantis* means that they must meet the requirements of merit as mentioned above. They must be in the state of grace, have a supernatural intention and assist at Mass in a suitable manner, i.e. fervently and reverently.

On a pastoral level, this means that the holier the congregation, the more they will be able to merit and therefore the better will be the pastoral life of both priest and faithful. Conversely, if any of the faithful are in the state of

---

[49]OCE, vol. 10, p. 19.

mortal sin, it affects everyone else since they are able to merit neither for the rest of the congregation nor for themselves. They become "dead weight," as it were. In an even worse scenario, if they are receiving Holy Communion in the state of mortal sin, they detract from the goodness of the Mass extrinsically and in this way affect everyone else. This is why the problem of the state of the faithful is such an important issue. The fact that a vast majority of Catholic couples are either using or have used contraception as well as the general moral and spiritual decay among the faithful in virtually all areas has left this aspect of merit regarding the Mass anemic, to say the least.[50]

E. The Decora

The next area which can affect the value of the Mass has to do with what we may call the decora.

> The priest who celebrates the Mass and the faithful who participate therein by hearing it, by serving at the altar, by giving a stipend, by procuring the requisite sacred vessels, etc., perform, without doubt, the holiest and most salutary acts of divine worship; for the Church herself says that there can be no other works so holy and so divine performed by the faithful than the celebration of the Eucharistic Sacrifice.[51]

Gihr mentions the procuring of sacred vessels. It is obviously meritorious for the faithful to provide the material means by which the Mass is offered, and this includes those sacred things that are used in the Mass. It is the pious custom and belief that those who procure the items used at Mass are remembered at each Mass, not necessarily by the priest, but by God who looks down from heaven and sees the objects which are used and knows who donated them.

Yet we have used the word "decora" for a specific reason. The term "decora" means a certain fittingness or becomingness about a thing. We use the word "decorate" to indicate the outfitting of a specific room or thing in a manner that suits its use. Here we see that this also applies to the liturgy. If

---

[50] Ott observes (*Fundamentals of Catholic Dogma*, p. 415) that the merit derived from the Mass on the part of the faithful does not work mechanically but is based upon the dispositions of the faithful. Also, the liturgical writers also indicate that the fruits of the Mass can be received more efficaciously by those properly disposed than by those not properly disposed. In this respect, for whom the Mass is offered also affects how efficacious the Mass may be.

[51] Gihr, *The Holy Sacrifice of the Mass*, p. 147.

we use objects that do not fit the majesty and the exalted nature of the Holy Sacrifice of the Mass, we can actually detract from the extrinsic value. Ugly things please God less and thus merit less. Also, if we give with the intention of being cheap, we tell God what we really think of Him, that retention of our money is more important than His glory.

Given the aforesaid, we can make a distinction between objective value and relative value regarding the decora. The objective value of the decora consists in the objects as they suit the nature of the Mass. Since the Mass is the highest act that can be performed in this life, then the best objects will increase its objective value. If we give objects that are made of the best and most noble materials fashioned by the best artists in a rightly ordered artistic fashion (and which admittedly may cost a great deal), those objects will give God the most glory and therefore we will derive the most merit in this regard.

Yet the artistic fashion in which the sacred objects are crafted, everything from the church to the vestments the priests wear, ought to suit the Sacrifice of the Mass according to the particular Mass that is said. This means that the best chalice should be used in more solemn Masses or on more solemn occasions. Part of the beauty of the decora consists in the objects being suited to the particular Mass that is being said. At low Masses one may not use the best vestments, whereas at high Mass he may desire the best vestments. This shows to God that we know which things suit which ritual. In the old rite there are various levels of Masses that can be offered, from the Pontifical High Mass all the way down to the low Mass of a simple priest. For the same reason that it would be unsuitable for a simple priest who is offering a low Mass to vest in vestments suited to a bishop, we ought to use objects ranging in beauty based upon the level of the Mass.

One of the primary difficulties of the new rite is the disappearance of this differentiation, with the ritual reduced to one form of the Mass with only very minor variations, usually in music and things of that sort. In the past it was understood that there were different feasts and occasions as well as priests who offered the Mass, and so one should offer different Masses as well as use different items suited to the Mass and the state of the priest who offers the Mass. While it is true that we can use different decora, even the simplest ought to be truly beautiful.[52] Often those who offer the new rite use ugly items because they think to do so pleases God. They argue based on the notion of simplicity.[53] Simplicity is not the same thing as ugliness.

Often priests feel obligated to use ugly liturgical items they receive from laity who may not have properly developed aesthetic senses. The first

---

[52]We will address this later in the book.

[53]We will show below this is not valid argument.

mistake is accepting ugly liturgical items in the first place. The second mistake is giving the laity the idea that they should go out on their own and purchase these items for the church. The laity should be told that if they want to donate an item, the priest should select the item based upon proper aesthetics in relation to the style of the church in which they will be used. The third mistake is the priest's belief that he is obligated to use an ugly item donated by a layman. While it is true that priests often do not want to offend the laity, nevertheless, those laity who donate ugly objects must be taught that such things do not suit the liturgy precisely because they detract from the extrinsic value of the Mass. They affect not only the others in the church, but even the layman who donates it because he is getting less fruit from the Mass as a result.

The relative value regarding the decora consists in the people, through a holy intention, donating a liturgical object which may not have the best material or best artistry but is still the best that they can afford. We are not speaking here of ugly objects, but simply ones that may be more simple and less ornate. Nevertheless God looks with great favor on these because of the faithful's sacrifice in donating what they can afford. We see this in relation to Christ's parable of widow's mite.[54] On the other hand those, who have money and yet out of miserliness do not seek to give God the best, detract from the extrinsic glory and, in the end, will not merit more for themselves or others. This is why the virtue of magnificence plays such an important role in church as well as other liturgical design.[55] Those who are miserly will never produce anything magnificent. The truly magnificent church or liturgical object pleases God both in itself and because a magnificent item more easily moves people to lift their minds and hearts to Him.

Objectively, then, we can say that offering Mass in a magnificent church with the vestments and sacred vessels that suit the level of Mass offered will have the most extrinsic value regarding the decora. This does not mean that we should always say the highest level of Mass all the time but whenever we offer any level of Mass, the decora ought to fit that level of Mass. On the other hand, lack of beauty in the decora will reduce the extrinsic value. Also, not saying Mass in a church will reduce the value of the Mass. This does not mean that a priest should forego offering Mass if he cannot get to a church, since there are all kinds of circumstances which may warrant not saying Mass in a church. Nevertheless, a Mass offered in a beautiful church will derive more fruit.

On a practical level, the laity and clergy must insist that the church and other decora be beautiful and properly suited to the Mass. This is not just

---

[54] See Mark 12:42-44.

[55] For a discussion of the virtue of magnificence, see ST II-II, q. 134.

a matter of aesthetics. As this section shows, it is a matter of spiritual import since it can directly affect the value of the Mass. This is so not only because the objects themselves merit more or less in the eyes of God but also because they will affect the clergy and the laity when they attend Mass. There is probably no layman who has not noticed the differences in their experiences of the Mass when they attended an ugly church as opposed to a beautiful one.

II. The Value of the Ritual Itself

We come now to the last area of extrinsic value, the ritual of the Mass itself.[56] The general contention among many who offer the new rite of Mass is that since it is valid it is just as meritorious as the old rite. Intrinsically, it must be conceded that this is true, and it is also true with respect to certain extrinsic aspects of value or merit. However, with respect to the ritual itself, given the traditional theology, Gihr argues that it is possible that one ritual may be more efficacious than another:

> The Church not only offers the Sacrifice, but she moreover unites with its offering various prayers and ceremonies. The sacrificial rites are carried out in the name of the Church and, therefore, powerfully move God to impart His favors and extend His bounty to the living and the dead. By reason of the variety of the formulas of the Mass, the impetratory efficacy of the Sacrifice can be increased in an accidental way, and the efficacy be directed in a special manner to different objects. The sacrificial fruit to be obtained by petition, through the mediation of the Church, is neither as to kind nor degree previously determined and limited. Therefore, the Church herself in her prayers is accustomed so to express her intentions and desires, that it can be known what benefits she wishes to obtain by the Mass and to whom she wills to apply them. Hence special prayers are more useful and more beneficial than general ones. Not only the degree of holiness of the Church, but also the nature of the prayers of the Mass and even of its whole rite exerts accordingly an influence upon the measure and nature of the fruits of the Sacrifice. From what has been said there follow several interesting consequences. Among others, that, on the part of the Church, a High Mass solemnly celebrated has greater value and efficacy than merely a low Mass; and also with regard to the Church's impetratory power a Votive or a Requiem Mass for a special intention is more valuable and efficacious than a Mass harmonizing with the Office of the day. At a Solemn High Mass the external

---

[56]There are a number of other distinctions made regarding value but they will not be covered here.

126

display is richer and more brilliant than at a low Mass; for at a solemn celebration the Church, in order to elevate the dignity of the Sacrifice, manifests greater pomp, and God is more glorified thereby.[57]

The full content of this passage needs careful unpacking. The different fruits are rooted in the very nature of the prayers. What the prayers ask for determines the fruits that will be derived. The very nature of the prayers and gestures that comprise the rite constitute the foundation for the value of the ritual and therefore determine whether one ritual is more efficacious or valuable than another. We shall return to this discussion in the next section.

This passage also notes that since different rituals have different fruits, we can say that it is not always best to offer the Mass that is generally the most efficacious. In other words, while a solemn high Mass said on the feast of the Immaculate Conception may have a greater efficacy when compared to a low Mass for the dead, it does not necessarily mean that one should offer a votive Mass of the Immaculate Conception as opposed to a Mass of the Dead. The prayers of the Mass of the Dead are ordered specifically to aid the dead. This is why the *General Instruction of the Roman Missal* of the new rite of Mass is problematic when it said that Masses for the dead should be said sparingly because the dead are already remembered during the Mass.[58] The actual Mass for the dead has fruits which specifically benefit the dead. In effect, this means that sometimes it is better to offer the ritual of the Mass more suited to the needs of the faithful, both living and dead, than to offer the Mass that is in general more valuable.

Another reason one ritual can be more efficacious than another is that it is offered with greater solemnity or, as Gihr puts it, pomp. The solemnity or pomp give greater glory to God, and are eminently suited to Him since He is the Majesty or Ruler of the whole universe. He is greater than any earthly king and therefore deserves a greater ritual than any earthly king.

Yet since a ritual is a combination of the prayers and gestures, then the more the gestures suit the one who offers the Mass, the action one is performing, and the person to whom it is directed (i.e. God), the more efficacious it will be.[59] Prayer itself has governing principles that make it

---

[57] Gihr, *The Holy Sacrifice of the Mass*, p. 144. Gihr, in support of what he has said here, notes the authors Quarti and Pasqualigo. Hence, it is not merely Gihr's opinion.

[58] *General Instruction to the Roman Missal*, 4th edition, 1975, para. 316.

[59] Some monastic rites contain less "pomp" because the rite is tailored or suited to the one who offers it, i.e. the members of the monastery. In other words, the degree and kind of pomp in monastic rites is based upon the particular spirituality of

meritorious, and these principles can likewise be applied to the ritual of the Mass. St. Thomas observes that vocal prayer is done in order to render God His due and to move man's mind and heart to Him.[60] Since prayer is an act of the virtue of religion, which is a part of justice, we pray in order to render to God His due.

The same principle can be applied to the ritual of the Mass. The ritual of the Mass ought to be ordered to God and not to man, except insofar as man is served in order to serve God. In other words, God is the end of the ritual, not man. This follows from the order of charity in which we love God and our neighbor for the sake of God.[61] The ritual should not have man as its finality, but God, for if it has man as its finality, it goes contrary to charity, which has God as its end. It will also go contrary to justice since one will not render to God through the prayers of the ritual what is due to Him.

St. Thomas describes additional conditions necessary to render prayer efficacious. As mentioned, prayer must proceed from charity,[62] and since it is a lifting of the mind and heart to God, it must have God as its end. Since charity is the virtue in the will which makes it possible to love God,[63] then charity directs us to God. The person praying must also have the requisite virtues, two of which St. Thomas names: humility and faith. Humility is necessary because we must recognize our unworthiness. Faith is necessary in order for us to know Who and What God is, so that we act rightly. Here the principle of *lex credendi lex orandi* plays a key role. St. Thomas says that prayers must be offered to God and with devotion.[64] Lastly, for the prayer to be meritorious, the person must be in the state of grace.

Applying these principles to a ritual, we conclude that it should inculcate love of God in the faithful as well as proceed from charity. In this way, the prayer will flow from a love of God. Since charity is directive of all

---

the monks of a particular religious order. Hence, in the case of the monastic rites, the value may be based more on suitability than pomp.

[60]ST II-II, q. 83, a. 12.

[61]ST II-II, q. 25, a. 1.

[62]All of these conditions can be found in ST II-II, q. 83, a. 4.

[63]ST II-II, q. 23.

[64]See also OCE, vol. 10, p. 18.

the other virtues[65] and since virtues moderate our actions,[66] a ritual that flows from charity will be a rightly ordered and moderated liturgy. It will neither be too long nor too short; St. Thomas observes that the measure or length of the prayer is ordered toward inciting interior devotion.[67] If it is too short, one does not have sufficient time to incite the devotion. If it is too long, it becomes difficult for man in his current condition, laboring under the effects of original sin, to sustain. The ritual must manifest the faith of the Church clearly and must dispose the people in such a way that they lead lives of grace. In the ritual, humility will be served and grace will be increased when the faithful make the proper acts of sorrow for their sins at the appropriate times. The ritual must seek to remove sin from the faithful so as to make them more pleasing to God and thereby increase the merit.

The prayer must also be said with attention,[68] and this also applies to the ritual, which is a collection of prayers. The people must be sure that they remain attentive to the sacrifice and the sacred mysteries that are occurring. This does not translate, necessarily, into being more physically active. Because man is a creature of habit, it is entirely possible to be physically active in something (because the physical acts are governed by habit) while the interior life is not at all connected to the activity. Therefore, a ritual must be one designed to maintain the attention of the faithful. Again, this does not mean it must be active and verbal. Rather, the ritual should be one of profound beauty that will naturally draw the worshipper to its contemplation. It should not be chatty and activist in nature so as to cause distractions that make it difficult for someone to maintain a focus on God. While activity can draw our focus since motion by nature draws our faculties, nevertheless the attention is drawn to the motion, not to God. This is why a ritual should not be activist in nature. Since all of the attributes necessary for prayer may also apply to the ritual, these conditions of prayer as they are rooted in the ritual will increase or decrease the ritual's value extrinsically.

Given these points, it is possible to see the truth of what Gihr said many years ago:

> The essential fruit of the Mass has its immediate and only source in the self-immolation of Christ, and is, therefore, independent of the contents of the formulas of the Mass Rite of the Church. Hence there

---

[65] ST II-II, q. 23, a. 8.

[66] ST II-II, q. 64.

[67] ST II-II, q. 83, a. 4.

[68] ST II-II, q. 83, a. 13.

is here a question only of the accidental, or subordinate, fruit, arising from the liturgical prayers of the Mass, but added to the essential fruit, and benefiting directly those for whom the Mass is celebrated.[69]

The accidental fruit derived from the ritual of the Mass is something real and consequently is something that must be taken seriously by those whose task it is to protect and administer the sacraments, viz. the Magisterium.

III. Is the Old Rite of Mass More Meritorious than the New Rite of Mass?

As mentioned above, since the new rite is valid, as to the intrinsic sacrifice, the agency of the Church and the agency of the priest as a public person, it is the same as the old. Also as mentioned, we cannot pass judgment on the priests or faithful who go to these respective Masses since we do not have access to their interior lives and cannot judge with certitude who is more holy. It is possible to have beautiful decora in the new rite of Mass, even though the decora used by many in the new rite is often lacking. However, when we consider the rituals themselves, it is possible to arrive at which is more efficacious.

The new rite is "streamlined" in the sense that those who wrote it sought to simplify the ritual. This resulted in less pomp, so in this respect we may say the old rite is more efficacious than the new. As we will slow in the next chapter, the old rite excels the newer rituals with regard to the virtues. Specifically, the old rite proceeds more from charity than the new insofar as the old rite is more ordered to God and less ordered toward the people. This is manifest not only in altar orientation (the new rite can be said oriented) but also in the fact that references to the supernatural virtues were reduced in the propers. Also, the new calendar reduces the glory of the saints. Since charity is love of neighbor for the sake of God, it is hard to see how charity could govern a reduction of the glory of God through the saints. The readings are said toward the people in the new rite, rather than as something offered back to God by facing God the Son Who shall rise in the east. In the old rite, the epistle and the Gospel are read facing God as in the form of a sacrifice offered back to Him. Many parts of the new rite are said facing the people (such as the introductory and penitential rites) rather than to God, as in the prayers at the foot of the altar in the old rite. In these and in other ways, the new rite is less ordered to God and therefore does not manifest the virtue of charity as well.

Some parts of the new rite are the same as the old. It is possible, provided the manners and gestures associated with these parts remain the same, that the new and the old rite can have the same value in respect to

---

[69]Gihr, *The Holy Sacrifice of the Mass*, p. 146.

these. Yet most of the parts that remained the same in the new rite (here we are thinking at least about the Latin versions of the prayers) had the gestures changed from the old rite. The Gloria in the old rite contains gestures that were dropped in the new rite, and the Gloria is not said facing God externally since the prayer is not said oriented. The first Eucharistic canon, which is in large part taken from the canon in the old rite, has had a vast majority of its gestures stripped away. These gestures derive an additional fruit, such as the gestures of the signs of the Cross made over the *oblata* and things of this kind.

The new rite, as a form of prayer, is hard to pray mentally since there are more things said out loud, and the general tenor of Vatican documents on the subject encourages a form of active participation that requires more things occurring on the side of the laity. The old rite of Mass, since it is less activist on the side of the laity, tends to make it easier for them to pray the Mass. While the old rite stresses a more interior active participation, the new rite, with a lack of periods of silence as exist in the old rite, makes the ritual less meditative. In fact, the periods of meditation in the new rite are somewhat artificial and are not integral to the ritual as such but serve to stop the ritual rather than being a part of it. In other words, the priest stops the rite so the people can meditate, rather than having the people meditate while the ritual is in progress, as is the case in the old rite. As a result, in the new rite it is harder for people to lift their minds and hearts to God. The requirement of attention as part of prayer is more difficult and so, in that respect, the new rite is less efficacious than the old because God is more pleased with those things that easily draw us to Him.

As will be seen in the next chapter, the old rite fosters greater humility than the newer rituals. This means that the newer ritual as a prayer has less of one of the conditions that make prayer efficacious. In this respect the old rite is more efficacious than the new. As will be seen in the next chapter, the old rite manifests the faith more clearly. In this respect the old rite is more meritorious than the new, since prayer has an efficacy based upon how the Faith is manifested in the prayer itself. In connection to the clarity of faith, it will also be shown below that the old rite is more beautiful than the new. The more beautiful a thing is, the more it pleases God. The more beautiful it is, the greater glory it gives to God. Because the old rite is more beautiful than the new, it is more efficacious than the new. In effect, the prayers of the old rite of Mass better express the desires and intentions of an authentic Catholic faith, since they contain the faith in a clearer fashion. The prayers of the old rite of Mass foster a greater sense of our unworthiness and need for humility and sorrow for our sins. The prayers are more ordered toward God and suit Him better since they contain a proper supernatural dimension.

Conclusion

It is safe to say that, objectively speaking, with respect to the ritual itself the old rite of Mass has an ability to derive more fruit than the new rite of Mass. While this value is accidental, since the essential or intrinsic merit of the Mass, which is the Sacrifice of Christ, is the same in both rites, it is nevertheless something serious. Since the faithful are the beneficiaries of the fruits derived from this aspect of the Holy Sacrifice of the Mass, we have a grave obligation to consider the impact that this factor may be having on the life of the Church. While it is not our intention to denigrate the new rite, we must recognize that the ritual of Mass used in the old rite is more efficacious and therefore more beneficial for the people who assist at it and for the priests who offer it.

Chapter 8: The Spirituality of the Ancient Liturgy[70]

Among liturgists and theologians, it is generally considered true that each form of ritual embodies a kind of spirituality which is proper to that ritual. Thus, for example, the Eastern rites tend to emphasize the mysterious aspects of the spiritual life as well as the role of icons in promoting devotion to Our Lord, Our Lady and the saints. The ancient rite of Mass embodies a spirituality and spiritual lessons that can appeal to every generation and time. By ancient ritual is meant that rite which was codified by St. Gregory the Great and which underwent a very slow organic development over the course of centuries. The last missal promulgated that enjoys that organic growth is that of 1962.

It is the common perception in the Church today that the liturgical development of the medieval period was, in fact, decadent and that we must return to the apostolic and early Church period in order to know what real liturgy is as well as God's will regarding the liturgy. This is, however, a fundamentally flawed notion. Aside from the fact that many modern liturgical experts (and by modern is meant of the last 100 years or so) were not accurate in their understanding of the liturgies of the early Church, the notion that medieval liturgical development was somehow an aberration is really a rejection of what was an authentic development based upon the understanding of the Mass as sacrifice. Moreover, such figures like to harken back to an era when the liturgy was supposedly "pristine," by which they usually mean that it conformed to their faulty theology of the Mass as a meal.

The point here is not to give a history lesson, but to explain that one of the premises on which this essay is based is that the ancient rite of Mass is actually the product of the hand of God Who used saints throughout history to develop it according to His holy intention. The desire to reject our liturgical patrimony seems to me to be in fact a desire to reject those things which God has done. Insofar as it is the work of God and the saints, the liturgy embodies certain spiritual principles in the very nature of the ritual that are worthy of reflection. Obviously, we cannot exhaust them all, so we shall limit the discussion to four: 1) the awareness of our sinfulness, 2) the need for self-denial, 3) perfection in virtue and 4) certain aspects about prayer. All of these are essential elements of any sound spiritual life.

I. Awareness of Sin

The first is, again, an awareness of our own sinfulness. The ancient

---

[70]This chapter first appeared as a two part article in *The Latin Mass* in the Summer and Fall of 2001

rite of Mass starts with the prayers at the foot of the altar, which begins the Mass with the priest orienting himself to the altar – the altar of his youth. The altar is, of course, the place where the sacrifice for our sins takes place, and the priest asks God to judge his cause. Immediately, there is a clear understanding that there are good and bad in this world. Since the *Confiteor* is required in every Mass, the ancient ritual makes it clear to us that we have sinned and the priest, and later the people, confess their sins not only to God but also to the whole heavenly court – i.e., to specific saints as well as to all the saints in general. The priest himself must confess his sinfulness independently of the people, both as an example for them and a sign that the priest needs to be keenly aware of his own personal sinfulness. The priest asks to be washed and forgiven repeatedly throughout the ritual in order to foster a sense of humility and unworthiness before God to perform the function that belongs to him. No priest who takes the prayers seriously can be overcome with pride. As the priest ascends to the altar, he asks for the sins of the people to be taken away and then as he reverences the altar he asks specifically that all his sins be pardoned.

There is of course the *Kyrie*, which is an appeal for God's mercy, and before the Gospel the priest asks again that his heart and lips be cleansed. Aside from the *Confiteor*, perhaps the most notable recollection for the priest for his sins is contained in the offertory prayer *Suscipe, sancte Pater*. The priest says during this prayer that he offers the spotless Host to "atone for my innumerable sins, offenses, and negligences."

It is necessary for the priest to remind himself regularly of his sinfulness and his proclivity to evil so that he will be motivated to root the sin out of his life. It is also necessary for the priest to do this so that he recognizes his unworthiness to offer the sacrifice and the need to strive for purity and holiness in order to offer it worthily. Since the first step toward sanctified perfection is to be aware of and admit to one's own sinfulness, these prayers are highly important for the spiritual lives of priests. None of us who are aware of the scandals and sins associated with priests over the past forty years should desire that these prayers be taken out of the offertory or Mass. The laity must desire that the priest be sinless, and one of the ways that is facilitated is by recognizing in the prayers at Mass that he is offering this sacrifice not only for the people but also for himself. If a priest has a sensitive conscience and knows that he must remain pure for the sake of offering the sacrifice, then he merits more graces from God for the people. Today people say that as long as the Mass is valid, the state of the priest does not really matter. While it is true that a priest does not have to be in the state of grace to offer the Mass validly, nevertheless, he has an obligation to be as holy as possible in order to merit more for those under his pastoral care.

There are of course two kinds of merit in the Holy Sacrifice of the Mass. The first is Our Lord's own Sacrifice in which, by the hands of the priest, He is offered to God the Father in expiation for our sins. Here we are referring to the fact that the Mass is the participation in the Sacrifice of Calvary and the merit flowing from this Sacrifice is infinite since That Which is offered is Infinite. But in addition to this essential or primary merit, there is a secondary merit that flows from three things: (1) the holiness of the priest, (2) the holiness of the people who join their own particular sacrifices to the Sacrifice of the priest and (3) the ritual itself. In order for us to gain more fruits from the Mass, we must do everything we can to aid the priest in being holy, e.g., by offering our prayers and mortifications for him so that he will obtain a holiness of life. But this is possible only when the priest is frequently reminded of his ability to fall into sin if he does not rely on the grace of God. It does not help us to ignore this reality and remove it from the ritual. Rather, the awareness of our sinfulness is absolutely necessary for our spiritual advancement, and the ancient ritual is not lacking in this regard.

The word culture comes from the Latin word "cultus." While our subject in this chapter does not allow us to go too far into the discussion, we should be aware of the fact that the cult – that is, the liturgy or rituals of the predominant religion – actually determines the culture of the society. We have seen this historically during the Protestant revolts and we have even seen it in our own lifetimes: when the Church changed the ritual of the Mass, the Catholic subculture in this nation collapsed. The point here is that if we want to transform our culture, we must have a ritual that possesses a keen awareness of our sinfulness; if we expect our society to have an awareness of sin, the priest when he approaches the altar must have a sense of his sinfulness. Since all graces come into the world by means of the Catholic Church, if our ritual is deficient, then perhaps we are cheating the world of the graces that the ritual we offer is meant to convey.

II. Self Denial, Detachment and Mortification

The second spiritual aspect of the ancient ritual that is manifest in a number of ways is the sense of self-denial and mortification. One of the clearest manifestations of this self-denial is the old rite's silence. When we meet someone who has the vice of loquacity, of talking too much, it is usually because the person is full of himself. It is a fact of human nature that any time we do something that is in accord with our physical dispositions, we get a certain pleasure from it. People often speak of being in the "mood" for certain things and not others, and when they get the thing that corresponds to their mood, they experience a certain pleasure in it. Talking is much the same way: the appetites can become attached to talking, and this is precisely what the old rite militates against. By requiring the silence of the people, it provides an opportunity for the appetitive desire to talk to be stripped from those in attendance.

Frequently, the laity who come to the old rite for the first time find an appetitive revulsion to the ritual because of the silence. They do not express it exactly that way, of course, but as they talk it becomes clear that they do not like the fact that they are not being talked at and not doing some of the talking themselves. St. John of the Cross used to say that before he would enter into mystical contemplation his "house," as he called himself, became all quiet; and by this he meant that all of his appetites and faculties had quieted down. This is a sign to us that we must be quiet, we must be stripped of self in order to ascend the heights of perfection, and the old Mass aids that understanding. Moreover, it teaches us that we do not have to be the center of attention by talking in order for the ritual to have a deeper meaning and significance.

The old ritual also fosters a sense of detachment on the side of the priest and the people because the ritual is completely determined by Holy Mother the Church. We see in the Old Testament that God gave very detailed instructions on how He was to be worshiped. This is key in understanding the liturgy in two ways. The first is that the liturgy is not our action, it is the action of God by means of the priest; it is not something we do, it is essentially something God does, for the consecration cannot take place without God Who is the first cause of the Sacrifice. The second way is that it is God, and not ourselves, Who determines how we will worship Him. This has been one of the most notable failings in modern times: a desire to determine for ourselves how we will worship God. It is erroneous because it is up to God to tell us the type of worship that pleases or displeases Him and, therefore, only He should be the one to determine the ritual. It was mentioned earlier that God had fashioned the liturgy over the course of time through the saints, who were filled with love of God – everything they did came from Him and led back to Him. The old rite teaches us the important spiritual lesson that if we are going to be holy and pleasing to God, then our task is to conform to the liturgy and not make the liturgy something of our own doing or make it conform to us.

Furthermore, since it is God who must determine the ritual, we learn that the Mass is not about us but about God. We are only a secondary aspect of the rite. This is made clear in the ancient ritual in that control over the liturgy is taken away from us, and we thereby recognize that it is not about us. While our desire is to benefit from the Mass, our benefit ultimately must be referred back to God; that is to say, we become holy because it gives God greater glory. So even the aspects that affect us are ultimately about God.

The traditional rite, by determining how the ritual is to be done, provides two important spiritual benefits for the priest. The first is peace, for he can go and conform himself to the will of God by following the rubrics of the Mass since they are predetermined; this provides for the priest a great sense of freedom. He does not have to fret over what he will choose and say because he is worried about what the congregation may think. He does not have to listen to a liturgical committee trying to tell him what to do. The second is that it teaches the priest self-denial and sometimes mortification when the ritual is out of his hands. The Mass is not about the priest; it does not have to be sustained by his personality. Obviously only a priest can offer the Mass, but he can lose and forget himself when the whole ritual is determined by the Church, which is the *Vox Dei*, the Voice of God. It makes it possible for him to forget himself and everything else so that he can perfectly enter into the mystery and the sacred realities present, and thereby derive the greatest benefit from them. In a most perfect fashion, he acts *in persona Christi* – in the person of Christ – because his own personality is minimized and he can become more like Christ. Since he says Mass facing God and not the people, his own personality, or lack thereof, is not what sustains the ritual. He is able to let his own personality fade into the background so that he can concentrate fully on attending to God. Here when we talk of service, the priest serves God first and foremost. Too often when the term "service" is used in conjunction with the priesthood, it usually means some type of social service, rather than its real meaning of service to God.

The old rite of Mass has only two kinds of options, both of which are heavily regulated. The first is that on certain days, according to certain conditions, votive Masses can be said; but that is something exterior to the ritual. The second is that under certain circumstances and on certain days, predetermined optional prayers may be added to the propers, e.g., to pray for rain, for peace, or something of this sort. But these are heavily regulated so that the priest understands that while he may choose to do them, when and how are not entirely up to him. The point is that options within the ritual should be minimized in order to foster obedience to superiors, self-denial and the reduction of self-will, all of which are necessary to the spiritual life. If many options are allowed, it actually militates against the priest's self-denial and it fosters self-will, since the ritual becomes subject to his choice. It also leaves him with the impression that the liturgy is really his doing rather than an action performed by God through him.

Lack of options teaches the priest detachment and it also teaches the laity self-denial because they know they cannot try to manipulate the priest to do in the liturgy what they want, since it is out of his hands. Detachment is key to any discussion of the liturgy and any sound spiritual life. Modern man has lost all detachment regarding the liturgy and he is constantly subjecting it to his appetites. But we need detachment, and any discussion of liturgical restoration requires that people first detach themselves from what they want so that they can know what God wants. Furthermore, the multitude of options and lack of detachment in the liturgy has led to a type of immanentism. Immanentism is a philosophy or notion which holds that everything of importance is about us and comes from us. If it is not from us, then it has no meaning or significance. Immanentism comes from the two Latin words *in* and *manere* which mean to remain in. Since man is incapable of reaching the heavens on his own (Babel and the Pelagian heresies have clearly demonstrated that), the liturgy must be from God and about God in order to draw us out of ourselves and to foster any sense of the transcendent, the striving for which is deeply rooted in the heart of man.

The ancient liturgy also provides a depth to one's spiritual life for three reasons. The first is that it takes us out of ourselves and brings us to God; if we remain in ourselves and if we fashion a liturgy that is at our whim and ultimately about us, then we are doomed to shallowness and superficiality. Rather, insofar as the liturgy is out of our hands, we recognize that it is beyond us, it is mysterious, and insofar as it is about God, it can forever be contemplated. The second is that it is founded on tradition. Tradition provides a mechanism in which man can abandon himself to God who fashions the tradition rather than taking control of it himself and jettisoning the tradition. In other words, tradition provides a mechanism by which the spiritual and liturgical patrimony of the saints can be given to each generation, who can use it to their spiritual benefit. Like someone who does not know his historical roots and therefore does not know himself, modern man has chosen to reject liturgical tradition and replace it with himself, only to be lost in self and never truly to understand himself. Tradition provides a way for the young to ground themselves in the wisdom of the past. This applies not only to cultural things but to the liturgy and the spiritual life as well.

The third thing that the ancient liturgy provides is repetition. Now modern man has rejected repetition because he has a fixation on novelty. Novelty, of course, gives our appetites delight but does not necessarily indicate depth. To enter into something in depth requires time and repeated considerations of a thing. *Repetitio mater discendi*, as we say in Latin: repetition is the mother of learning. This principle applies not only to learning but to our spiritual lives as well. By repeating a prayer, its meaning becomes more known to us and therefore is able to be entered into more perfectly and with greater depth. Since the ancient rite allows not for novelty but repetition, it provides a way in which people can focus on the mysteries present rather than the new things that are constantly popping up. With the silence quieting our faculties and the repetition that characterize each Mass, we are able to participate in and enter more perfectly into the mysteries of the Mass. Too often participation is equated with physical activity rather than the higher and more active form of participation which is spiritual participation.

Novelty begets spiritual gluttony. By spiritual gluttony is understood the spiritual defect by which one takes delight and concerns oneself only with the physical and spiritual consolations sent by God rather than using the consolation as a means to growing more holy. Spiritual gluttony occurs when people do spiritual or religious things because of some consolation or delight they derive from them and so the delight, rather than God, becomes the end of the action. Novelty begets spiritual gluttony because people tend to think that newer is always better, and so each new thing brings them some new delight. Here we see that novelty can easily degenerate into keeping people entertained, but the danger is that insofar as it prompts one to stop looking at God and fixating on the new thing that sates our appetites, it impedes our spiritual growth. All of the saintly spiritual writers warn that spiritual gluttony is very dangerous for the spiritual life.

The ancient ritual actually destroys spiritual gluttony on three levels. First, all of the silence takes away from our appetites the desire to talk. It is a fact that some people like vocal prayer because of the "spiritual high," to use a degenerate sixties and seventies term, that comes from doing the talking. Second, the repetition ensures that the appetites, which constantly want something new, are not satisfied. Repetition in a spiritual good is something that is appreciated on an intellectual level, not an appetitive level. Our appetites can get bored when we experience the same thing; the intellect, on the other hand, is able to see the value of the thing each time it encounters it. Third, a certain pleasure comes from being in control of something. This is another reason that the ritual must be fixed or determined by the Church and not by ourselves. For insofar as the ritual is determined by our choice among options and not according to the universal laws of the Church, we take a certain pleasure in being in control. But this is to subordinate a spiritual good to our natural desires.

Moreover, while it is not part of the newer rituals themselves, some of the forms of music employed in them are used because of some sensible or appetitive pleasure derived from the music rather than for their usefulness in drawing the mind and will into closer union with God. This leads people to confuse the pleasurable experience with actually experiencing God. In effect, it leads people to think that authentic experiences of God are always pleasant. While in the next life they are, in this life the experiences of God are often arduous and exceedingly painful for us – not because of some defect in the way God handles us, but because of our imperfections and sinfulness which cause our pain. As St. Theresa of Avila once said, "God, if this is the way you treat your friends, no wonder you have so few of them."

The point is that music and all of the other aspects of the ritual should be geared toward weaning people off sensible delights and consolations as the mainstay of their spiritual lives. This is why Gregorian chant which, has an appeal to the intellect and will, naturally begets prayer, which is defined as the lifting of the mind and heart to God. Gregorian chant does not appeal to one's emotions or appetites; rather, the beauty of the chant naturally draws us into contemplation of the divine truths and the mysteries of the ritual.

To return to our discussion of liturgical options, by having a predetermined ritual by the universal laws of the Church, one avoids having one person force his disposition and his own spiritual life or lack thereof on the rest of the people attending Mass. In other words, it avoids having someone impose himself or intrude on the spiritual lives of the laity by the choices he makes which flow from his own interior dispositions and spiritual life. Since people naturally differ in disposition, when the ritual becomes the product of one individual or even a few, it loses its spiritual appeal to the rest of the people, who may not share the same dispositions.

The traditional rite, on the other hand, avoids this pitfall by determining the ritual itself. One of the advantages of the ancient ritual is that it does not matter which parish you attend; it is everywhere the same. Insofar as the options of the new rite allow for the particularization of the ritual, it ceases being catholic (meaning universal). In fact, in an age of hyper-mobility, it seems especially imprudent to have changed the ritual. The author realized this when he went to Rome and attended Mass in Italian. Had the Mass been in Latin according to the ancient rite, he would have felt right at home at Mass; instead, he was left with the impression that he was merely an onlooker from the outside. This is why Latin and a fixed ritual allow the Mass to have a universal appeal: one can attend it in every country, in every parish in the world and still feel right at home. While we may not understand the homily or sermon when we are in a foreign country, we can nevertheless enter into the ritual in the same depth and fervor that we can at our home parish. This also avoids the unfortunate problem of people parish shopping, as it were, trying to find a priest whose choice of Mass options suits their own dispositions.

Latin also provides a form of self-denial by taking the translation of the ritual out of the hands of questionable agencies. Inclusive language is a classic example of what we have been describing: the desire of a small group to impose its own spirituality on everyone else. The desire for inclusive language is a manifestation of the expectation that the ritual should conform to the group rather than vice versa. Latin undermines this idea because everyone, as Pope John XXIII says in *Veterum Sapientia*, is equal before the Latin language. Latin forces a type of self-denial on us because we cannot manipulate the language to our own ends. It also thwarts the inclination of the priest to *ad lib*, foisting his own personal disposition on those attending the Mass.

The Latin, the fixed rubrics, these things strip us of our selves so that we can become nothing. St. John of the Cross often noted that we must be nothing so that God can become everything in us, or, as in the words of St. John the Baptist (which we can apply to the ancient ritual), "I must decrease, so that He may increase." Stripping ourselves of self, which the ancient ritual does, is a requirement for any authentic spirituality.

III. Perfection in Virtue

This brings us to the next topic: perfection in virtue. The old rite of Mass, insofar as it strips us of self, humbles us. This is necessary, since every one of us suffers from pride. Moreover, by not giving us control over the ritual, the old rite begets meekness, the virtue by which one does not go to extremes in one's reactions or actions. There are countless stories of laity and priests being furious after attending the new rite because of something the celebrant did. The priest should not be the cause of anger during the Mass. By becoming the cause of anger, he erodes the meekness of the laity. Having a fixed ritual, provided the priest follows the rubrics and says the Mass reverently, minimizes the chance that the priest will anger the laity. In this way, the old rite assures meekness.

Humility is the root virtue in the concupiscible appetite, i.e., the thing in us that inclines us toward bodily goods. Humility is the virtue by which one does not judge oneself greater than he is. St. Thomas Aquinas tells us it is the root virtue of all the other virtues and that no other virtue can exist without it. The old rite of Mass roots out pride and begets humility because it is not our action or our product but the product and action of God. Moreover, by coming up against the mysterious which for us in this life is insurmountable, it naturally causes in us a sense of our smallness in comparison to God. This in turn tempers the way we behave because we are in the presence of someone who causes "awe," which is an overwhelming sense of wonder or admiration. "Awe" naturally causes us to stop and consider ourselves in the light of that which is awesome; it captivates us and therefore moderates what we do. The ancient ritual, in begetting humility and meekness – upon which all the other virtues rest – reminds us of the words of Christ, Who said, "Learn from Me, for I am meek and humble of heart." In other words, " I conform myself to the truth, I am not proud and do not judge myself greater than I am, I do not go to extremes in my reactions." This is what we must desire in any ritual. The ritual should speak to us – not in our own words, but in the words of Christ. In this way the ancient ritual can be seen to be saying metaphorically, "Learn from me, for I am meek and humble of heart."

Once meekness and humility are in place, the virtue of reverence naturally follows. Reverence is the virtue contained under the more universal virtue of justice, and more particularly religion, in which one holds in honor and esteem some thing, usually sacred. The ancient ritual helps us to honor those things that are holy because, first, we are humble and recognize the greatness of sacred things. Secondly, we approach God in a sense of self-denial and subservience, and in this respect the ancient ritual excels. For the priest bows his head, genuflects and humbles himself often in the prayers that God might look upon his actions and be pleased.

Fortitude is also taught in the ancient ritual, if in no other way than that it is clear that it is spiritual warfare. At the very beginning, when the priest vests by putting on the amice, he says a prayer in which he asks Our Lord for the helmet of salvation so that he can fight off the incursions of the devil. Also, since the priest is not subject to a liturgical committee in making decisions on what should and should not be done, the traditional rite strengthens the priest and reaffirms the masculine aspects of being a priest.

Here we highly recommend the article by Fr. James McLucas on the emasculation of the priesthood,[71] in which he argues that the newer rituals have, in fact, taken away from the priest those things that are masculine: e.g., the role of providing for and protecting his spiritual family. In the ancient ritual, he alone feeds his spiritual family by distributing Holy Communion. This also means he can protect the sacred mysteries. The systematic removal of all these things that emphasize the masculine and fatherly role of the priest has weakened our vision of the priesthood. Moreover, we tend to get what we offer as an example. Thus, if we place before people a weakened view of the priesthood that has little or no virtue of fortitude, then we can expect priests to become weak and effeminate, and attract seminarians who follow suit. Fortitude is defined as engaging the arduous good and the ancient ritual provides an avenue for the priest to obtain the greatest and most difficult type of fortitude: self-discipline through self-denial.

The ancient ritual also avoids violations of justice. The new Code of Canon Law states that the laity have a right to attend the liturgy said according to the rubrics. Now all the options have eroded the sense that the priest must render to the people their due; the flow of the Mass is at his discretion. This leads the priest to think that he can do whatever he likes. While Church documents are clear that he cannot do so, the fact is that all these options contain the implicit principle of "do what you want." This is why, when the ritual is out of the hands of the priest, it naturally begets a sense of the requirement of justice in all of us. For when the priest does something that is contrary to the rubrics, or even in the rubrics but included as optional, it gives people a sense that the priest is concerned not so much about what God wants as about what he wants, especially if one attending the Mass does not like the particular option. Ultimately, the ritual of the Mass is about God, and ought to seek the best way of rendering to God His due. This comes through a deep sense of justice. Through the sacrifice to God and the conformity of the ritual to that sacrifice, we recognize that with respect to God, we have no claim of justice insofar as we are mere creatures. Therefore, the Mass must be about God and not ourselves. The ancient ritual helps us to forget and lose ourselves in the rendering of justice to God through the Sacrifice.

---

[71] *The Latin Mass*, Spring 1998.

The ancient rite begets faith, hope and charity. It begets faith because it excels in its expression of Catholic theology. Faith comes through hearing and we hear the Faith in the very prayers of the ancient ritual. It begets hope because of its deep sense of the transcendent and our participation in the transcendent. It begets charity because it helps us to realize that worship is about God, not us. Charity is defined as love of God and neighbor for the sake of God. Even when we love our neighbor, it must be for the sake of God. Hence the ritual helps us to focus everything on God, thereby giving a proper direction to our spiritual lives. Even if this were not the case, the ancient ritual begets charity if for no other reason than that it keeps people's imperfections at bay by taking away the ability of one person to impose himself on another, thereby averting anger, hurt feelings and the like.

IV. Ascendance in Prayer

The last aspect is ascendence in prayer. We have already mentioned the silence that is necessary to ascend the heights of prayer. While it is not required for vocal prayer, it is required for mental prayer and the other seven levels of prayer. St. Augustine said that no person can save his soul if he does not pray. Now it is a fact that mental prayer and prayer in general have collapsed among the laity (and the clergy, for that matter) in the past forty years. It leaves one with the impression that this development actually has to do with the ritual of the Mass. Now in the new rite, everything centers around vocal prayer, and the communal aspects of the prayer are heavily emphasized. This has led people to believe that only those forms of prayer that are vocal and communal have any real value. Consequently, people do not pray on their own any longer.

The ancient ritual, on the other hand, actually fosters a prayer life. The silence during the Mass actually teaches people that they must pray. Either one will get lost in distraction during the ancient ritual or one will pray. The silence and encouragement to pray during the Mass teach people to pray on their own. While, strictly speaking, they are not praying on their own insofar as they should be joining their prayers and sacrifices to the Sacrifice and prayer of the priest, these actions are done interiorly and mentally and so naturally dispose them toward that form of prayer. This is one of the reasons that, after the Mass is said according to the ancient ritual, people are naturally quieter and tend to pray afterwards. If everything is done vocally and out loud, then once the vocal stops, people think it is over. It is very difficult to get people who attend the new rite of Mass to make a proper thanksgiving by praying afterward because their appetites and faculties have habituated them toward talking out loud.

The ancient ritual also gives one a taste of heaven, so to speak. Since the altar marks the dividing line between the profane and sacred, between the heavenly and the earthly, and the priest ascends to the altar to offer Sacrifice, the traditional rite leaves one with a sense of being drawn into heaven with the priest. This feature naturally draws us into prayer and gives the sense of the transcendent and supernatural that are key in the spiritual life. The numerous references to the saints foster devotion rather than minimizing it. The Latin provides a sense of mystery. The beauty of the ritual, the surroundings that naturally flow from the ritual itself (such as the churches that are designed for the ritual), the chant – all of these things lead to contemplation, the seeking after that which is above.

Conclusion

Clearly we have not exhausted all the spiritual aspects of the ancient ritual, but the four areas we covered demonstrate that the ancient ritual and the newer forms have different spiritualities. If the Church is to capture the sense of the transcendent for the laity, if we are to have humble and saintly priests, if we are to have a ritual that is driven by charity and therefore has God as the sole focus of our longings and desires, it must restore that liturgy that God Himself fashioned both when Christ was on earth and through the loving hands of the saints throughout history. We cannot be satisfied with a liturgy that is the work of our own hands. For this reason, we ought not subscribe to the theory that we need to produce yet another ritual. We need the work of God back, because if the ancient ritual does anything, it teaches us that we do not need our own self-expression. We need God.

Chapter 9: The Order of Charity[72]

In the *Summa Contra Gentiles*, St. Thomas Aquinas argues for the existence of God based on what can be known by the natural light of reason, i.e. what can be known by human intelligence without the aid of revelation. From the principles and reasoning laid out in his argument for God's existence, St. Thomas unpacks what else we can know about God through the natural light of reason. One of the things He observed is that God is infinite[73] and intelligent.[74] He goes on to say:

> That thing alone is primarily and essentially known by the intellect by whose species the intellect understands; for an operation is proportioned to the form that is the principle of the operation. But... that by which God understands is nothing other than His essence. Therefore, the primary and essential object of His intellect is nothing other than Himself.[75]

What St. Thomas is saying is that the proper object of God's knowledge is Himself. In other words, the primary thing that God knows is Himself. Interestingly, St. Augustine says that God the Son is the knowledge of God the Father of Himself.[76] St. Thomas says that God does know other things but He knows them by virtue of the fact that He is there cause.[77] So we may say that God knows us insofar as He knows Himself and, in knowing Himself, He sees Himself causing us.

According to St. Thomas, "the understood good is the object of the will... But that which is principally understood by God is the divine essence... The divine essence, therefore, is principally the object of the divine will."[78]

---

[72]This article first appeared in *The Latin Mass* (Summer 2006).

[73]SCG I, c. 43.

[74]SCG I, c. 44.

[75]SCG I, c. 48, n. 2: illa enim solum res est primo et per se ab intellectu cognita cuius specie intelligit: operatio enim formae quae est operationis principium proportionatur. Sed id quod Deus intelligit nihil est aliud quam sua essentia, ut probatum est. Igitur intellectum ab ipso primo et per se nihil est aliud quam ipsemet.

[76]St. Thomas observes this as well in ST I, qq. 34 and 35.

[77]SCG I, c. 49.

[78]SCG I, c. 74.

Here St. Thomas is basing his observations on the fact that the will is a blind faculty and can will something only when it is presented its object by the intellect. In other words, we cannot will something unless we know it. Since the proper object of God's knowledge is Himself, the proper object of God's will is the same divine essence, i.e. Himself. Now the proper act of the will in relation to the good (God is goodness itself[79]) is love, for love is "willing the good of another".[80] Therefore, the proper object of God's love is Himself. Yet St. Thomas goes on to say that God does will other creatures to exist and that He wills the good for them,[81] but He does so only insofar as He wills Himself.[82] So St. Thomas is saying that God loves us insofar as He loves Himself. Yet, this very order of loving God, i.e. Himself and us insofar as He loves Himself, is the very foundation for the reflection of that love in the creature. In other words, this order of loving God and then loving creatures for the sake of God is the very order of charity in us. Our Lord gave two precepts of charity,[83] and so St. Thomas asks whether the object of charity consists in God alone. He then answers:

> since the species of an act is taken from its formal notion and that which is born in the object under such a notion... The formality of loving one's neighbor is God, as we ought to love our neighbor as in God. Hence it is manifest that the same species of act is that by which God is loved and that by which one's neighbor is loved. And because of this, the habit of charity not only extends itself to love of God, but also to the love of neighbor.[84]

---

[79] SCG I, c. 38.

[80] See Aristotle, *Rhetoric*, II, c. 4 (1380b35); ST I-II, q. 26, a. 4 and SCG I, c. 91, nn. 2 and 3.

[81] SCG II, passim.

[82] SCG I, c. 75.

[83] See Ripperger, *Introduction to the Science of Mental Health*, vol. II, pp. 66f.

[84] ST II-II, q. 25, a. 1: cum autem species actus ex obiecto sumatur secundum formalem rationem ipsius, necesse est quod idem specie sit actus qui fertur in rationem obiecti, et qui fertur in obiectum sub tali ratione.... Ratio autem diligendi proximum Deus est, hoc enim debemus in proximo diligere, ut in Deo sit. Unde manifestum est quod idem specie actus est quo diligitur Deus, et quo diligitur proximus. Et propter hoc habitus caritatis non solum se extendit ad dilectionem Dei, sed etiam ad dilectionem proximi.

Charity does not merely consist in love of God and love of neighbor, but in the love of God and the love of neighbor *for the sake of God* (*propter Deum*). One's neighbor is not loved for his own sake but for the sake of God and God constitutes the formality, i.e. the perspective taken on one's neighbor. Hence the virtue of charity is ultimately about God, even when one loves one's neighbor for the sake of God.

Therefore, the order of charity in us follows the order of God's love in Himself. God loves Himself and He loves us for His own sake (*propter Seipsum*); we love God and our neighbor (and self) for the sake of God (*propter Deum*). We become like God insofar as we love everything from the point of view of God. It may be thought that somehow God is selfish by loving Himself and loving us only insofar as He loves Himself. We must not forget that God is goodness itself and so it is proper for God to love Himself. We are not goodness itself, but are good only by virtue of the fact that we participate in some way in God's goodness. Therefore, our love should not rest on ourselves but upon God, who is the source of our own goodness. For God, to love everything for his own sake is right order; for us to love other things only insofar as we love ourselves is disordered, because we are not goodness itself; God is.

Sanctified perfection is reached when the will is moved by nothing other than God or created things when looked at from the point of view of God. Since God created man for His (i.e. God's) sake and for his own glory, then our entire reason for existence is for the sake of God. Our entire lives are for the sake of God.

This applies *a fortiori* to the liturgy. The liturgy, if it is to follow the order of charity, must ultimately be about God. It can be about us only insofar as it is about God. The liturgy is a means for us to reach God, to give God greater glory, to worship God and in the end to help us to orient ourselves entirely to God. To the degree that we make the liturgy about ourselves without it being about God, we deviate from the order of charity and turn away from God. For this reason, any liturgy that focuses on man for his own sake destroys the order of charity and will therefore afflict the life of the Church and its members.

Chapter 10: Teaching Modesty[85]

St. Thomas Aquinas defines modesty as the virtue in which exterior actions, either in deed or in words, due mode is observed.[86] Modesty is the virtue that restrains our exterior gestures.[87] It is thus a broader virtue than that conveyed by the modern use of the term *modesty*, which deals only with the dress and actions in relation to the Sixth and Ninth Commandments. The medieval use of the term takes into consideration *all* of our exterior actions and motions.

Yet, what does it mean to observe due "mode" in our actions? St. Thomas says in his commentary on Peter Lombard's *Sentences* that it consists in three things:[88] 1) "first is the discussion (*collocutiones*) with those with whom we live, and, in these, mode posits austerity." For St. Thomas austerity is a moderation of delights, so that when we speak of austerity in relation to exterior actions we refer to restraining and moderating the pleasures or delights we take in our exterior actions. This is why random, irrational or foolish behavior is contrary to the virtue of modesty: these kinds of actions are often done for the pleasure they bring rather than for a virtuous end.

When we consider the old rite of Mass, we see that it does engender an austerity in those who attend it. Its music is moderated and ordered toward lifting the mind and heart to God rather than giving sensible delights. Yet, St. Thomas says that austerity does not exclude all delights but only excessive and disordered delights. The use of incense and bells, for instance, while giving us sensible delight, orders us toward God and, in this sense, provides an example of the old rites austerity with respect to order and moderation. The old rite likewise requires a certain austerity with respect to our neighbors, by the mode of conduct expected of the laity in attendance. This austerity, as it were, prevents the Mass from degenerating into a social or festive occasion.

The second thing pertaining to the mode of modesty involves "exterior goods, such as clothes, horses, and things of this kind and in these, mode posits humility so far as to the quantity and use. Hence,... humility is the habit of not exceeding in cost and preparation; but simplicity so far as to the motive seeking, which... is the habit of being content in those things which happen, for there is not much care of such things. Here St. Thomas's observing two

---

[85]This chapter first appeared as an article in *The Latin Mass* (Fall 2006).

[86]ST I-II, q. 70, a. 3. See also *Super ad Galatas*, c. 4, l. 5; ibid., c. 5, l. 6; *Super II ad Cor.*, c. 10, l. 1; *Super ad Colas.*, c. 3, l. 3 and *Super ad Titam*, c. 3, l. 1.

[87]III Sent., d. 33, q. 3, a. 2a.

[88]These three are taken from III Sent., d. 33, q. 3, a. 2c.

things. The first is that modesty helps us to moderator exterior goods, i.e. we have neither too many of them nor to few; we give neither too much concern nor too little to the things we own; we spent neither too much nor too little. Our circumstances sometimes govern these considerations; hence, someone who buys a luxury car when he cannot make the payments on his meager house is immodest. This is also why the Church has traditionally taught us that we must come to Mass dressed in suitable apparel, not to showy or ostentatious but modest, dignified and orderly.

The third thing that pertains to the mode of modesty involves "one's own actions which pertain to the body; and, in these, mode posits ornateness to acting, which... is knowledge about what is suitable in motion and dress; so far as to externals, which are considered according to due time, place and order." This profound passage requires some explanation. Here St. Thomas says that the person with modesty acts so that his action suit time, place and order. Obviously the person who talks in the church before Mass is not observing due time and place for talking, and thus we may say that his actions are immodest. St. Thomas also mentions *order*, and by order he means that our actions are proportionate and directed to a truly good end.

The virtue of ornateness teaches us the congruity between our externals, our actions and person and even gender.[89] Andronicus calls this ornateness in the proper sense. But ornateness should be suited to affair, person or place in which one's actions manifests the best order. In effect, the person's very actions become "ornate" by being "dressed" with proper order and suitability of person to circumstances. We should never say anything or do anything that is out of place or does not suit our state in life as individuals.

The old rite teaches us modesty in this respect by being ordered to God and not earthly things. The fact that the Mass is oriented – i.e., facing interior east (not necessarily *geographical* east but rather with all participants in the Mass facing the same direction) – means that we are concerned about God more than ourselves. This is itself a kind of modesty. We do not offer Mass facing each other or worry about what people are going to think of how we have arranged the liturgy. Holy Mother the Church instructs the priest how Mass is to be offered and, by following what the Church requires, the priest moderates his actions and actions of the faithful towards each other.

As for the order or truly good end of the Mass, we know that it must be God.[90] In reference to Proverbs 22: 4, St. Thomas observes that the end of modesty is Fear of the Lord.[91] Fear of the Lord for St. Thomas is the gift of the

---

[89] See ST II-II, q. 168, a. 1.

[90] See previous chapter.

[91] *Super ad Titum*, c. 3, l. 1.

Holy Spirit by which we turn away from depraved delights and earthly things and towards God. Since modesty restrains us from inordinate delights and actions, it will direct this to this salutary fear of God in the form of a fear of offending Him by our disordered passions, appetites and emotions. The old rite excels in teaching us this, for it is not about us but about God; its motions direct us to God and by its sublime content it lifts our minds and hearts from earthly things to God.

St. Thomas also says that modesty (*pudor*[92] *honestatis*) is equal to a pure and stable authority.[93] In other words, modesty is a virtue by which we approach[94] an authority in a proper and restrained manner. In this respect the old rite is most modest, for it restrains man from following his passions – i.e. what *he* wants – in his approach to God, Who is almighty, infinitely just, magisty itself, and inscrutable in His omniscience. When one approaches someone who has power over our very lives and their every aspect, great moderation in our actions is necessary; it is best if we consult wise people as to how to approach that person. It is for this reason that the old rite is most excellent, for it was begun by Christ and fashioned slowly over the course of centuries by Saints whose Fear of the Lord was perfect, whose approach to making changes in the liturgy solicitous of the gravity of what they are doing and whose keen sense and desire was not to offend God but to give him the greatest glory and honor that they could.

The fact that the old rite is predetermined in virtually all of its parts by holy mother the church, leaving virtually nothing to the discretion the priest, trains all of us in a profound sense of modesty. It teaches us that when we approach God we do so not on our terms but on God's. It teaches us that we must approach Him modestly, with a keen understanding of who we are and how our actions, prayers and externals relate to God. Thomas à Kempis observes:

> Oh, how clean those hands should be, how pure the lips, how sanctified the body, how immaculate the heart of the priest to whom the Author of all purity so often comes. No word but what is holy, none but what is good and profitable ought to come from the lips of the priest who so often receives the Sacrament of Christ. Single and modest should be the eyes accustomed to looking upon the Body of

---

[92] St. Thomas calls *pudor* a certain exterior composition (III Sent., d. 33, q. 3, a. 2a, ad 4).

[93] III Sent., d. 33, q. 3, a. 2a.

[94] ST II-II, q. 120, a. 2, ad 3. The words St. Thomas uses to refer to approaching is "in accessu".

Christ. Pure and lifted up to heaven the hands accustomed to handle the Creator of the heaven and earth. To priest above all it is written in the law, 'be ye holy, for I, the Lord your God, and holy.'[95]

The Church therefore requires that the priest practice custody of the eyes, an integral part of modesty: we should never let our eyes fall on anything that would distract us from God or lead us into sin. This is why the priest, when he turns to say *Dominus vobiscum*, does not look at the people, for his eyes as Thomas à Kempis says, must be accustomed to look upon the Body of Christ. In other words, his eyes must be directed to God and not earthly things. Moreover, the priest is directed as to when he is to look at the crucifix and when he is not. Out of humility at the beginning of Mass, he does not look at the crucifix when the *Gloria* is said but at other times the Church directs him to look at the Cross as an act of humility, in which we show to God through this action, this form of modesty, our humility, our lowly place in relation to Him. Even the actions of the priest are determined by the Church, for the rubrics determine the placement of the hands during each part of the Mass. This begets modesty and his gestures.

The old rite regulates and thereby trains the priest when to remain silent and when to speak in relation to things of God. Lapide observes in his commentary on the book of Leviticus that "the praise of silence is a certain thing, in which the interior of the soul as well as the external in sacred things venerate God, since it excites others to praise God, they see so much modesty and religion."[96] This is a profound insight into human psychology. Silence in the church and during the Holy Sacrifice of the Mass expresses the virtue of modesty by teaching others in our exterior and interior quiet – by which we mean the traditional spiritual sense of the term, in which nothing created occupies our thoughts and actions – that we are to be directed to God. Here we see the wisdom of the Church in placing silence in a large part of the rite of the Mass; the faithful are hereby directed not toward each other, as talking does, but to God alone. The interior (and exterior) silence is manifested indirectly by women who always wore veils in the church as an act of modesty, insofar as the veil was an outward sign to others that the beauty of the woman was not the object of consideration during this most sacred event (i.e., men were to practice custody the eyes and interior silence by not looking upon or thinking about earthly beauty of women). It was also a sign to the woman of her need of humility. Insofar as the Mass is not about her, people's attention should be directed not to her but to God alone.

The silence in connection with these other externals of the faithful

---

[95] *Imitation of Christ*, b. 4, c. 10.

[96] Lapide, *Commentaria in Scripturam Sacram*, vol II., p. 12.

associated with the old rite begets in others a profound sense of the sacred and that something serious is happening here. We are approaching God, the God Who could destroy us in a single act, the God who can condemn us to eternal punishment and whom we must therefore approach in reverence, in awe, in silence – in a word, in modesty. It is for this reason that the song "let all mortal flesh keep silence" is one of the most profound we have, and should be song often to remind us that in fear and trembling we stand before God, pondering absolutely nothing earthly.

According to St. Thomas Aquinas and other historical authors, there are four parts or sub-virtues to the virtue of modesty, and we may even say also to the Fruit of the Holy Spirit of Modesty.[97] The first is humility, which restrains and moderates one's desire for his own excellence. Clearly the old rite begets profound humility, as has been mentioned above. The second virtue under modesty is studiosity. This is the virtue in which one applies oneself to study those things that suit his state in life. Curiosity is the vice opposite to studiosity and is the vice in which we seek useless and profane knowledge. Chapel veils are great for cutting the curiosity of males. In the past, people were instructed not to "rubberneck" during Mass or while in the church, since it showed a lack of modesty with regard to one's exterior glances and a neglect of custody of the eyes. The old rite, by focusing all in the direction of God by the orientation of priest and people, teaches us to direct our eyes and not to be looking around. If the priest does not face interior east, then the tendency arising from human psychology is to start looking at each other. That in turn will spill over into a lack of custody of the eyes during Mass, and when Mass is not going on in the church. This is also why churches were not built to be "theaters in the round" in which everyone could see each other.

The third virtue under modesty is eutrapelia. This is the virtue of right recreation in which our bodily actions and motions are decorous or decent and manifest a striving for all of the virtues (*honestia* in Latin). Eutrapelia serves to moderate the delights of play and recreation.[98] Eutrapelia not only helps to moderate how much recreation or play we do, but also the very actions in the recreation and play are subordinated to virtue. In this respect the old rite teaches us that worshiping God is serious business and not a matter of recreational entertainment. It is not a matter of whether we are deriving from it some appetitive delight but whether due worship is being given to God.

The fourth virtue under modesty is modesty in the modern or stricter sense as referring to exterior apparel or clothing. St. Thomas knows that this

---

[97] These four are taken from ST II-II, q. 160, a. 2. As for modest being a Fruit, see ST I-II, q. 70, a. 3 and Ripperger, *Introduction to the Science of Mental Health*, vol. II, p. 121.

[98] See II Sent., d. 44, q. 2, a. 1, ad 3.

sense of modesty serves to moderate delights with respect to the senses.[99] This is the virtue that helps us with respect to two things: 1) whether our clothing leads others into sins regarding the Sixth and Ninth Commandments, and 2) whether or clothing fits due circumstances – i.e. befitting person and place. For example, it is immodest for priest to engage in his priestly work without being dressed like a priest. Modesty, in this respect, is engendered by dress codes, such as existed at Catholic schools in the past. Uniforms or certain kinds of dress express something about the interior life of the individual who is wearing them. If a person wears sloppy and unkempt clothes, that is a sign of interior disorder and spiritual sloth. If a person refuses to wear clothing according to the legitimate custom of the place, he acts contrary to modesty and commits the sin of *admiratio*.[100]

Yet the old rite also teaches us modesty in this second respect. It determines the vestments the priest must wear. The alb, for instance, is white as a sign of the purity necessary to approach the most holy Eucharist. Consider also that the priest wears the stole crossed underneath the chasuble. It is crossed as a sign that the stole, which is the sign of the office of the priesthood, is intimately connected to the self-denial on the Cross of Christ. It is under the chasuble because the chasuble is often a remote sign of the Church – it is a sign of the public act performed by the priest in relation to sacrifice, and that public act is to be done within the Catholic Church alone. The colors of the vestments teach the priest modesty and appropriateness insofar as his dress should suit certain occasions, e.g. the color black as a sign of death in morning, the color violet as a sign of penance and the color white is a sign of the purity of the Saint or mystery of the day. The colors of the vestments should be modest as well, ordered toward worship of God and not signs of inculturation, personal preference, and the like.

Here we begin to see the intimate connection between a ritual and the behavior the priest who offers it. If the ritual begets modesty and restrains the actions of the priest, the other decora, such as church appointments, vestments, and the like, will also manifest restraint, for the priest will develop the virtue of modesty by the very ritual that he offers. If the ritual does not demand modesty of the priest in all of its aspects, the decora will slowly slip into disorder as the lack of modesty in approaching God in the ritual makes its way outward into the priest, the faithful and finally in the monumental patrimony of the Church, i.e. in the physical things used in the worship of God.

St. Thomas says that modesty helps us to have due maturity in

---

[99] II Sent., q. 44, q. 2, a. 1, ad 3.

[100] *Admiratio* is a sin or vice against modesty in which one causes wonder and thereby draws undue attention to oneself.

observing exterior gestures,[101] a point the old rite likewise teaches us. It teaches that the ritual must be a manifestation of spiritual maturity and not one of the emotion or puerility. The old rite was slowly fashion over centuries, giving it a certain age, wisdom and grace. Maturity is a form of completion in which a person not only reaches a certain stage and physical growth but also a certain stage of the interior life. That stage is marked by self-denial, mortification, virtue and a striving for excellence. Spiritual immaturity, on the other hand is marked by selfishness, self-indulgence, and a lack of holiness and virtue. The old rite of Mass, in teaching us a profound sense of modesty, demands of its participants a spiritual maturity because the ritual is not, for virtually all parts of the Mass, at the discretion or indulgence of the priest or people. It teaches that a ritual itself must demand self-denial and austerity on the side of the people, for only in this way can we approach God in Fear of the Lord and in a manner worthy of his Divine Majesty.

---

[101] III Sent., d. 33, q. 3, a. 2a, ad 3.

Chapter 11: Aesthetics and God[102]

Traditionalists are often told by those committed to the *Novus Ordo* that the only legitimate reasons for going to the old rite are aesthetic. Often they state that it is merely a matter of personal preference; and by reducing the discussion to merely one of subjective aesthetic sense or taste, they think they can keep at bay intellectual arguments that hold the old rite to be superior to the new. However, they fail to realize that the argument from aesthetics is actually one of the most cogent of the arguments in favor of the old rite.

In a chapter later in the book, how aesthetics relates to culture is addressed. In that chapter, a basic look is provided at what beauty is and the attributes of beauty, viz. clarity, symmetry and completion or perfection. Since these attributes of beauty constitute whether the *thing* is beautiful, something is objectively beautiful or its not, if it possesses the attributes or not. The aesthetic sense, which we developed regarding those things that are beautiful, must therefore be in conformity with the beauty of the things as they are, since the aesthetic sense must be based on truth.

Truth is defined as the conformity of intellect and thing. This means that one's ideas are true when they are in conformity with the way things are in reality. If a man thinks the grass outside is green when it is green, then his mind conforms to the things as they are and so he knows the truth about the grass. However, if he thinks that the grass is violet when it is really green, that he does not have the truth in his mind since his mind does not conform to reality. Aesthetic sense is the ability of the intellect to grasp what is *truly* beautiful. Given the aforesaid, an aesthetic sense is either true or false; one either finds pleasing that which is truly beautiful by having a true aesthetic sense or he finds things that are not truly beautiful as pleasing and thereby has a false aesthetic sense.

The Catholic Church teaches us that God is intelligent and all-knowing; and since he is the cause of all things, He knows exactly the way they are because He is causing them to be as they are. Now since God is intelligent and since beauty is that which is pleasing to a cognitive faculty, then God is pleased with those things that are truly beautiful. In other words, God, like man, is pleased with things that are beautiful. A thing can have more or less beauty if it has more or less being (since beauty is convertible with being) or if the attributes of beauty are possessed more or less, e.g. the cathedral at Chartres is more beautiful than the new cathedral of Los Angeles, which is built-in abstract forms and thereby lacks the clarity of the cathedral of Chartres. Many of those committed to the *Novus Ordo* will admit that the

---

[102]The chapter first appeared as an article in *The Latin Mass* Fall 2002.

old rite Mass is more beautiful. The music is more beautiful, the ritual is more beautiful, and so on. However, in order to avoid being accused of speaking for them, let us consider a few examples out of the many that could be given that demonstrate that the old rite is in more beautiful than the new rite. One way in which the old rite is more beautiful than the new is that it possesses superior clarity by virtue the fact that it manifests Catholic dogma more clearly, both in its prayers and its liturgical gestures.

Another attribute of beauty in which the old rite is superior to the new is according to the attributes of symmetry or proportion. Since the new rite of Mass is customarily said *versus populum* rather than oriented (or *ad orientem*), one is left with a slight theological problem, well expressed in the words of Cardinal Medina in response to a question regarding n. 299 of the third edition of the *General Instruction of the Roman Missal* of the new rite, in which the position of the priest facing the apse (oriented) is addressed:

> However, whatever may be the position of the celebrating priest, it is clear that the Eucharistic sacrifice is offered to the one and triune God… The physical position, especially with respect to the communication among the various members of the assembly, must be distinguished from the interior spiritual orientation of all. It would be a grave error to imagine that the principal orientation of the sacrificial actions is [toward] the community. If the priest celebrates *versus populum*, which is legitimate and often advisable, his spiritual attitude ought always to be *versus Deum per Jesum Christum*, as a representative of the entire Church.[103]

The Cardinal then continues by noting that the tradition, with some exceptions, was to offer mass oriented, since Christ rises in the east. Those interested in a more thorough development of this notion can read Klaus Gamber's book, *The Reform of the Roman Liturgy*, in which the author discusses the issue of orientation as a way of facing God, Whose Son will rise in the East.

The point is that even the Cardinal is essentially admitting that what is occurring exteriorly, when the Holy Sacrifice of the Mass is offered *versus populum*, is not what *should be* occurring interiorly, since the priest is to face God interiorly. In the new rite, there exists a lack of symmetry or proportion between what the priest is doing interiorly and what he is doing exteriorly, if he offers Mass *versus populum*. It is possible to name numerous other instances in which what occurs in the new rite is not clearly reflective of what Catholics believe, but for the sake of brevity, we shall move on to the next

---

[103]Prot. No. 2036/00/L – 9/25/2000.

attribute of beauty.

We have already seen an instance in which the old rite possesses greater clarity and proportion, so what remains of the attributes of beauty is perfection or completion. With regard to this, some argue that the offertory of the new rite, practically speaking, is missing, since there is no real offering of the gifts in a proper fashion. However in order to avoid the liturgical complexities of that argument, we shall take a look at something more obvious, which the average reader can verify. In a book entitled *Problems with the Prayers of the Modern Mass*[104], Anthony Cekada shows that the prayers or propers of the new rite were often taken from the old rite and rewritten (intentionally?) in order to exclude the miraculous, supernatural and the sacred. If this is the case, then the new rite lacks something that is proper to the sacred liturgy which is addressed to God, Who is the font of all holiness and sacredness. Therefore this lack of something that should be there is a lack of completion, perfection or wholeness, which constitute a necessary attribute of beauty. In this respect, the old rite possesses more of the attribute of perfection or completion.

Since the old rite possesses all three of the attributes of beauty and to a greater degree than does the new rite in the respects discussed above as well as many others, and since beauty is in the *thing*, then the old rite is *objectively* more beautiful than the new rite. Let us recall at this stage that God is an intelligent Being. Since beauty is that which is pleasing to a cognitive faculty and the old rite is more beautiful than the new, then the old rite is objectively more pleasing to God than the new rite. Here we see the cogency of the argument. It is not based on subjective likes and dislikes but on the objective nature of beauty, and the fact that the old rite is indeed objectively more beautiful than the new rite.

Traditionalists and non-traditionalists alike should strive to conform their aesthetic sense to the objective beauty of things. While this argument may be disagreeable to those who have appetitive attachments to the new rite and may be disagreeable because of its rather formal and logical formulation, nevertheless we hope that they are willing to follow reason more than appetite. In conforming our aesthetic sense to the objective beauty of things, we shall come to appreciate and be ever more pleased with the ancient rite of Mass. Accordingly, we will be more like God, Who finds the old rite of Mass pleasing because of its excelling beauty.

---

[104] Available through TAN Books.

Chapter 12: The Priest and the Mass[105]

Much of the chapter on the "Spirituality of the Ancient Rite of Mass" applies to the priest and the laity alike, but certain dimensions of the ancient rite of Mass speak directly to the heart of the priest. These dimensions may speak to the faithful as well, but they have a particular aspect about them that is proper to the priest alone, if for no other reason than that he is the one offering the Mass in a manner in which the faithful are not.

There are common qualities in all good priests. Among those common qualities are purity, sacrifice and devotion, all three of which are sustained and increased in the priest who says the ancient rite of Mass with fervor. This chapter is reflection on those three qualities from the point of view of the priest. These aspects do not speak to the heart of the priest committed to mediocrity or complacency, even though he be orthodox. They speak to the priest whose desire it is "to be absorbed in Christ" and to follow in the way of spiritual perfection witnessed by St. Paul: "and I live, now not I: but Christ within me".[106]

A. The Priest and Purity

In a priest who truly loves God there is a burning desire for purity, and purity is one of the constant themes throughout the ancient rite of Mass. From the very beginning, when the priest says the mandatory vesting prayers, purity is at the fore, reminding the priest of the necessity to be pure in order to approach the altar of sacrifice. In fact, according to the old rite of blessing of vestments, the very vestments themselves are blessed with the petition that they may be purified (*purificare*).[107] Hence the very vestments the priest wears indicate that he must be pure to don them. The priest then washes his hands by saying the *Da, Domine*, asking that every stain be washed away so that without pollution of mind and body he may worthily serve God at the altar. The first required prayer that the priest must say tells him he must be free from every stain in order to serve God worthily.

St. Thomas tells us that:

a stain is properly ascribed to corporeal things, when a comely body loses its comeliness through contact with another body, e.g. a garment, gold or silver, or the like. Accordingly a stain is ascribed to

---

[105]This chapter first appeared as an article in *The Latin Mass* (Advent 2005).

[106]Gal. 2:20.

[107]*Rituale Romanum*, Tit. VII, c. 20.

spiritual things in like manner. Now man's soul has a twofold comeliness; one of the refulgence of the natural light of reason, whereby he is directed in his actions; the other, from the refulgence of the divine light, viz. of wisdom and grace, whereby man is also perfected for the purpose of doing good and fitting actions. Now, when the soul adheres to ther things by love, there is a kind of contact in the soul: and when he sins, he adheres to certain things, against the light of reason and of the divine law... Wherefore the loss of comeliness occasioned by this contact is metaphorically called a stain on the soul.[108]

What St. Thomas is saying is that any time one sins, through an act of love of the sin, the soul's brightness is diminished. This diminishing is left in the soul in the will, since sin is in the will.[109] St. Thomas also says that what remains is a disposition or habit to sin and that this is what detracts from the brightness.[110] Divine grace will restore the brightness, but it is necessary to have an act of hatred for the sin to go contrary to the first motional love of the sin, for hatred separates us from our sin since hatred is a certain dissonance of the appetite of that which is apprehended as repugnant or harmful[111] and we naturally turn away or flee from that which is repugnant or harmful. This is necessary to purify the faculties that are left with the effects of sin. Once the soul is purified of all the effects of sin, its first brightness is achieved. As long as there remains any habit, disposition or attachment to sin, the soul is not pure; its brightness is not fully there.

For this reason, the priest washes his hands to ask God to take away, by grace, the stain of sin so that he may be pure. The act of washing is an

---

[108]ST I-II, q. 86, a. 1: macula proprie dicitur in corporalibus, quando aliquod corpus nitidum perdit suum nitorem ex contactu alterius corporis, sicut vestis et aurum et argentum, aut aliud huiusmodi. In rebus autem spiritualibus ad similitudinem huius oportet maculam dici. Habet autem anima hominis duplicem nitorem, unum quidem ex refulgentia luminis naturalis rationis, per quam dirigitur in suis actibus; alium vero ex refulgentia divini luminis, scilicet sapientiae et gratiae, per quam etiam homo perficitur ad bene et decenter agendum. Est autem quasi quidam animae tactus, quando inhaeret aliquibus rebus per amorem. Cum autem peccat, adhaeret rebus aliquibus contra lumen rationis et divinae legis...
Unde ipsum detrimentum nitoris ex tali contactu proveniens, macula animae metaphorice vocatur.

[109]ST I-II, q. 74, a. 1.

[110]ST I-II, q. 86, a. 2, ad 1.

[111]ST I-II, q. 29, a. 2.

action that goes contrary to the love of sin and therefore helpes to purify him, not just in the order of grace, but in his very faculties. There are constant reminders to the priest that he must do little acts of penance, even during Mass, so that as he approaches the "Holy of Holies" his soul may be purified. He must be pure even to wear the vestments which are pure. When we have just washed a white shirt, we make sure we avoid getting stains on it. In like manner, the priest should not even don the vestments of Mass without having done everything he can to purify himself, so that he does not defile the very vestments he wears. Obviously, the term *defile* is meant spiritually; only that which is pure should touch the things consecrated and purified for divine worship. So important is it that the priest be pure that Fr. Garrigou-Lagrange observed that no man should be ordained who has not entered the illuminative way.[112] The illuminative way is the second stage on the way to perfection, the stage entered once one has done everything he possibly can to purify his soul. He should have stop sinning by this stage. He should have rooted out every possible vice and imperfection. Only in this way is the man suited to wear the vestments which are so pure. As we shall see, only in this way is a man worthy to stand at the altar.

While this is what God deserves, we still need priests, and if we ordained only men who have reached this stage in the spiritual life, there would not be anywhere near the number of priests we have now. For that reason, Holy Mother the Church has always declared that the minimum standard is that no man should have a grave moral defect. In other words, only those who are habitually staying out of mortal sin should be ordained, and no man with any spiritual imperfection or habit ordered toward moral sin should be ordained. This is why the very concept of homosexual clergy is inherently contradictory and utterly unacceptable, since homosexuality is itself a grave moral defect.

After the priest vests, he approaches the altar and begins the prayers at the foot of the altar. After he has made his confession, the priest says the *Indulgentiam* which is a prayer which remits venial sins. This is important because it helps to purify the priest and restore the brightness to his soul. Having completed the prayers at the foot of the altar, the priest says the *Aufer a nobis* as he ascends the three steps to the altar: "take away from us our iniquities, we beseech the, O Lord, that we may be worthy to enter with pure minds in the Holy of Holies. Through Christ our Lord. Amen."

One of the ways to purify the soul is through prayer since it mortifies our faculties and subordinates them to reason which, by the lifting of the mind and heart, is joined to God, Who is Purity Itself. This prayer not only mortifies

---

[112] See Garrigou -Lagrange, *Three Stages of the Interior Life*, vol. 1, p. 219. The requirement to be a bishop is even stricter. According to Garrigou-Lagrange (loc. cit)., the person who becomes a bishop should be in the unitive way.

the senses and heart of the priest, but also purifies his mind by reminding him, as he asks for purity of mind, that he may be worthy to enter into the Holy of Holies, i.e. to ascend to offer sacrifice at the altar.

Here we see the importance of liturgical principle *lex orandi, lex credendi*. We recognize as Catholics that only what is pure and holy may enter into the company of God. That the priest might not defile the sacred mysteries that he dispenses and protects through the Holy Sacrifice of the Mass, he himself must be pure. If he suffers stain, he will defile the very mysteries entrusted to his care. This is why, among other reasons, it is so important for the faithful to pray for the holiness of their priests. For if the priest is a defiled man, he will defile that he comes into contact with and he will defile the things of God, procuring God's wrath rather than his mercy.[113]

As the priest kisses the altar he asks that all of his sins may be forgiven in the prayer *Oramus te*. The next time the cleansing of the heart occurs is during the *Munda cor meum*, the prayer said by the priest before he sings or recites the Gospel: "cleanse my heart and my lips, O God Almighty, Who didst cleanse the lips of the prophet Isaias with a burning coal; and vouchsafed through Thy gracious mercy, so to purify me that I may worthily proclaim Thy Holy Gospel. Through Christ our Lord. Amen." Fr. Gihr explains this passage:

> First comes the petition for the interior purification (*Munda cor meum*). A thought of frequent occurrence with the Fathers is that the soul should receive the word and truth of God with the purity similar to that of the Blessed Eucharist. Only the clear fountain is the image of the sun reflected: in like manner, it is only in a perfectly pure heart that the light of heavenly truth can be reflected fully and unobscured. Wisdom enters not into an unclean soul nor does it dwell in a body subject to sin... The heart is not only sullied by sin but its purity is likewise dimmed and lessened by passion, distraction, earthly inclinations and worldly attachments. Hence the humble petition of the priest, that the Lord would purify anew his heart; for only a stainless heart is a vessel worthy of divine truth and wisdom... This petition has its foundation and development in a symbolic reference to mysterious event in the life of the Prophet Isaias [Isaiah 6:5]. He relates his call, consecration and mission to exercise the office of a prophet. In a marvelous vision he beheld the glory of the God of hosts

---

[113] By defile one does not mean that the holiness of the priest affects the validity of the sacraments. The sacraments work *ex opere operato* which means that if a validly ordained priest intends to confect the sacrament and says the right form over the right matter, then the sacrament is confected. In the context of the Mass, the holiness of the priest does not affect the validity of the Mass.

and heard the canticle of the angels in His praise; filled with his holy awe, he acknowledged and confessed his sinfulness and unworthiness. Then a seraph took from the heavenly altar of incense a live coal, touched therewith the lips of the Prophet, burning away all its defilement, saying these words: "Behold! this hath touched thy lips, and thy iniquities shall be taken away, and thy sin shall be cleansed." Then only did Isaias say: "Lo, here am I, send me!" – The live coal in the Prophet's vision is a symbol of grace and of its efficacy. Grace is like unto a spiritual fire which so consumes and destroys all earthly dross in the soul, that it becomes more brilliant and radiant than the finest gold and silver. The fire of the grace of the Holy Ghost not only purifies the heart, but also enlightens the mind with exalted wisdom and inflames the soul with heavenly love.[114]

The next time we encounter the notion of purity is in the offering of the host during the offertory. The priest says the prayer *Suscipe, sancte Pater*:

Receive, O Holy Father, Almighty, eternal God, this spotless host which I, thine unworthy servant, offering to thee, my living and true God for my own countless sins, offenses, and negligences, and for all here present; as also for all faithful Christians, living and dead; that it may avail for my own and for their salvation unto life eternal. Amen.

The spotless host, which in Latin is *immaculata hostia*, indicates that what is offered God must be spotless. This will provide for us the understanding of why the priest must be pure. As we will discuss below, when the priest sacrifices himself to God, he too must be an immaculate host.

During the *Lavabo* (the washing of the priests hands), the priest prays that he may wash his hands among the innocent and that he will stand around the altar of the Lord. We are beginning to see why there exists a certain dissonance between the priest who is not holy and offering the ancient rite of Mass. How can any man who is in the state of mortal sin offer this rite and not be an utter hypocrite? Only a man in the state of grace can offer this Mass with any clarity of conscience. Moreover, any priest reflects upon what this ritual is saying recognizes that he must strive for purity so that there is a congruity, harmony, a symmetry – in a word, a certain beauty in his presence at the altar.

During the Canon, the priest blesses the host many times, preparing it for transubstantiation, that most holy act by which bread becomes God. Under normal circumstances the priest does not touch the host during the

---

[114] *The Holy Sacrifice of the Mass*, p. 472.

offertory and the Canon until right before the consecration. Yet, before he takes the host in his hands, the ritual requires the priest to purify his fingers, which will hold the precious Body of our Lord. The priest does so by wiping his fingers on the corporal.[115] This is a last sign to the priest that he ought to be pure, not just physically, but spiritually, to sustain God in his hands.

It is here that we see the primary meaning of why the priest ought to be pure. He is about to perform the most sacred act of the most sacred rite given to man by God. He is about to hold Purity Itself in his hands. We know, by the metaphysics of St. Thomas Aquinas, that no created thing can act or touch upon God. Even when God is intimately involved in our lives, He remains entirely undefiled. God is pure act, as St. Thomas and Aristotle say. He is pure existence, pure goodness, pure benignity and pure mercy, and the priest is about to turn bread into Purity Itself. For this reason, the priest must strive to be absolutely pure so that he worthily performs the sacred action entrusted to him by God. A sinful priest, a priest who lives a life filled with impurity, a priest whose spiritual life is at best second to his worldly concerns, is not worthy to turn bread into Purity Itself and hold It in his hands. This is why the priest hands are consecrated, for they are set apart and dedicated to hold God. This is why in the old rite, when the priest is anointed when he is sick or dying, not the palms of his hands but rather the tops of his hands are anointed. All other people have their palms anointed. In reverence and respect for the holiness of the hands of the priest, which have already been consecrated[116] that they may hold the Consecrated, his palms are not anointed.

The next time the notion of purity is encountered in the Mass is in the prayer *Unde et Memores*, where the sacrificial victim is offered to God. This sacrificial victim is "a pure victim, a holy victim, an immaculate victim." Again, the priest, who acts *in persona Christi*, must be pure and immaculate like the Victim he offers to God the Father in expiation for sins.

Later in the Mass, during the preparatory prayers for the priest for Holy Communion, the priest asks that he may be delivered from all iniquities. He then consumes the precious Body and Blood of our Lord. In order not to be guilty of the condemnation warned of by St. Paul, the priest must be sure that he is in the state of grace so that he does not commit sacrilege in receiving holy Communion in the state of mortal sin. The more pure he is, the more efficacious is his reception of Holy Communion and the more worthily does he complete the ritualistic sacrifice of our Lord. After Holy Communion, he asks that what he has received he may receive with a pure mind and no

---

[115] See *Ritus servandus in celebratione Missae*, VIII, 4.

[116] The priest is also reminded of this when he takes the host to be consecrated and says "who the day before he suffered, took bread into his holy and venerable hands..."

stain of sin may remain in him "whom thy pure and holy sacraments have refreshed." The priest is asking that he may be pure as the sacrament is pure.

B. The Priest and Sacrifice

In this part of the chapter we will not recount how well the sacrificial aspect of the Mass is expressed in ancient rite of Mass. Instead, we shall consider certain aspects of the ancient rite of Mass so that we may see how the priest is called to offer himself sacrificially. We begin with one aspect that is common to all rites, viz. the priest acts *in persona Christi.* Christ, when He offered the sacrifice on Calvary in a bloody manner, once and for all, lay down his life in propitiation for the sins of men. In like manner, the priest himself must be a man a sacrifice, willing to lay down his life for the sake of those under his pastoral care. This laying down of his life may not entail martyrdom – although in certain parts of the world, such as China, that is entirely possible. Rather, for most priests, it means a sacrifice that comes through the august life of the priest, such as when he must practice self-denial to get up in the middle of the night to annoint someone, to hear the extra confession even though he is physically and psychologically exhausted, to take that phone call from the parishioner that tests him to the point of making him a saint and so on.

But the sacrificial aspect of the life of the priest is nowhere more perfectly manifest then when he offers the ancient rite of Mass and it is in this context that he acts *in persona Christi* in a unique way. Just as Christ offered himself to God the Father in expiation for sins, as He offered His life upon the cross, so to the priest, when offering the Holy Sacrifice of the Mass, offers the second Person of the Blessed Trinity to God the Father in expiation for sins. The Mass is, of course, an atemporal participation in the Calvary sacrifice.

The ancient rite of Mass contains sacrificial dimensions that remind the priest of his likeness to Christ and that in an efficacious manner joined the heart of the priest to the Sacred Heart of Christ in such a way that the two hearts become one. But first we must make a short recursus on the nature sacrifice. St. Thomas Aquinas teaches us in the *Summa Theologiae* that justice is a virtue by which we render to others what is due to them.[117] He also says that justice, as a virtue, resides or is in the will because through justice we willingly render to others what we ought.[118] St. Thomas then notes that religion is part of justice, because through the virtue of religion we render to

---

[117]See among others the tract on justice, ST II-II, q. 58-122.

[118]Ibid., q. 58, a. 4.

God was due to Him.[119] It is through the virtue of religion that one fulfills his obligations to God. St. Thomas observes that reverence pertains to the virtue of religion. Reverence is a virtue by which one renders honor to someone for some excellence that he possesses. Now God created us, keeps us in being, maintains the order of the universe, and gives us everything that is good, and so He excels above every other thing.[120] So we know that to God alone belongs a special form of honor and, for this reason, it belongs to God alone to be worshiped. St. Thomas then notes that sacrifice is the proper act of religion and reverence and it is to be offered to God alone, for sacrifice is the highest form of honor that may be given.[121] In sacrifice, the thing sacrificed is rendered to God, because, out of justice, we owe him every honor as well as the greatest honor. Sacrifice is the greatest honor we can give to God because we must give from ourselves the first fruits, the highest goods, in order that we may render to God something proportion to His excellence and greatness.

St. Thomas then tells us, and we know from the old and new Testaments, that sacrifice is that which is offered by a priest: for the essence of the priesthood is to offer sacrifice.[122] Now there are two kinds of sacrifice. The first is that which the sacerdotal priest offers, which is the sacrifice of Jesus Christ Himself during Mass, which is the making present of the Calvary sacrifice. The second kind of sacrifice is that which those who are not sacerdotal priests offer. We know through pious encouragement of the Church that those who are not sacerdotal priests ought to offer up their prayers, sufferings and good works in union with the sacrifice of the Mass, so that their sacrifices may be efficacious and meritorious in the eyes of God. This is what is meant by the priesthood of the laity, that they offer their sacrifice to God.[123] The greatest thing we can give, the highest first fruit, is our own will, for by sacrificing our wills to God we give him everything that is proper for selves, for nothing that we do on our own comes about except through our free wills.

---

[119] See ibid., q. 81.

[120] All of these assertions can be known through the natural life of reason, as is evidenced in SCG, I and II.

[121] See ST II-II, q. 85.

[122] See Hebrews 8:3 and Council of Trent, Sess. 23, c. 1 (Denz. 1764/957).

[123] The priesthood of the laity consists in the indelible mark which they receive at Baptism, which gives them the power to offer up their sacrifices in union with the priest who offers Mass. The indelible mark of the sacerdotal priest and the priesthood of the laity differs not in degree but in kind, since the indelible mark of the sacerdotal priesthood makes it possible for him to confect certain sacraments which the laity cannot.

Therefore, the proper sacrifice of the laity is the offering of the will back to God, and since justice is in the will, the greatest act of justice is to give the will to God.

The priest offers Mass in a twofold way. First, he does so as a public person acting on behalf of the Church. This is not properly his own sacrifice, but that of the Church. The second is the sacrifice of himself as a private individual. This sacrifice is done in Mass by offering his will to God, an act he performs principally by sacrificing himself to God by following the commands of his superiors. The priest follows the commands of his superiors, in turn, principally by obedience – which, within the context of the Holy Sacrifice of the Mass, involves offering the ritual according to the mind of the church, i.e. by following the rubrics. In other words, the way the priest sacrifices himself at Mass is not by doing *his own* will but the will of God through his superiors. Since the ancient rite of Mass leaves virtually nothing within the rubrics of the Mass to the discretion and the will of the priest, and since it gives great detail to the manner in which the Mass is to be offered, it offers a profound means by which the priest can sacrifice his will completely. In other words, the desire of the priest of pure heart is to be totally forgetful of self and placed himself perfectly at the service of God. This is achieved by having the Church predetermine how he is to offer the Mass. Once the elements of the Mass are subject to the priest's will, it ceases being something to which the priest can sacrifice himself perfectly.

If the priest is to act *in persona Christi* (and Christ during the agony the garden said "not as I will but as thou wilt"),[124] the priest most perfectly emulates Christ by entering the sacrifice of the Mass by not doing his will but the will of God, as manifested by the Church, in a ritual that is "not his own", i.e. not of the priest's making. It is true that Christ's offering of His life was voluntary; He did not have to hang up on the cross.[125] But in choosing to do the will of the Father, He sacrificed His own will.[126] In like manner, when a man chooses a life of the priesthood, which involves offering the Holy Sacrifice of the Mass, he ought to do so by being able to surrender his will to God totally. This is most perfectly accomplished by the priest's relinquishing control over the rite of the Mass so that he may perfectly join his heart to the totally sacrificial heart of Christ. Fr. Nicholas Gihr observes:

---

[124] Matthew 26:39.

[125] Christ said (John 10:18), "And I have power to lay it [my life] down: and I have power to take it up again."

[126] Since Christ has two wills, it is by means of the human will that Christ offers himself even though the human will and the divine will in Christ are in perfect accord.

St. Teresa was ready to sacrifice her life for even the least ceremony of the Church. In the service of the Almighty, in the most Holy Sacrifice of the Mass even the smallest thing has its meaning and importance; and, therefore, the Church has so exactly and minutely regulated by her rubrics the entire department of the priest at the altar. Whosoever conscientiously complies with these ecclesiastical regulations, has the special merit of practicing the virtue of obedience in all his actions and movements when celebrating.[127]

When the priest offers a rite of Mass in which he can totally surrender his will in obedience to the determinations of how the rite is to be offered, the motions of the liturgy becomes the motions of the priest's heart. What the liturgy asks for, the priest asks for. What the liturgy prays in desire becomes the desire of the priest. The joy of the feast becomes the joy in the heart of the priest. In a certain symmetry of hearts, the heart of the liturgy and the heart of the priest moves one.

Since "to make changes in the liturgy is the prerogative of Saints" and since saints are those whose hearts are perfectly subordinated to God, then the development of the ancient rite of Mass throughout history became a manifestation of the will (heart) of God. This culmination in the liturgy of the saints makes it possible for the heart of the priest to be perfectly sacrificed to God.

What do the ancient rituals suggest regarding the nature of the sacrificial elements and therefore the sacrificial spirit of the priest? The first is that it must be a pure sacrifice. We pray in the *Unde et Memores* immediately after the consecration: "[We] offer unto Thy most excellent Majesty of Thine own gifts bestowed upon us, a pure victim, a holy victim, an immaculate victim, the holy bread of eternal life and the chalice of everlasting salvation." If the priest is to be of one heart with Christ, he too must be a pure, holy and immaculate victim. In other words, he must not only be willing to sacrifice himself during the Mass, but he must also be willing to sacrifice himself for his people outside of Mass. Sometimes when babies are crying, he is sacrificing himself even during Mass. Yet, to sacrifice himself as Christ did means that he must be willing to suffer, he must have a spirit of mortification, he must have a profound humility and he must not have any desire for human respect. This becomes abundantly clear to the priest when he is offering the Holy Sacrifice of the Mass for the very parishioners who are offending God with their daily lives and on occasion even offending the priest himself. Any priest who has been ordained for any length of time can tell stories of having

---

[127] *The Holy Sacrifice of the Mass*, p. 342.

to sacrifice himself for those under his pastoral care who are also the very people who make them suffer by their insults, their chiding, the displeasure at his work and his sacrifices and even in some extreme cases by their accusations and attacks. In this way, the priest becomes like Christ, and no priest can ever expect to be loved by all of the people. He must be willing to be hated by the people as long as he is willing to sacrifice himself so that they may be saved. Just as Christ hung upon the cross to save the very people who crucified Him, so the priest must be willing to be "crucified" by the very people for whom he daily sacrifices.

In the *Supplices te rogamus* we pray that the offering may be borne by the hands of God's holy angel to his altar on high in the sight of his Divine Majesty. The priest, too, must desire to be borne into heaven by the Angels by his sacrifice and ultimately at the time of his death. As was mentioned in a prior chapter, when the priest offers the Holy Sacrifice of the Mass, his personality is able to fade into the background. Since he says the Mass facing East, people do not have to look at him during the entire course of the Mass. His personality is hidden because most of the actions are hidden. Moreover even the actions are determined by the Church, for the rubrics determine the placement of the hands during the Mass. The rubrics require the priest looked downward when he turns to the people both in order not to distract him and in order not to permit his "self-expression" to affect people's ability to enter into the Mass. The rubrics determine what is contained in the rite of Mass so that his personality does not come through in the choices made regarding the various parts of the Mass. In other words, as the priest's personality fades into the background and he obeys the laws of the Church on how he is to offer Mass, it becomes hard to distinguish how one priest says a Mass as opposed to another. The rite of Mass tends to universalize the experience of the faithful, and even the priest, have of the Mass by minimizing the priest's personality. While Christ's personality is everywhere and in all cases amiable and approachable to all people of goodwill, not every priest's personality is. Since often the priests' personalities are nothing to get very excited about, the fact that their personalities are minimized provides a buffer for the faithful who must attend their Masses. As the priest's personality fades and he takes on a universal personality by following the rubrics, he is more able to enter and portray the personality of Christ is more able to act *in persona Christi*. But this can occur only if the priest is willing to sacrifice himself and his own personality in order to "assume the personality of Christ".

This sacrificing of the personality of the priest reminds us of three scriptural passages. The first is that which is spoken by St. John the Baptist, "he must increased: but I must decrease."[128] The second is the words of St.

---

[128] John 3:30.

Paul, "and I live, now not I: but Christ lives in me."[129] The last of the words written by St. Paul are the inspiration the Holy Spirit: "I became all things to all men, that I might save all."[130] This passage can seem as if St. Paul is suggesting that one be fake, superficial or even duplicitous. But what St. Paul is instructing us to do is to become perfect. As the author has detailed in another work,[131] this actually means that as a person becomes perfect, reason, which is a universal power, universalizes our personality by instilling virtue in us. Virtue takes away those peculiarities of our personality that make it difficult to be in the company of others. It is not difficult to notice that a very virtuous man can be in anyone's company, whereas the vicious man can be in the company only of those who share his vice, and even then only sometimes.

As the priest acts more and more *in persona Christi* his personality becomes universalized.[132] In other words, the peculiarities that make his personality difficult to sustain fade in the background as he adheres faithfully to the determination of the rite of Mass by Holy Mother the Church. In other words, the priests personality becomes universalized like Christ and so, through the sacrificing of his own personality and taking on Christ, the priest and the rite of Mass take on a universal appeal. In this way the priest can "be all things to all people".

As the priest's personality fades into the background and as his heart becomes one with the motions of the liturgy he himself begins to become like Christ, a pure oblation offered to God. To the degree that he is not pure, to the degree that he does not sacrifice himself and he tries to control the liturgy, to that degree will there be a dissonance with the ritual he offers and to that degree his private offering at the Mass is not perfect. The offering which he does on behalf of the Church (i.e. as a public person or agent of the Church) is perfect since it is none other than offering of Christ to God the Father Who is perfect. But the private offering he makes may not be pure because his sacrifice itself may not be pure, and this will affect not only the spiritual life of the priest but also his very priestly identity.

The very nature of the priest is to offer sacrifice. Since the sacrifice the priest offers at the Mass is twofold (one the offering of Christ and the

---

[129] Gal. 2:20.

[130] I Cor. 9:22.

[131] Ripperger, *Introduction to the Science of Mental Health*, vol. III, chpt. 16.

[132] That Christ's personality is universal and therefore is not subject to psychological analysis is the general theme of the book by Romano Guardini entitled *The Humanity of Christ*.

other his own private sacrifice), the identity of the priest will undergo a confusion. Confusion is defined as the mixing of two distinct, or we may say even contradictory, elements. When the priest offers the perfect sacrifice of the Church but does not perfectly offer his own private sacrifice, he will undergo a confusion. His identity will be unclear. The more he glorifies himself outside of Mass and becomes perfect and the more he sacrifices himself in the Mass, the clearer will his priestly identity be to himself and others. In fact, we may say that as a private person, the perfection of the sacrifice of the priest occurs when, having rid himself of all spiritual imperfections and unholiness before Mass, is able to sacrifice himself perfectly during the Holy Sacrifice of the Mass so that he may perfectly join himself and his sacrifice to that of Christ. While the faithful may also join their sacrifices to the priest's so that they may have their true efficacy, they will never enjoy the intimacy of the sacrifice of the priest that he has with the Sacrifice of Christ upon the Cross as he offers Mass in the intimacy of his action in the ritual.

C. The Priest and Devotion

> The worthy celebration of Mass, as well as the devout attendance thereat, independently of the graces to be obtained, belongs to the chief means of virtue; for the liturgy of the Mass is by its nature calculated to impress and to move deeply all those who take part in it with faith and attention, to excite and awaken in the celebrant and the faithful present pious thoughts and feelings, wholesome affections and resolutions and acts acceptable to God of the different virtues. The Eucharist Sacrifice is so constituted as to be a school, in which the most manifold virtues are awakened and nourished, strengthened and purified. From the altar proceeds the impulse to all striving after higher virtues, after a life of perfection.[133]

Many priests have found that when offering the ancient rite of Mass there is a deepening of devotion to God and to His saints. St. Thomas tells us that devotion comes from the Latin word *devovere*, which means "to vow".[134] Hence, devotees are those who have vowed themselves to God as being totally subject to Him, and so devotion is nothing other than the will (since it proceeds from justice) promptly giving itself to that which pertains to the service of God (*cultus*). St. Thomas goes on to say that the exstrinsic cause of devotion is principally God. Yet the intrinsic cause that is in ourselves

---

[133] Gihr, *The Holy Sacrifice of the Mass*, p. 210f.

[134] See ST II-II, q. 82.

requires meditation or contemplation. Since devotion is an act by which one promptly gives his will over to God, this can only occur when the will is presented the object by the intellect to contemplate or meditate. So devotion is prompted by the consideration of the divine goodness and His good works as well as by consideration of our defects, which show us our unworthiness of God. This latter meditation destroys presumption, a vice that causes us not to be subject to God, and so prompts us to virtue.

When considering the ancient rite of Mass, we begin to realize the rite is meditative in the silence of the Canon. It is meditative in the content of its prayers. We also see a healthy yet balanced reflection on our own sinfulness and unworthiness throughout the prayers of the Mass, such as the *Confiteor* with its threefold *mea culpa*. We see this in the offertory in the prayer *Suscipe, sancte Pater* in which the priest offers the host to God for his innumerable sins, offenses and negligences. The beauty of the Mass draws us to an inward contemplation.[135] All of these things contribute to the inner silence and strong devotion of those who participate.

Yet one of the areas in which the ancient rite excels is in the devotion to the Saints. "The church has connected with the divine sacrifice a copious rite, in which the veneration of the saints finds manifold expression."[136] The devotion to the saints finds itself in the ancient rite in four ways. The first is the mentioning of the saints in the various prayers throughout the Mass, such as the *Confiteor* and the *Suscipe, sancta Trinitas* in which our Lady, St. John the Baptist, St. Michael and Sts. Peter and Paul are mentioned. Of course, there is the mentioning by name of the many saints in the Canon both before and after the consecration. The relics of the saints that lie in the altar are mentioned in the *Oramus te Domine* as the priest venerates the altar after he has ascended following the prayers at the foot of the altar. There is the mention of St. Michael the Archangel during the blessing of the incense prior to the offertory. During the *Libera nos, quaesumus* after the *Our Father* there is the mention of the Blessed Virgin Mary, Sts. Peter, Paul and Andrew.

The second way is by virtue of the magnificent sanctoral calendar of the ancient rite of Mass. The number of the feast days of the saints fills the calendar year, providing the priest a constant reminder of the example of the saints. Also, the division of the saints into categories such as confessor and virgin provides the priest with an understanding of the will of God in the lives of individuals, i.e. that He does not distribute His graces evenly but "as He

---

[135] See the chapter in this work entitled, "Aesthetics and God".

[136] Gihr, *The Holy Sacrifice of the Mass*, p. 190.

will".[137] In the calendar, with what is effectively a seven class system,[138] one gets a strong impression of the hierarchy of grace and the different perfections of God as manifested in different saints. One gets a strong sense of the hierarchy that we will see once we enter into heaven. Moreover, the fact that the sanctoral cycle at times takes precedence over the temporal cycle provides a profound understanding of venerating God through His saints. Even though the Sundays after Pentecost are second-class, some of the feasts of the saints take precedence over the Sunday. Since the Resurrection has already given the most solemn of the feast on Easter itself as well as an octave, it is not necessary to celebrate the commemoration of Easter on *every* Sunday. Since most Catholics do not attend daily Mass, if the temporal cycle always or for the most part takes precedence over the sanctoral cycle and Sundays are always a celebration of the Resurrection of our Lord, the laity are left without a sense of the place and the devotion of the saints in the life of the Church. With a balanced table of precedences, one is left with a strong understanding of the harmony of the temporal feast and how they relate to sanctoral feasts. Further, the propers that are assigned to the feast of saints revealing a truly supernatural vision, and they provide depth as well as direction to the spiritual life of those who pray. The third way in which devotion to the saints is fostered is in the recognition of their role in the development of the ancient rite. As Gihr points out:

Already Pope Innocent I (402-417), in writing to Decentius, Bishop of Gubbio, about ritual matters, traces the origin of the Roman liturgy to the Prince of the Apostles: "Who does not know," he writes, "that what has been handed down by Peter, the Prince of the Apostles, to the Roman Church is still observed unto this day, and must be observed by all?" St. Peter, consequently, must be regarded (in a more general sense) as the founder of the Roman liturgy, for the method of celebration followed and introduced by him was, without doubt, the essential and permanent foundation for its latter development and form. "This liturgy, as yet a tender plant, was brought by St. Peter, the Prince of the Church, into the garden of the Roman Church, where by his nursing care and that of his successors, assisted by the Holy Ghost, it has grown to a large tree, and although the trunk has long ago attained its full growth, it nevertheless shoots forth in every century

---

[137] I Cor., 12:11.

[138] Even though there are only four "classes" in the old rite calendar of 1962, there are seven *de facto* since there are feasts of the same class in which some are privileged and some are not.

new branches and new blossoms."[139]

As was mentioned before, to make changes to the liturgy is the prerogative of saints. The priest enjoys a certain devotion to the saints who slowly fashion this venerable rite though time. From the beginning as with St. Peter and its relatively obscure history for the first couple of centuries, it had a slow growth until the codification of St. Gregory the Great. Then from that time on the ancient rite of Mass remained relatively unchanged except in a few accidentals until 1964. In other words, the Mass had minor modifications made by saints, such as Pope St. Pius V. The priest recognizes his indebtedness to the saints who, by the hand of God, fashioned the rite slowly over the course of centuries.

The fourth way in which the devotion to the saints is fostered is in the consideration of the saints who attended and offered this Mass. In substance, this is the same rite of Mass offered by such great saints as Albert the Great,[140] Gregory the Great, Alphonsus Ligouri, Ambrose, Anselm, Augustine, Robert Bellarmine, Benedict, Bonaventure, Charles Borromeo, Dominic, Ignatius, John of the Cross, Louis Marie de Monfort, Pius V, Pius X, Thomas Aquinas, John Marie Vianney and a whole host of other priests who were saints. This is the rite of Mass attended devoutly by saints such as Bernadette Soubirous, Catherine of Siena, Faustina, Margaret Mary Alacoque, Scholastica, Theresa of Avila, Teresa of the Child Jesus, and one of this author's favorites, St. Hermenegild. When the priest considers himself in the company of the lineage of saints, martyrs and holy virgins whose devotion to this rite of Mass was exemplary, his devotion and affinity for the saints is strengthened.

Is this not also the case in favor of an accidental efficacy of the Mass as well? When someone does something for us, we tend to like not only what he did but *how* he did it. So when someone does the same thing, we can enjoy it when we see the person do it in the way in which it was done in the past. God sees all of time before Him at a glance and so He sees all the saints who offered and participated in what is substantially the same rite of Mass throughout time. When God looks at all of the saints who offered and assisted at the ancient rite of Mass, He sees all the merit of the saints and effects that came from the rite of Mass via the saints. Therefore, when we offer in substance the same rite of Mass as the saints, God looks with favor on the offering according to the merits of the saints. In other words, there accrues to the specific rite of Mass the merits of the saints who have offered and attended that rite of Mass. For this reason, attending and offering the ancient rite of

---

[139] Gihr, *The Holy Sacrifice of the Mass*, p. 335.

[140] The various western rites such as the Dominican, the Carmelite, etc., are generally considered to be organically connect to the proper Roman rite.

Mass provides a value or efficacy that is not enjoyed by a rite that is not organically developed or connected to the ancient rite of Mass. If one were to argue that the new Saints would offer and assist at a rite that is not organically developed or connected to the ancient one, and thus will have its hagiological efficacy as well, this we could not deny. But on the other hand, what is the point in splitting the lineage enjoyed by the ancient rite of Mass? In other words, why would we establish two different lineages of hagiological value? Why not build on the one that we already possess actually?

Another aspect that fuels the devotion of the priest is the consideration of the very prayers of the Mass. In this connection, Fr. Gihr comments:

> Fr. Faber styles the Church's Rite of the Holy Sacrifice "the most beautiful thing this side of heaven," and, as he remarks, "it came forth out of the grand mind of the Church, and lifted us out of earth and out of self, and wrapped us round in a cloud of mystical sweetness and the sublimities of a more than angelic liturgy, and purified us almost without ourselves, and charmed us with celestial charming, so that our very senses seem to find vision, hearing, fragrance, taste and touch, beyond what earth can give." The Church prayers of the liturgy are superior to all other prayers; no "human genius can hope to attain their beauty and sublimity." In these two qualities, the Mass differs from all other offices in remarkable manner. It has not merely flights of eloquence and poetry strikingly displayed in particular prayers, but it is sustained throughout in the higher sphere, to which its divine purpose naturally raises it. If we examine each prayer separately, it is perfect; perfect in construction, perfect in thought, and perfect in expression. If we consider the manner in which they are brought together, we are struck with the brevity of each, with the sudden but beautiful transitions, and the almost stanza-like effect, with which they succeeded one another, forming a lyrical composition of surpassing beauty. If we take the entire service, as a whole, it is constructed with the most admirable symmetry, proportioned in its parts with perfect judgment and so exquisitely arranged, as to excite and preserve an unbroken interest in the sacred action. No doubt, to give full force and value to the sacred rite, its entire ceremonial is to be considered.[141]

It is here that this chapter comes together. When the priest strives for purity so that his sacrifice maybe perfect, the old rite aids him with its beauty.

---

[141]Gihr, *The Holy Sacrifice of the Mass*, p. 337.

Because of his devotion to the perfect style of the Mass, he is able to give himself completely to God by surrendering himself entirely to the rite of Mass. In other words, his devotion, which arises "naturally" out of his attention to the prayers of the rite of Mass, aids him in striving for and desiring purity and in sacrificing himself perfectly. In other words, a rite which comes from God and the saints should be the kind of rite to which a devout person, a person who puts himself aside, can totally surrender himself and a rite to which his sacrifice can be perfectly added. If a rite comes from human hands, either by the priest's choice of what will be in the Mass or by the construction of a rite by men who are not saints, it will not have a universal appeal. In the end, the purity of heart of the priest and his desire to sacrifice himself will be at variance with the rite that does not allow him to do so by making him choose what will be in the rite. While in a certain sense any rite can undergo perfecting, nevertheless no rite should contain elements that are at variance with the priest's ability to sacrifice himself totally to God through the rite, if the priest has a pure heart. As Fr. Gihr observed, the rite should make him go out of himself, not bind himself to himself. It should be a thing of devotion and, as we saw, devotion is that which makes us more subject to God and not ourselves. When the rite of Mass is predetermined and yet fashioned by God through the hands of saints, the priest can enter into it devoutly, i.e. the rite of Mass will give rise to devotion in the priest. But if the rite of Mass is a thing of his own making, his subjection to God (i.e. his devotion) will have to be something he attempts to supply on his own, rather than something elicited by the rite itself.

Even those of bad will must admit it, says Fr. Gihr:

> That overruling influence of the Spirit of God, that directs even in secondary matters the affairs of the visible Church, nowhere else appear so marked and evident as in the arrangement of the rite of the Holy Mass, which, although only monumental, yet in its present state forms such a beautiful, perfect whole, yea, a splendid work, that it excites the admiration of every reflecting mind. Even the bitterest adversaries of the Church do not deny it; unprejudiced, aesthetic judges of good taste admit that even from their own standpoint the Mass is to be classed as one of the greatest masterpieces ever composed. Thus the momentous sacrifice is encompassed with magnificent ceremonies: it is our duty to study to penetrate more and more into their meaning, and to expound what we have learned to the people according to their capacity.[142]

---

[142]Ibid.

The problem today, of course, lies in the fact that so many people are prejudiced judges who are not capable of looking at each rite of Mass objectively. Even priests whose holiness of life should detach them from a desire to control the liturgy often are not able to consider the monumental patrimony that exists in the ancient rituals.

We shall end this chapter with the following reflection. Purity of life and heart of the priest drives him to want to sacrifice himself totally to God. Sacrificing himself totally can be done only when he does not do his own will. The subjugation of devotion will drive him not to do his own will but only the will of God. The ancient rite of Mass provides that opportunity to the priest. But this is only the beginning. The total devotional sacrificing of the priest to God only opens the door for the rite of Mass to further instruct the priest:

> This glorious rite of the Sacrifice of the Mass is an unfailing mine of religious instruction and edification; it is like an immensely rich mine, where always new gold veins are disclosed to the searching look. Even if we were to devote our entire life considering in our meditations and prayers the mystical liturgy of the Mass, they would still remain for our heart and mind new treasures, still new riches would reveal themselves and new beauties would be disclosed. And yet though it be so deep and impenetrable as to prove inexhaustible to even the greatest contemplative saint, it is, at the same time, so clear and easy of comprehension, that the most artless child as well as the most simple of the faithful finds therein light, incentive, strength and nourishment for his religious life.[143]

---

[143]Ibid., 338.

Chapter 13: Modern Philosophy and the Liturgical Development[144]

Perplexity often surfaces when a Catholic, who seeks to conform himself to the teachings and mind of the Church, walks into a recently built or renovated Catholic church and sees in the "worship space," as it is now called, at the front or in the center of the church, two separate altars of equal size. The confusion occurs because in his knowledge of Catholic theology, there does not appear any necessity for two altars. Those who construct the altars see them as an expression of the fact that Christ is present both in the Eucharist and in the Word. Clearly, this is why philosophical distinctions within the liturgy are of prime importance: if one is not capable of making the distinction between substantial and implicit presences of things, then one is going to fall into error regarding how the "worship space" should be arranged. But the problem appears to run deeper, for without a clear grasp of philosophical notions, it is virtually impossible to engage in a discussion about the liturgy in a truly Catholic sense. For this reason, we will consider the impact of modern philosophical thought on the liturgical development.

A. Metaphysical Cause

Since the Church, in her wisdom, has pointed Catholic philosophers toward Thomism[145] as a way of avoiding error[146] and providing a truly perennial Christian philosophy,[147] we ought, therefore, to look to the philosophy of St. Thomas as the principle by which we judge modern philosophical thought. Yet, in connection to the relationship the liturgy has to philosophical thought, we can ask ourselves why there are so many liturgical variances and opinions. The first logical possibility, which seems ever more to be the case, is that people do not believe what the Church believes and, consequently, there is a disparity as to what they do and what should be done

---

[144]This article first appeared in *Christian Order* in the August/September 2000 issue.

[145]The possible citations are numerous, but among others see: Leo XIII, *Aeterni Patris*, passim, but especially paras. 21, 25 and 33; Pope St. Pius X, *Pascendi Dominici Gregis*, para. 45; CIC/83 can. 252, §3 and Sacred Congregation For Catholic Education, *Ratio Fundamentalis*, paras. 79 and 86.

[146]Among other see: Leo XIII, op. cit., paras. 18, 21 & 29 and Pope St. Pius X, loc. cit.

[147]See the two works of Pope St. Pius X, loc. cit. and *Studiorum Ducem*, passim.

liturgically in a Catholic church. That is to say that because some do not believe the teachings of the Church, their liturgical actions do not suit the mysteries present. Rather, their liturgical actions reflect a different belief and, consequently, what they do liturgically is unsuitable. Conversely, because many priests have systematically abused the liturgical laws of the Church, the laity have become confused, not only as to what is liturgically appropriate, but more so and even consequently, they have become confused about what pertains to the Catholic Faith since the Faith itself is not being revealed through the liturgical action.

Even though this is true, we must ask the obvious question: why is it that those who are faithful and loyal to the Church and by all intents and purposes love, promote and seek after orthodoxy, do not agree on what should be done liturgically? There are two possibilities: the first is quite legitimate, viz. there are a variety of suitable ways of revealing the same mystery through liturgical action[148] and so different but not contradictory liturgical actions can suit the mysteries contained in the liturgy. The obvious fact of the various rites within the Church is a demonstration of this truth. The second logical possibility for the differing liturgical views is that those who are orthodox have been affected by modern/non-realist metaphysics and philosophy which has governed the last seventy years of liturgical change.[149] In the last forty-five years, the role of non-realist metaphysics and philosophy has actually accelerated and has become an integral part of the liturgy and consequently there has been an erosion of suitability in the liturgy.

There seem to be four modern metaphysics or philosophies governing the current forms of the liturgy and consequently causing the lack of suitability. The first is a type of nominalism in which the knowledge of the essences of things is completely uncertain or rejected. This metaphysics finds its place in a type of "syncretizing" of the liturgy in which a liturgical action is never to offend anyone since in the final analysis we cannot know what

---

[148]Clearly this notion must be handled prudently so as to be sure that the best form of the liturgy arises and that liturgical minimalism or excess do not occur.

[149]Here, reference is made to the fact that the liturgical variations in this century seemed to increase with the rise of the liturgical movement, in France and German in the 1920s. Historically, it appears that the more widespread the liturgical movement became, the more the modern philosophy seemed to govern the liturgical life of the Church. One could even argue back further, referring to the Modernist crisis which began in the last century and whose liturgical legacy we are currently living. But even though there was a discussion about the liturgy, the actual "experimentation" with the liturgy and rapid changes did not begin until after Pope St. Pius X stopped purging the seminary and university faculties of Modernists.

God really revealed or anything else of importance for that matter.[150] Consequently, contradictory things are introduced to please people on the emotional level so that what they believe will not be left out or offended.

The second form of metaphysics is that of rationalism. This has caused an abstraction to occur not only in religious art as it finds its place in Churches, vestments, statuary, etc., but also in the very architectural styles that are utilized. If a realist metaphysics is not employed, then the liturgy, and consequently the "worship space," will not be designed to conform with reality. This is why sanctuaries now find themselves in the middle of the Church rather than at the front and elevated to signify the heavenly court.[151] Moreover, since the senses are not important, they will not be used to lift the mind and heart to God during the liturgy. This is one of the reasons why bells and incense have all but faded out. The bells provide a mechanism which not only harks of heaven but also draws the person's attention into the liturgical action by means of the auditory faculty. Moreover, the incense provides a sweet odor to give the mind the impression of the heavenly sweetness of God's mercy and the rising of our prayers to God.[152]

The third influential philosophy, which has had a great impact, is empiricism. This philosophy essentially states that there is nothing beyond the senses and so pursuit of those things beyond the senses is futile.[153] This philosophy leads to a horizontalizing effect and emptying out of the transcendental dimensions of the liturgy[154] which is nowhere better expressed

---

[150] One of the more important ways this can be seen is the lack of distinction between the priestly and lay roles. Since we cannot really know the nature of anything, it does not seem fitting for one person to take a higher role and imply that he is by nature somehow different from the rest.

[151] It should be noted that while these reasons are proffered, it is possible that a variety of causes from various metaphysical and philosophical tenets be operative.

[152] The intention is not to fix absolute interpretations on the liturgical actions or things since that is neither within the competence of the author nor his intention. Moreover, since each thing in the liturgy is capable of many complementary interpretations, each interpretation should be given its due.

[153] One of the ironies of the new forms of the liturgy is that while denying the use of sensory images and language to lift the mind and heart to God, at the same time they use the senses to bring everything down to a banal and 'appetitive' level; a cursory reflection on some new forms of liturgical music bears this out.

[154] This is perhaps why the New Mass has little appeal to the youth. The youth in our age have been subjected to the modern metaphysics and philosophy in every aspect of their lives and when they see a liturgy which is likewise governed by these

than in the lack of proper altar orientation.[155] Moreover, if there are no real supernatural realities to which we must adhere, then it is not right that the priest performs all of the functions and this is why the role of the laity has become exaggerated; in a word, the role of the laity has been misunderstood because of a materialist/empiricist philosophical influence which finds no place for the transcendent. If a priest is not signed with a (spiritual) indelible mark, then he is no higher than anyone else and ought not to "dominate" the liturgy. If one's understanding does not include the transcendent/spiritual teaching of the Church about the nature of the priesthood, then one will not believe there is anything really different about him and so he is not to assume a role which by nature implies a difference from the laity.

One last metaphysics, which has become very widespread and seems to affect even the best intentioned, is the historicist metaphysical reflections of Hegel. Hegel essentially taught that there was one substance which is in a constant state of flux. This flux was a process going from a thesis to an antithesis which is the opposite of the original thesis and then finally to a synthesis of the two. It means that everything is changing and it cannot help but change. Consequently, to try and go back to a previous state of affairs is impossible, futile and foolhardy to imagine.[156]

This historicism has led to catastrophic effects. It seems to have been adopted almost as a whole, not necessarily as an explicit principle or

---

philosophies, they find it, like many other things they experience in modern society, to be vacuous. Consequently, they tend to seek the transcendent outside the Church since it does not seem to provide it, or they reason themselves back to a time and liturgy which embodied a realist metaphysics and philosophy and thus provides a fulfilment to the desire for the transcendent. Perhaps this is why the Mass of Pope St. Pius V has so much appeal to the youth and where that Mass is said the medium age is quite young.

[155]Klaus Gamber's book *The Reform of the Roman Liturgy* clearly indicates the proper understanding of the orientation of the altar. But suffice to say that if the Son of God, like the natural sun, rises in the east (*oriens*) and providing that the Son is God, then it is only fitting that we should face God during the Mass. To say that the previous liturgical rite said Mass with its back to the people is to exhibit a fundamental lack of understanding of the nature of sacrificial ritual and liturgical history; one always faced the one to whom the sacrifice is offered. To face the people signifies a horizontal understanding of God or it puts people in the place of God.

[156]The notion of the outmoded or outdated past, i.e. to put the past in a pejorative light, seems to have taken deep rooting in the fact that except among a few there is a general distrust for tradition.

philosophy, but at least as an implicit principle.[157] The adoption of this principle leads to a constant changing of the liturgy and the ensuing mentality that it must be novel or changing in order to be relevant and true to the wholly historical nature of liturgy. This also meant an immediate eradication of ecclesial laws since they cannot accommodate the necessity for constant change and they inhibit the liturgical "growth" of a particular place.[158]

B. Liturgical Effect

The new rite of Mass, unfortunately, did not escape the non-realist metaphysics and philosophies. Even if we do not consider post ritual promulgations[159] as part of the original new rite of Mass, nevertheless, the horizontalizing effect is clear. Comparisons of prayers have shown that the sacred and supernatural have been removed from the propers.[160] The Hegelian

---

[157]A principle does not have to be explicitly grasped in the mind of the knower to be operative. Moreover, because people learn by imitation, there is a strong drive in man to imitate or adopt what other people think. Consequently, it appears that many have adopted this historicism without a clear reflection on what they were doing. Moreover, it must always be kept in mind that operative principles tend to have a life of their own. Even if the one under its sway does not desire to follow the principle to its logical conclusion, the principle itself will drag the adherer to that conclusion and this has been clearly demonstrated by the liturgical principles adopted by the earlier liturgists and the fact that those principles only recently are finding their full expression.

[158]Perhaps, this is where the document *Sacrosanctum Concilium* failed to see that it contained diametrically opposed principles. It said first that any change must be an organic development (para. 23) which is a true and valid principle and it reflects a proper understanding of how things developed historically on the liturgical level. But then the document employed vocabulary which embodied a Hegelian metaphysics, e.g. while the word "change" appears only several times in one form or another, what is affected by the changes includes virtually every aspect of the liturgy (see paras. 63-82). When changes of that magnitude are ordered, there should be no wonder why the Hegelian metaphysical principle of change took over.

[159]Such as the permission of the use of altar girls, Communion in the hand, etc. These observations would be applicable to the 1969 and 1970 editions of the Sacramentary. However, if the Vatican were to include these in the *General Instruction to the Roman Missal*, the point is even more cogent.

[160]See the text of Anthony Cekada, *Problems with the Prayers of the Modern Mass* (currently published by TAN Books and Publishers, Inc.), or Denis Whitehouse's summary article about this text in the March 2000 *Christian Order* ("Liturgical Cleansing").

metaphysics finds its place in the numerous options allowed since the options facilitate a constant changing of the liturgy. While it is true that certain options were allowed in the previous rite such as votive Masses, etc., the option was not an integral part of the ritual as it appears to be in the newer forms of the liturgy.

Moreover, there is a rationalistic strain that runs very deep when extra-mental realities and signs (language being one of them) mean very little, e.g. the changing of the Communion rite from its previous form[161] to "Corpus Christi," with the communicant saying "Amen." The reason this is a difficulty is because if we understand the Hebrew meaning of the term, it can imply something which can lead people to believing something materially heretical. When the priest shows the host and then says "The Body of Christ," the communicant responds with "Amen" which is in the subjunctive[162] which implies some lack of certainty about the fact of it actually being Christ's Body. Many believe it is a contracted form of the previous Communion rite but the previous Communion rite did not imply what is implied here.

Our intention is not to make a point by point analysis of the new ritual since such an analysis would be far too extensive for our present discussion but our hope is that the modern philosophies may be seen as active in the new ritual[163] as promulgated.[164] The ritual of the Mass, any Mass, is a very powerful form of intellectual formation on all those involved in it, from the priest who offers the Mass to the laity who attend it. It also means that if a non-realist metaphysics or philosophy has sway over elements of the Mass, the people and priest will likewise be influenced by that metaphysics or

---

[161]That is "Corpus Domini Nostri Iesu Christi custodiat animam tuam in vitam eternam. Amen," i.e. "May the Body of Our Lord Jesus Christ preserve your soul unto life everlasting. Amen."

[162]Amen is Hebrew for "so be it." See Podradsky, *New Dictionary of the Liturgy*, 1966. See also *The Catechism of the Council of Trent*, p. 588.

[163]This is not to imply that the new rite of the Mass is invalid.

[164]This implies that even if the ritual is said according to the rubrics, it still has some fundamental difficulties. The fact that Cardinal Ottaviani and several other cardinals and high ranking ecclesial officials warned Pope Paul VI of the (theological) problems inherent in the new ritual prior to its promulgation in 1969 is significant. Moreover, the fact that Paul VI and subsequent liturgists and theologians all but ignored the observations made by the cardinals and others is quite perplexing considering their high rank within the Church. The text of Cardinal Ottaviani is currently published by TAN Publishers under the title *The Ottaviani Intervention* and it draws attention to the fact that the problems inherent in the new rite of Mass were perceived long before their effects were felt in the Church.

philosophy. In fact, the entire discussion of the liturgical renewal and now the "reform of the reform" has been a complete witnessing to the different philosophies involved. For example, those who think that we need to have a new ritual other than the ordinary form, due to the inherent and associated difficulties it bears, often reject the idea of "reconnecting to tradition" and assert that "we cannot go back." These suffer from a Hegelian metaphysical influence.[165] In other words, they don't want the Mass of Pope St. Pius V (thesis), nor the Mass of Paul VI (antithesis) but a new rite of Mass which is often referred to as a combination (synthesis) of elements of both rituals.

The difficulty appears to be the very fact that they are saying the new rite. Because the liturgy is a very powerful form of intellectual formation, those who say it consistently or with any intellectual and volitional involvement cannot escape its formative effects. In other words, even though they do not wish to be affected by the modern metaphysics and philosophies implicit in the new rite of Mass, they cannot escape the modern philosophies taking an implicit role in their deliberations about what should and should not be in the liturgy.[166]

What should be evident is the fact that since the realist metaphysics has collapsed, there are disparities between what is taking place liturgically and what the Church believes, since there are aspects of the liturgy in which the actions *(orandi)* and the beliefs *(credendi)* are not congruent. Without a realist metaphysics and epistemology, one cannot strive for suitability in the

---

[165]It is nothing short of Hegelianism to assert that modern man is fundamentally different than his predecessors and therefore a new ritual is needed in order to appeal to modern man. The fact is that since man's essence does not change, all essential and virtually all accidental liturgical forms will have appeal to every generation.

[166]This perhaps is the most telling sign of the modern problem, viz. that there are those who see themselves as worthy of making the changes who are not in positions of ecclesiastical authority. While those in authority will be aided by their office, those who do not have authority will not. Moreover, the very fact that there is in the liturgical discussions a great deal of language embodying expressions such as "I want" and "I think" is a sign of the inevitable subjectivism which results from the rationalist metaphysics present in the liturgy. Moreover, if one has a realist metaphysics, one quickly realizes that one is not worthy of determining what is and should be part of the liturgy. For there is a fundamental lack of humility about someone who cannot see the awesome responsibility of determining the intellectual formation of the faith of billions of people. Only those endowed with the proper ecclesiastical office, after prayer, sacrifice and mortification ought to approach the sacred mysteries and even then with only slight changes in mind, remembering how the saints formed the liturgy under the guidance of God's Most Holy Hand. Moreover, we must recoup the humility which teaches us that we must conform ourselves to the liturgy and not the liturgy to ourselves.

liturgy since there is no intention to ensure that our sensory signs and actions 'congrue' with the spiritual realities.[167] Only a realism, which maintains that man can know things through his senses, will ever provide an adequate approach to liturgical matters.

C. Philosophical Solution

Where does this leave the members of the Church? It seems that the only solution is to reconnect with the tradition in a living manner.[168] Not

---

[167]What this means is that if one does not hold to a realist epistemology, and consequently, a realist metaphysics, one will not hold that we can come to true intellectual, universal and conceptual knowledge by means of the senses. Consequently, there is no psychological motivation to ensure that there is a congruity between what one believes and what one does exteriorly. Rationalists use abstract art and signs since, for them, there is no real need or use of the senses. The empiricists do not believe in anything spiritual, so the sensory signs to do not point to anything beyond sensible reality but focus the attention on the 'appetitive' and human. Hegelians want a constant changing of the signs to reflect the constant changing of beliefs. Clearly, then, only a realist metaphysics realizes that essences do not change and that our conceptual knowledge of those unchanging essences is acquired by means of the senses. Therefore, only a realist metaphysics will grasp the changelessness and spiritual reality of the Deposit of Faith and the nature of a man and therefore recognize that a liturgy must be something which does not change essentially or substantially over time. Rather, like accidents in general, the liturgy would change only accidentally and slightly over the course of a long period of time. This is why organic development of the liturgy is crucial because it recognizes that if a liturgy reflects the teachings of the Catholic faith, it will not need major modifications. Rather, only slight changes from time to time will be needed as a deeper grasp of that same Deposit becomes clearer. Therefore, suitability in the liturgy will only occur when a realist metaphysics is insisted upon and when the changes in the liturgy are not wide sweeping but only slight. Moreover, it will not accept a completely newly designed rite since that implies that essences somehow change and that the prior liturgy did not reveal the essence of the Faith. But in point of fact, the traditional Rite did reveal the Faith and therefore there is no need to create an "essentially" new and different rite.

[168]Some have mistakenly concluded that those currently in the Church are bound by the precepts of the Second Vatican Council to make liturgical changes. While this may have been true for those who immediately followed the Council, it does not necessarily apply to those currently in the Church. Commands are given by a competent authority and are to be carried out with a certain set of circumstances in mind, but these commands bind as mediated by the circumstances under which the command was given; when the circumstances fundamentally change, one is no longer bound by the command. This moral principle is employed in the CIC/83: "Can. 41: The executor of an administrative act to whom the task of execution only is entrusted, cannot refuse to execute it, unless it is quite clear that the act itself is null, or that it

through taking and adapting it to some new form of the liturgy, but reconnecting with our tradition in the fullest sense and offering only those forms of the liturgy which were not imbued with non-realist philosophy. Once the realist metaphysics and philosophy operative in the ancient liturgies has taken root in those most intimately connected with the liturgy,[169] then with "fear and trepidation," the Church can consider whether any changes are really needed. It would seem only at that point that suitability as contained in the liturgical *agere sequitur esse* would be grasped and employed as an operative principle in the proper sense and would be applied to any liturgical deliberations.

---

cannot for some other grave reason be sustained, or that the conditions attached to the administrative act itself have not been fulfilled. If, however, the execution of the administrative act would appear to be inopportune, by reason of the circumstances of person or place, the executor is to desist from the execution, and immediately inform the person who issued the act." Consequently, because the liturgical situation and life of the Church have changed in such a serious manner since the closing of the Council in 1965, we today are no longer bound by the requirement of the Council to make the changes since it cannot be sustained without more confusion besetting the already clouded minds of the laity and clergy, and, consequently, it would be inopportune by reason of the circumstances.

[169]If St. Paul (Romans 10: 17) is right that faith comes through hearing, then it must also be the case that if the Faith is expressed clearly through the liturgy, the faith of the laity will also be revitalized. Moreover, many more people would be converted to Catholicism if more witnessed the Mass of Pope St. Pius V which by its very forms of expression "preaches" the faith by the very nature of its *orandi* to those who will hear it. But if the liturgy does not "preach" the Faith, it will not convert anyone.

Chapter 14: A Historical Juncture in Liturgical Development

With the promulgation of the *motu proprio Summorum Pontificum* by the Holy Father and subsequent clarification *Universae Ecclesiae*, there is renewed interest in an authentic liturgical development. This is said in light of the Holy Father's statement that:

> "For that matter, the two Forms of the usage of the Roman Rite can be mutually enriching: new Saints and some of the new Prefaces can and should be inserted in the old Missal. The "Ecclesia Dei" Commision, in contact with various bodies devoted to the *usus antiquior*, will study the practical possibilities in that regard.[170]

Article six of the *motu proprio* observes that "in the Masses celebrated according to the missal of Blessed John XXIII with the people, the readings are able to be proclaimed also in the vernacular language, using editions recognized by the Apostolic See."[171] The formulation of this article indicates two things: (1) that when Mass is said *with the people*, one may read the readings in the vernacular. (2) However, the Latin indicates by the use of the term "etiam" that this is not a substitution but that the readings may be read in the vernacular *in addition to* the readings done in Latin at the altar at the normal time.[172] It appears that the Holy See is allowing for what has become the custom in many countries where the readings are done in the vernacular at the time of the homily after they have been said at the altar.

However, as was observed in the *Latin Mass Magazine*, Monsignor James P. Moroney on EWTN[173] used a set of statistics to argue for the use of

---

[170]Benedict XVI, Letter accompanying the *motu proprio Summorum Pontificum*, July 7, 2007.

[171]Benedict XVI, *Summorum Pontificum* (July 7, 2007 - translation mine): Art. 6. In Missis iuxta Missale B. Ioannis XXIII celebratis cum populo, Lectiones proclamari possunt etiam lingua vernacula, utendo editionibus ab Apostolica Sede recognitis.

[172]The word "etiam" is defined (Charlton T. Lewis and Charles Short. A *Latin Dictionary*. Claredon Press. Oxford. 1975. p. 662) as: "annexes a fact or thought to that which has already been said, *and also, furthermore, also, likewise, besides* (syn. quoque)."

[173]"The World Over" with Raymond Arroyo, July 9, 2007.

the 1970 Lectionary with the 1962 Missal. While the legislation of the *motu proprio* does not seem to allow for the use of the readings of the ordinary form in the extraordinary form of the Mass as was noted above, the question remains as to whether the lectionary of the ordinary form *should* be used in the extraordinary form of the Mass in the future by the granting of permission from the Holy See.

One of the arguments in favor of using the lectionary of the ordinary form in the extraordinary form of the Mass is that the new lectionary contains more of Scripture than does the prior missal. In the *Newsletter* of the Committee on the Liturgy,[174] it is observed that the ordinary form includes 14% of the Old Testament and 71% of the New Testament. While use of statistics can have a place even in the use of liturgical studies, nevertheless, to imply that readings in the ordinary form should be the used in the extraordinary form because the ordinary form has statistically more of the Scriptures in it, is to fall prey to the false principle that "more is always better". It is true that the document of Vatican II *Sacrosanctum Concilium* (para. 51) called for an increase in the amount of Scripture, the question is not merely just a matter of amplification of the number of readings.

The question is about the *principles* that govern the selection of the readings for the particular Mass of the day. Mere quantitative increase often appears to be the principle that is governing the discussion on the amplification of the readings and other parts of the Mass in relationship to the extraordinary form. However, just as one would not wear a purple tie with pink polka dots with a pinstripe suit to work, certain things in one form of the liturgy will not be suited to the other form. In other words, it is not merely a matter of quantity but a matter of quality of the readings in relationship to the particular theme of the Mass or feast in relationship to the Mass. For example, on the last Sunday of October in the old rite, it is the feast of Christ the King. In the new rite (2007), it was the 30th Sunday in ordinary time which has for its reading a passage from the Gospel according to St. Luke (18:9-14) in which Christ gives the parable of the tax collector who asks God to be merciful while the Pharisee who is in the temple with him looks down upon the tax collector. This reading has no suitability or correspondence to the feast of Christ the King.

A. *Conveniens* or Suitability

This brings us to the broader question of suitability in the liturgy. Since the Church, in her wisdom, has pointed Catholic philosophers toward

---

[174] Volume XLIII, May/June 2007, p. 27.

Thomism[175] as a way of avoiding error[176] and providing a truly perennial Christian philosophy,[177] we ought, therefore, to look to St. Thomas to learn how he understood the metaphysical notion of suitability. Saint Thomas does not say too much about suitability, and like many other terms and notions in his philosophy and theology, they are used in such a way as to imply a certain grasp on the side of the reader as to their content. Nevertheless, there are a few places and ways he uses the term which gives us a clear idea of what it means for one thing to suit another. In the *Tertia Pars* of the *Summa Theologiae*, St. Thomas delineates how one thing suits another:

> what suits (*conveniens*) each thing is that which suits *(competit)* it according to the notion (*rationem*) of its proper nature; as it suits man to reason because this suits him insofar as he is rational according to his nature.[178]

From this passage we can see a few things operative. The first is that suitability includes two things, viz. the thing and that which is said to suit that thing. Secondly, that something suits something because it suits or befits the notion or concept of its proper nature. In other words, there is a correspondence between the essence of the thing and the other thing that befits or suits it.

What exactly St. Thomas means by one thing suiting another thing, based upon some correspondence between it and the nature of the thing, can be seen in some of his other works where we see him employing the term:

> something is reduplicated in some proposition when insofar as it is that through which the predicate suits the subject; whence it is necessary that in some way it is the same with the subject and in

---

[175]The possible citations are numerous, but among others see: Leo XIII, *Aeterni Patris*, passim, but especially paras. 21, 25 and 33; Pope St. Pius X, *Pascendi Dominici Gregis*, para. 45; CIC/83 can. 252, §3 and Sacred Congregation For Catholic Education, *Ratio Fundamentalis*, paras. 79 and 86.

[176]Among other see: Leo XIII, op. cit., paras. 18, 21 and 29 and Pope St. Pius X, loc. cit.

[177]See the two works of Pope St. Pius X, loc. cit. and *Studiorum Ducem*, passim.

[178]ST. III, a. 1, a. 1: unicuique rei conveniens est illud quod competit sibi secundum rationem propriae naturae, sicut homini conveniens est ratiocinari quia hoc convenit sibi inquantum est rationalis secundum suam naturam.

some way it is the same in the predicate.[179]

Here the term "suits" is used to indicate that in a proposition, the predicate suits the subject because they are the same in some way. In other words, suitability implies some type of identity or sameness between the two things.[180] This is born out in his statement in a lesser known work on the operations of nature:

> Indeed, some hidden operations are found in certain bodies which similarly suit all those which are of the same species, as all magnets attract iron. Hence, it remains in this way that operations follow some intrinsic principle which is common to all having the same species.[181]

Here the notion of suitability indicates that those of the same species have something in common and those operations are said to suit those things. One last text that gives us an idea of St. Thomas' notion of suitability has to do with proportion:

> proportion is nothing other than a certain condition of two things suiting each other in something, according to which they suit or are different. Moreover, they are able to be understood to be suitable in a two fold way. In one way, from the fact that they are suited in the same genus of quantity or quality, as the condition of the surface to a surface or numbers to numbers, insofar as one exceeds the other or equals it or even heat to heat, and in this way proportion is not able

---

[179]III Sent. d. 10, q. 1, a. 1, aa. 1a: in aliqua propositione reduplicatur cum hoc quod dico, secundum quod, est illud per quod praedicatum convenit subjecto; unde oportet quod aliquo modo sit idem cum subjecto, et aliquo modo idem cum praedicato.

[180]Another text which indicates this is that of *In libros physicorum* (I. 3, c. 5, n. 11) where he says: "for it is not necessary that all things suit each other in every way that are in some way the same, but those which are in the same subject or thing and from the same perspective" (non enim oportet quod omnia eadem conveniant iis quae sunt quocumque modo idem; sed solum illis quae sunt idem subiecto vel re et ratione.) Here Aquinas links up the notion of identity, i.e. something which is the same either in the subject or thing and according to concept or notion.

[181]*De occultis operibus naturae*, un.: quaedam vero operationes occultae in quibusdam inveniuntur corporibus, quae similiter conveniunt omnibus quae sunt eiusdem speciei, sicut omnis magnes attrahit ferrum. Unde relinquitur huiusmodi operationes consequi aliquod intrinsecum principium quod sit commune omnibus habentibus huiusmodi speciem.

to be between God and creature, since they do not come together (*conveniant*) in a genus. In another way, they are able to be suitable when they are suited to some order, and thus proportion occurs between matter and form, making and made, and other things of this kind, and thus proportion is required between the knower and knowable, since the knowable is as if the act of knowing potency.[182]

For Aquinas, something is suitable either because it is in the same genus or there is something between the two things according to some order. In the case of being in the same genus, the same thing is found explicitly in the one as in the other. But while St. Thomas does not mention it, in the case of order, one things suits another because again there is some type of "sameness," viz. implicitly or in some other way.

The ability to grasp suitability in things implies that there is a rational power which has the capacity to see them as being the same either explicitly or implicitly, e.g. if one knows what a pen is, one knows explicitly that writing and the pen suit each other. Whereas, some things are suitable in an implicit way, i.e. the rational power has to draw out of the two the similarity that exists. For example, one must draw out of the way we treat dignitaries a few facts before knowing what kind of action is proper to a dignitary, i.e. one must know what and who are dignitaries and what kind of actions both absolutely and according to local customs suit dignitaries. Once one knows what a dignitary is and what certain forms of action imply dignity, one is then able to bring the two together and know which suits the other, since what is the same in both is the notion of "dignity." Without the knowledge of both, it is likely that one would do something which is unsuited to the dignitary. But this capacity to grasp the two is a sign of the intellect's power to penetrate the natures of things.

B. Different Liturgical Forms

In the context of the readings at Mass, the readings in the ordinary

---

[182]*De Trinitate* p. 1, q. 1, a.2, ad 3: proportio nihil aliud est quam quaedam habitudo duorum ad invicem convenientium in aliquo, secundum hoc quod conveniunt aut differunt. Possunt autem intelligi esse convenientia dupliciter. Uno modo ex hoc quod conveniunt in eodem genere quantitatis aut qualitatis, sicut habitudo superficiei ad superficiem aut numeri ad numerum, in quantum unum excedit aliud aut aequatur ei, vel etiam caloris ad calorem, et sic nullo modo potest esse proportio inter Deum et creaturam, cum non conveniant in aliquo genere. Alio modo possunt intelligi convenientia ita quod conveniant in aliquo ordine, et sic attenditur proportio inter materiam et formam, faciens et factum et alia huiusmodi, et talis proportio requiritur inter potentiam cognoscentem et cognoscibile, cum cognoscibile sit quasi actus potentiae cognoscentis.

form of the Mass are *unsuited* to the extraordinary form. This follows from the fact that they are on different cycles (the old rite has an one year cycle which includes both the feasts and the Saints and the liturgical year, whereas the new rite has a Sunday cycle, a weekday cycle, and a sanctoral cycle.) It also follows from the fact that because they are on different cycles the readings simply will not fit the themes of the Mass in the extraordinary form. This would not exclude the possibility of amplifying the readings in the extraordinary form but the readings must suit particular feasts and the cycle that is present within the extraordinary form.

Some argue that the readings should be done in the vernacular and facing the people since the readings are there for the education of the faithful. In relationship to this assertion, we quote at length from the text *The Holy Sacrifice of the Mass*:

> The use of the Latin language in nowise prevents the faithful from participating in the fruits of the Sacrifice, notwithstanding assertions to the contrary. The demand that the Mass should everywhere be celebrated in the vernacular, is based for the most part on ignorance, or on an entire misconception of the real nature and object of the Eucharistic Sacrifice. The liturgy of the Holy Sacrifice contains "much that is instructive" (*magnam eruditionem* - Trident.), but instruction is by no means its principal object. The altar is not a pulpit, the Holy Mass is not primarily a doctrinal lecture or an instruction to the people. The Sacrifice is essentially a liturgical action performed by the priest for propitiating and glorifying God, as well as for the salvation of the faithful.[183]

The liturgy is not principally and foremost for our instruction but for the giving of glory and praise to God and for the propitiation of our sins. This includes all of the Mass and not merely the Canon. The Epistle and the Gospel are part of a sacrifice of praise offered to God and this is why the Church offered them in Latin since Latin being a sacred language is more pleasing to God by that very fact. For this reason also the readings are announced at the altar as a form of sacrifice of praise given back to God for the good (i.e. the very epistles and Gospels themselves) that He is given to us.

Final Observations

Development has been part of liturgical history from the beginning, but that development of the liturgy always followed certain principles.

---

[183] Gihr, *The Holy Sacrifice of the Mass; Dogmatically, Liturgically and Ascetically Explained*, p. 325

Among those principles are: (1) while the liturgy in its totality is educational, nevertheless it is principally about God and not us. (2) The parts of the Mass must suit each other. (3) Making liturgical changes is the prerogative of Saints and this is precisely because of the fact that they, being holy, know what suits God Who is holy; a holy man is a principled man and will therefore approach the liturgical changes in a principled manner. (4) liturgical changes were done organically which indicates that they were done slowly over the course of time.

Given the aforesaid principles, a discussion to foster liturgical changes at this time appears inopportune for a few reasons. (1) Since this is the age of immanentism, it simply is not possible to fulfill the first principle that the liturgy is principally about God because we are too focused on ourselves. (2) Since the study of metaphysics which rested upon a philosophical realism has collapsed within the Church, a proper metaphysical understanding of suitability and how it should play itself out in the liturgy is not present at the current time except among only a few. (3) The Holy Father himself observed:

> ... in many places celebrations were not faithful to prescriptions of the new Missal, but the latter actually was understood as authorizing or even requiring creativity, which frequently led to deformations of the liturgy which were harder to bear. I am speaking from experience, since I too lived through that period with all its hopes and confusion. And I have seen how arbitrary deformations of the liturgy caused deep pain to individuals totally rooted in the faith of the Church.[184]

Because there have been deformations based on a lack of proper understanding of the principles that govern the liturgy as well is difficulties regarding obedience to the Magisterium who has repeatedly warned priests that they were not to make liturgical changes to the liturgy, it is hard to see how we can hope for a principled approach to the liturgical development. (5) When liturgical changes are discussed, often there is a lack of understanding of how we are bound to the tradition that went before us. Liturgical discussions often call for whole scale changes which manifest a lack of understanding of the nature of *organic* development. In a word, many of the liturgical discussions lacked piety.

While the Holy Father's desire to have an authentic liturgical development is commendable, it does not appear that now is the time for such a development. There is no guarantee that the development would follow a principled approach nor can we claim that this is the age of the Saints who would ensure a principled approach. Not all of the principles are fully

---

[184]Benedict XVI, Letter accompanying the *motu proprio Summorum Pontificum*, July 7, 2007.

understood which have governed the liturgical developments of the past and this can also create difficulties for a current liturgical development. Therefore we cannot but recommend that no major changes are made to the extraordinary form of the liturgy for two generations or so. In the meantime, we can hope that the upcoming generations will have the reverential dispositions necessary to have an authentic organic development of the liturgy.

Part IV: Quodlibetals

Chapter 15: Christian Art and Culture[1]

Among traditionalists there is a great deal of discussion about culture and art, but it has proceeded without a clear discussion of how the two are related. In order to understand the relationship of Christian art to culture, one must have a grasp of four things. The first is the nature of art; the second, connected to the first is: what is beauty? Third, what is truly "Christian" and, lastly, what is culture? It appears, at least to to this author, that our contemporaries are so confused about all four of these that we should briefly discuss each.

The first is art. St. Thomas Aquinas says that "art is nothing other than right reason of some produced works."[2] In other words, art is the application of right reason toward producing some kind of work. There are different kinds of work and so there are different kinds of art.

> While *mechanical* arts aim at the production of things useful, the *fine* arts aim at the production of something beautiful, i.e. of works which by their order, symmetry, harmony, splendor, etc., will give apt expression to human ideals of natural beauty as to elicit aesthetic enjoyment in the highest possible degree.[3]

The mechanical arts are there to produce things which we can use for the sake of our physical and spiritual benefit, such as cars, modern kitchen appliances, computers, etc. Here we see that technology is a branch of the mechanical arts.

The fine arts, on the other hand, are there to give expression to the beauty of the natural order which we see around us. This comes from Aristotle's observation that "art is the imitation of nature." It is fact that any art whatsoever is always in some way imitative of nature. For even the most creative of artists take things which they have experienced and use them in different ways to express some idea or image which they have in their minds. For in order for us to have anything in the imagination, it must in some way come from what we sense in reality. Even those works of art which seem to have nothing in common with reality, the artists takes colors and shapes which he gets from real things and fashions them according to his concept or idea. Nothing is in our imagination that was not first in the senses and so art has a connection to reality which is not able to be denied.

---

[1] This chapter was first published in *The Latin Mass* (Spring 2002).

[2] ST I-II, q. 57, a. 3: ars nihil aliud est quam ratio recta aliquorum operum faciendorum.

[3] Coffey, *Ontology or the Theory of Being*, p. 204.

We therefore ask ourselves this question. If art is the imitation of nature, how are we to imitate it? Is good art merely a replication of some real thing? Is good art merely the art which expresses most clearly the conception of the artist? What if the artist is morally depraved and so his mode of thinking tends to distort everything according his bad character? In order to address this, we must answer our second question: what is beauty?

There are a number of definitions of beauty; many of them are true since they express different aspects of beauty. However, the best definition of beauty, in my opinion, is that used by St. Thomas Aquinas, viz. "beauty is that which is pleasing to a cognitive faculty."[4] Sometimes St. Thomas says it is that which is pleasing to sight (*visa*) but sight is of different kinds. There is physical sight which is a type of sense knowledge and there is intellectual sight and so we may say that beauty is that which pleases something which has the capacity to know. To demonstrate the truth of this definition, let us consider the following example: most women desire to be beautiful in order to please their husband or fiancé and that is why at their wedding women dress in a fashion to accentuate their beauty in such a way as to appear acceptable and pleasing so that he will say "I do" at the altar rail. No normal person wants to be ugly and this is natural to all of us: we desire to be beautiful in order to be pleasing to ourselves and others.

While all agree that we want to be beautiful, very few can agree on what is beautiful and for that reason we must take a look at what the attributes of beauty are so that we can identify them in art. Beauty is called, according to some metaphysicians, a transcendental. A transcendental, without going into all of the abstract details, is something that can be said of everything that exists. Metaphysicians do not always agree regarding the number of transcendentals, but we will only concern ourselves with just a few. We can say that of all things that exist, everything that exists is a being, i.e. it is something which has existence. Everything that exists is also one and by this we understand that everything that is exists as an individual. We are distinct from each other and that is because we are separate beings. Everything that exists is good and this is because God created it and since everything that God creates reflects some perfection in God, then everything that exists is good since God is all good. We say that something is bad because it lacks some good or perfection and so we can say that insofar as something lacks being, it is evil. Some metaphysicians hold that beauty is a species of the good and without going into all of the complexities of the issue, this author thinks it is possible to say that beauty is different from the good. For example, one might see a beautiful painting and recognize it as such, but that does not mean that person desires to possess the painting. "The good is that which all

---

[4] See ST I-II, q. 27, a. 1, ad 3 ("pulchrum autem dicatur id cuius ipsa apprehensio placet") and Coffey, op. cit., p. 193.

things desire" and with respect to the painting, we do not necessarily desire to possess it.

If there is something lacking which should be in the thing, it is bad and this is also applicable to beauty, insofar as if there is something lacking in something that should be there, it is not beautiful. In fact, something is ugly because it lacks beauty. For example, we would say that a person who has one eye that is significantly lower on his face than another or whose nose is bent to one side is ugly. This is because the person's face lacks symmetry which is one of the attributes of beauty. In fact, there are three categories of attributes which a thing must possess in order for it to be beautiful. The first being symmetry, which is an attribute in things in which two or more parts are well arranged according to a proper order. It is sometimes called proportion and, in music, we call this harmony.

The second attribute is integrity, sometimes called perfection. Integrity or perfection means that the thing is whole; that there are no parts of it missing that should be there. For example, if we see a person who is missing part of his face, we say the person is ugly, whereas the person, who has all of the parts of his face, assuming he has the other attributes of beauty, is beautiful. The third attribute of beauty is clarity or splendor. This attribute is present when something is beautiful is easily known or makes itself known. We can see this when we are in a crowd of people that someone who is very beautiful tends to naturally draw our attention. Aristotle used to call this amplitude insofar as a thing had be of a certain size in order to make itself easily known. Things that are too small are hard for us to know.

The reason we have gone into all of this is to point out that beauty is in the *thing*. In other words, beauty is the existence of these three attributes in the thing. All know the dictum "beauty is in the eye of the beholder," but the common understanding of this phrase is actually false. For we have just seen that beauty is something in the thing itself, for something is beautiful because in *it* are symmetry, proportion, clarity, etc. Let us do a short test to see if beauty is in the thing and not in the eye of the beholder: imagine if men who are married told their wives that they are not *really* beautiful. Each husband should tell his wife that beauty is in the eye of the beholder and so it is merely in his mind, not in her. If beauty is in the eye of beholder, women ought to forget doing all those things which accentuate their beauty and just find some guy dumb enough to think they are beautiful. No. The fact is that beauty is in the thing and so the husbands can reassure their wives that they are beautiful; provided they really are.

The problem is that people do not distinguish between beauty which is in the thing and the aesthetic sense which is in the person beholding the beauty. The aesthetic sense consists in the person's ability to grasp what is truly beautiful. Some people, as Aristotle says, are depraved and this affects their ability to see what is truly beautiful. There are several things which affect our ability to see what is beautiful. The first is our disposition; if we are in an angry mood, what we think is beautiful may be different from when we are in a good mood. We see disposition playing a roll in that some people are naturally more attracted to people who are blond haired than they are people who have black hair. Another thing that can affect what one thinks is beautiful is one's virtue. For certain virtues temper our appetites which have a capacity to affect our intellectual judgment. We often see people who are angry doing things they would not do outside that moment of anger and so the passion of anger tends to affect their judgement. Now beauty is something which we grasp or understand intellectually, so if our passions are disordered, it will affect our ability to judge whether something is really beautiful or not. This is why a good character in an artist is absolutely critical for him to be able to produce truly beautiful art. The last thing that we will discuss regarding those thing which affect our aesthetic sense is our mental habits. If we are prone to error and we are habituated in thinking erroneously, our judgment about what is truly beautiful will be affected. This is why mental hygiene is important for grasping what is beautiful. Many of us have watched movies where the mentally disturbed villain observes that something is beautiful when in fact it is grotesque. It is here that we can also say that the more mentally ill the members of a society become, the more they are prone to error. The more they are prone to disordered passions and the living of their lives, the more will their art become grotesque.

Another attribute of beauty is that it naturally draws one to contemplation. Whenever we see something really beautiful, it naturally draws out intellect into considering it. For example, take the average male. If a beautiful woman walks into a room full of men, the men will follower her around the room with their eyes. If an ugly woman walks into the room, they will tend to keep doing what they are doing. The point is that beauty naturally draws us to consider the thing which is beautiful. This is also why we can sit for a long period of time looking at a sunset or a view of a range of mountains. On the other hand, we tend to ignore or be repulsed by things that are really ugly.

This brings us to Christian culture. We cannot exhaust all of the dimensions of culture but we can say that the word culture is ultimately derived from the Latin word *cultus*, which means worship. It is fact that the predominate cult determines the culture in which we live. The cult determines the culture because the cult specifies what are morally acceptable ways of behaving. If the predominate cult says that it is evil to lie, then members of the society will not lie, as a general rule. As a result, the culture would be different from one which says that lying is good. This also helps us to see in what culture consists. Culture does not consist in how many cheeses you have in your country, although that maybe a small part of it. Culture consists in (1) the public habits of the society and (2) the effects of those public habits. In other words, the various artistic things we see in a particular culture, the buildings, the statues, the music, the fine arts, what people eat, how they eat, how they greet each other are actually the effects of the cult. If our cult holds that purity and modesty are good things to be pursued, then publically acceptable dress, the rules of courtship, the statues, etc. will all reflect modesty and purity. If our cult is the cult of the self, then the public dress will degenerate into what our passions want here and now.

The last question we want to answer before we tie it all together is what does it mean to be truly Christian. Since a Christian is one who follows Christ, this means that a Christian will follow the religion which Christ Himself established and told us to follow and that is the Catholic religion. A truly Christian culture is a Catholic culture and here we mean Christian in the fullest sense. To the degree that a specific culture is not *Catholic*, it is to that degree not *Christian*. Some Protestant cultures, one could argue, are Christian, but it could be argued that they do not possess the fullness of truth regarding the teachings of Christ and so their culture can never be fully Christian. Therefore, true Christian culture is one which adheres to the cult established by Christ which is the Catholic cult. This also indicates that we must submit to authority which has the right to interpret the deposit of faith so that we may know the truth. For that reason, only an orthodox Catholic faith hallmarked by its proper adherence to the Magisterium of the Church can be a foundation for a truly Christian culture.

How does all of the aforesaid fit together. As we mentioned, beauty is that which naturally draw us to contemplation. If our art has both a Christian theme, i.e. it is about Our Lord, Our Lady, an angel, a saint or some mystery of the faith, *and* it is beautiful, it will naturally draw people to contemplate that which is extolled by the art. The beauty of the art will draw them to contemplate the art and the Christian theme will provide the subject matter of contemplation. For example, how many of you have walked into a Catholic Church and seen a statue which lacked clarity, i.e. you could not figure out what the statue was? What happens? You end up spending all your time trying to figure out what or who it is rather than kneeling in front of the statue and the beauty of the statue naturally drawing you to contemplate the mystery or virtue portrayed. Contemplation and prayer are intimately connected, in fact sometimes prayer is called contemplation. Often contemplation has a more restricted sense within the various levels of prayer but the point is that contemplation is naturally an activity of the mind. Prayer is the lifting of the mind and heart to God and so if the statue is beautiful, it will naturally draw one's mind and so it is much easier for one's will to follow because of the beauty. But if the statue is ugly, then my prayer is done in spite of the statue, not because of it.

We must comment, therefore, on the current artistic and architectural practices of certain members of the Church. It appears as if some members of the Church have no aesthetic sense or very little aesthetic sense because they are building Churches which are ugly and they are putting statuary in the churches which are equally hideous. We build churches which do not draw people to contemplation and then we wonder why mental prayer has collapsed among the laity. We put in statues that are unrecognizable and we wonder why the cult of saints has imploded. The fact is that people are moved by what comes into the senses. If we present people with statues that lack clarity, proportion and symmetry and then we wonder why people do not go up to the altar rail and pray before the statue, we only have ourselves to blame. Let us not forget that the aesthetic sense is often determined by our mental habits. Faith is a virtue which resides in the intellect by which one gives assent to those teachings revealed by Jesus Christ and taught by the Church, commonly called the deposit of faith. The Catholic cult teaches that purity, modesty, truth and temperance are virtues. If they are, why do some of the new churches being built not contain statuary to give one the impression of purity by the clarity of statues? Why are the statues not representing modesty and humility by portraying saints with hands folded like the humble slave? We, as Catholics, believe that the desire to lead a life according to truth is necessary for salvation and yet we have statues and churches which do not have any resemblance to the true beauty of the doctrines of the Church, Our Lady or the virtues and perfections of the saints. We must conclude that the aesthetic sense of those who are uglifying the churches do not have the same habits of mind that we do. In fact, we dare say that they do not believe the same things we do. Here we see how crucial authentic orthodox faith in submission to the teaching authority of the Church is to Christian art. Art is, again, right reason applied to certain produced things. If we do not have right reason, if we do not have the right faith, we will not have the right art. There is an intrinsic connection between right belief and beauty. While it is possible for a pagan artist to produce beautiful art, true beauty is know when we are able to look at the natural order the way God sees it and this is done through faith. It is in this way that our aesthetic sense is perfected because we see things the way God sees them and so truly Catholic artists who lead lives of virtue have a much greater potential to produce beautiful art than someone whose beliefs are distorted, which in turn distorts his view of reality.

Here we use the term *potential* because it is possible for someone who is morally degenerate to produce beautiful art. Yet, this is because there is something else compensating for their lack of good character. For instance, a right faith may help one to see reality properly despite one's lack of moral virtue and so they can produce beautiful art because it flows from their faith. Or in those who do not have right faith, we cannot deny that there are some who can produce truly beautiful art, e.g. Mozart. But in these cases one cannot deny, or so it appears, that God has given then a particular gift or genius (not given to most) and so what may normally come through intellectual and moral virtues in some artists actually is able to be compensated for by the genius given to them by God. The problem today is that many artists think they are a genius (but really are not) and have no virtue and it shows in their art.

What of culture? If part of culture consists in the public habits of a society which is expressed in its art, then the art has a capacity to express the beliefs of a given society. If the society fills the public places with Catholic art, the art becomes something which all of the members of the society can contemplate. If the art is beautiful and Catholic, then it will have the effect of drawing people to think about what the art is portraying. Many of us who do not live in a Catholic culture have gone to other countries which were or are Catholic and the public devotion of the society which is manifest in its art is edifying and spiritual transforming. For example, in Bavaria, which is heavily Catholic, one often finds along the roads a beautiful crucifix with a small roof over it. It naturally draws one to think about Christ and for a good Catholic, seeing the statue brings great joy. If our statuary actually draws us to the truth and we are lovers of the truth, the statuary and art can actually contribute to joy and happiness of a society.

Our modern situation, however, is not so Catholic. Since the onslaught of modern philosophy, there has been a tendency to divorce man from reality. It is a fact that man comes to true intellectual knowledge of things by means of the senses. This means that what one puts in reality before men will often determine what they think. While men have free will and so they can choose to reject what they see in reality, for either good or ill, nevertheless, most men are formed, both when they are young and when they are old, by what they see day to day. As modern philosophy divorced us from reality, we have begun thinking things which are contrary to reality. Our way of thinking has become detached from reality and has led to art suffering from several defects. The first is that art has become abstract. Our architecture and art is no longer based on what we find in reality but abstract forms and shapes. Instead of having a building made of natural materials adorned with beauty, imitating things which we see, we are now seeing buildings made of glass and plastics in abstract shapes and forms. Again, mental habits affect our aesthetic sense. As man began laboring under the bad ideas, he formed habits which resulted in his art becoming ugly and yet he thinks it is beautiful. It no longer has clarity as just mentioned; there is no proportion any more, there is no symmetry. In fact, art and architecture today seem to be hallmarked by their disproportion and dissymmetry: the more of it, the better, or so it seems. This abstraction in our way of thinking and in art has actually affected the members of the Catholic Church and it is one of the many factors which has eroded the Catholic subculture in this country and the Catholic culture abroad. If one's art does not remind him of any Catholic doctrine or if one sees no

Catholic art at all, how is it going to encourage him to live a Catholic life?

This is the problem with modern society. The abstract way of thinking and the constant manipulation of created things has now intellectually formed two generations and is currently forming another generation because most of what they see is abstract architecture and art. The younger children are not having their imaginations filled with beauty and so they are less pleased and there is less joy. They are not having their senses filled with Christian art and so there is less of a natural tendency in them to seek those things pertaining to contemplation. The irony of it is that while we are not filling our senses or the sense of our children with beautiful art which naturally draws us to intellectual considerations, we are leading lives which are immersed in sensuality.

If our culture is to be healthy; if it is to be truly Christian, we must recapture a proper philosophy of reality, of how we know and of art. Art is not only the expression of Catholic culture; but it is also one of the causes of Catholic culture by placing before us those things which we are to contemplate. If we want a Catholic culture, we must produce beautiful Catholic art in all its forms. Which brings us to the practical aspects which we can implement in our own daily lives.

First, parents must remove any art which is inimical to the moral and religious formation of their children. This includes everything from the types of programs they watch, which is part of the fine arts to the music they hear, to the statuary that they have in the house. For the benefit of their children, they should adorn their houses with pictures, statues and other forms of art which will naturally draw their children to contemplate the mysteries of faith so that the children will develop the proper habits of mind and in turn will be able to judge what is beautiful from a properly developed aesthetic sense. Adults must do likewise, whether they have children or not. They should have Christian art in their homes and if possible in their place of work. Nothing forbids art which does not have a specifically Catholic theme to be in our homes provided it is truly beautiful, for in the beauty alone it will reflect God and develop the aesthetic sense of the children.

Pastors must stop gutting the churches of their beautiful adornments. The vestments and other liturgical items should be beautiful as well. They should place in their churches those statues and pictures which will aid their parishioners in leading good Catholic lives. Sometimes you will hear people say that the churches must be very simple since the more simple a thing is the more Godly it is since God is strictly speaking simple. While it is true that God is absolutely simple in the sense that His being is absolutely simple, our churches must not be too simplistic. Clearly, some churches are simple because the people cannot afford much. But often, pastors will gut a church and then spend thousands, and in some cases hundred of thousands, of dollars beautifying the rectory. It logically moves one to wonder what they really think.

The problem with this notion is that while something that is simple is beautiful insofar as it is like God, we as humans find it difficult to contemplate beauty which is simple. The reason is that beauty has order and since we, who are complex beings both in our nature and in our way of understanding, need a certain amount of complexity in a thing in order for us to see the order among the various parts of the thing. So we need a certain amount of complexity in the art in order for us to easily see the beauty of it. Practically, this means that churches which have a certain degree of complexity actually aid the faithful more in their spiritual life than churches which are utterly bare. This also means that while moderation must be observed, pastors should ensure that their churches are adequately decorated with art which will aid their faithful.

Sometimes the faithful will complain that they are spending all this money on building a new church which is ugly. There is a moral of the story: the faithful control one thing and one thing only in the church and that is the money. If your pastor is spending money to rip out the statuary in the Church or to build an ugly church, give your money to support the building of other beautiful churches. If you are a major benefactor, insist that your money goes toward building churches that really are beautiful and encourage the pastor or bishop to do so.

Moreover, pastors must employ music in the liturgy which adheres to proper aesthetics. It must be music which moves us to contemplation, not to emotion. We said before that our passions or emotions can blind us and so we must be sure that our music in the Church is based on orthodox teaching and true beauty and not one how much it placates or moves us emotionally. By doing so pastors will affect the aesthetic sense of parishioners who will in turn take that into their daily living in public. By doing so we will begin to affect the culture. If our music is truly beautiful, while taking its proper place in the liturgy by enhancing it and not replacing the worship as it often does, then we will affect people's attachment and love to the doctrines and liturgy of the Church. Parents must also not allow their children to listen to music unless it is truly beautiful. We cannot change the aesthetic of our culture over night but we can transform it by the aesthetic formation we give to our children who will one day be leaders in our society.

On the societal level, if we want to have Catholic culture in the United States of America, as strange as that may sound, there are two things, among others, which we must do. Obviously we must propagate the faith so that by teaching the faith others will follow it. The second is that we must erect churches that inspire even the pagan. We can erect statues of Our Lady, Our Lord or some other saint in own yards so that passers-by will be drawn to consider the Catholic faith and for Catholics to lead a public life according to the faith. We can erect beautiful statues along highways and in the streets.

The moral of the story is that we can begin transforming this culture into a Catholic one by inundating the senses of the members of this society with art that is truly Catholic. If we want them to think in a Catholic way, we must fill their senses with Catholic things. We must see that beautiful art truly is a means of propagating the faith. We must see that beautiful Christian art is a means to shaping a culture into a Catholic one. We must see that all beautiful Christian art is ultimately there to lift our minds to God, Who is that for which all things strive.

Conclusion

Where we stand in the history of the Church is a question that we cannot help but ponder. The last 50 years have left the Church in a state which is never been seen before. Yet, it will remain in this state as long as men of the Church do not take serious count of the impact that the intellectual work done in the 150 years has had on the life of the Church. We are, without doubt, at a crossroads. As the generation which ushered in the changes in the Church wanes in its years and as the new generation of priests are ordained and the younger laity are seeking something to which they can attach a serious and substantial spiritual life, the question of the Sacred Tradition will be seen as one of the greatest import.

Even as the question of how the members of the Church relate to the Sacred Tradition finds its answer, we have come to a point in the Church were the pieces of the doctrinal, moral and spiritual aspects of the Church must be taken up. But those pieces, in many respects, do not come to us as an integrated whole, for that can only come through a living tradition in which the tradition as a whole is passed on intact to the next generation. By way of commentary, this is not the luxury of our generation. We are left with the prospect of fighting for the tradition without the aid of having been passed the tradition to us intact. While the Sacred Tradition is not a case of Humpty-Dumpty, picking up again the living Sacred Tradition is fraught with difficulties when it is not handed to on intact. We are already seeing this problem rear its ugly head, even among certain traditionalists.

In a time when the living tradition, except in a few isolated areas of the Church, has died and those who are trying to recoup it must go back to sources of the tradition and, inmost cases, they are returning to the monuments which have remained. We can only have gratitude to God for having kept most of them in tact. But therein lies a rather substantial problem. We live in an age imbued by the principle of immanence and it would be disingenuous to think that traditionalists, many of them raised in the secular culture imbued with that same principle as well as raised in the modern Church overrun by the principle, will, in an objective fashion, put aside the subjectivism and take up the intellectual cause of the Sacred Tradition having put themselves completely aside. The point: when recouping the tradition, there are already signs of the principle of immanence operative among certain traditionalists. We see this when discussions of the liturgy are dominated by the sentences with words in the first person. This is exacerbated by the fact that many of those committed to the tradition have been seriously hurt and wounded by the lack of compassion on the side of those who follow the principle of immanence. The confluence of the woundedness arising from the pain of seeing the Church in many of its aspects attacked and dismantled, the woundedness arising from Original Sin and the principle immanence does not bode well for recouping of the tradition. Again, this is often seen when the discussion of the liturgy is met by people who, considering themselves experts because everyone in the modern world dominated by the principle of immanence is an expert in his own feelings, makes choices and selections among ceremonials when there is a question of what is to be done in the liturgy. There are also signs of those who want to mix the rites because that fits their disposition. We are also seeing the signs of ignoring rubrics even in the old rite, making things up as they go along due to ignorance or distaste for the way things were done in the tradition, a disregard for the principles and canonical law that dictate how customs are revived and when they are revived. But we are also seeing the signs of a lost historical memory. When the tradition is not passed on in a living manner, aside from the vicissitudes in recouping the Sacred Tradition by those who suffer from Original and Actual sin, we are left with the fact that that the monuments do not contain everything.

On the other hand, there is God. He created the world, established the Church and fashioned the liturgy literally over the course of millennia in order to achieve His desire: rightly ordered worship from a loving creature. He has not abandoned the tradition because He started it and fashioned it over the course of thousands of years. He has also provided the correction within the tradition when the members of the Church deviated from the Sacred Tradition and what He had bequeathed to the Church. In word, while man labors under Original Sin and lives in a secular and religious culture dominated by the principle of immanence, God is stronger than that. His grace is a force, not just to be reckoned with, but one which will eventually win. If it be the will of God that this is not the age of Christ's return, the outpouring grace on the side of God to bring the Church into an even greater glory than we have seen in the past is assured. For those who love the Sacred Tradition, who honor those who in a selfless manner sacrificed even their very lives in some instances, for the preservation and the continuance of the tradition, who in the desire of their heart seek the full restoration of the Church and the NOW required reform of its members, we await the coming glory of a fully restored Sacred Tradition.

Agius, George. *Tradition and the Church* (The Stratford Company, Boston, 1928)

Ante-Nicene Fathers [henceforth ANF – Hendrickson Publishers. Peabody, Massachusetts. 2004.]

Attwater, Donald. *A Catholic Dictionary.* The McMillan Company. New York. 1941.

Bernard Wuellner. *Summary of Scholastic Principles.* Loyola University Press. Chicago. 1956.

Bernardi, Peter J. "Maurice Blondel and the Renewal of the Nature/Grace Relationship." *Communio.*

Billot, Ludovico. *De Immutabilitate Traditionis contra Modernam Hæresim Evolutionismi.* Apud Aedes Unversitatis Gregorianae. Roma. 1929.

Blondel, Maurice. *The Letter on Apologetics and History of Dogma.*William B. Eerdmans. Grand Rapids, Mich. 1994.

--------------------. *L' Action Essai d'une critique de la vie et d'une science de la pratique.*

Bonneterre, Didier. *The Liturigcal Movment: Guéranger to Beauduin to Bugini.* Angelus Press. Kansas City, MO. 2002.

Catechism of the Catholic Church. editio typica. Libreria Editrice Vatican. 1997.

Catechismus Catholicae Ecclesiae. Editio typica. Libreria Editrice. Vaticana. 1997.

Catholic *Encyclopedic Dictionary.* The Gilmary Society. New York. 1941.

Chervin, Rhonda and Kevane, Eugene. *Love of Wisdom: An Introduction to Christian Philosophy.* Ignatius Press. San Francisco. 1988.

Christian Order. London.

Christian Pesch. *Praelectiones Dogmaticae.* Herder & Co. Friburgus. 1924.

Code of Canon Law Annotated. E. Caparros, M. Thériault and J. Thorn., ed. Wilson & Lafleur Limitée. Montreal. 1993.

Coffey, P. *Ontology or the Theory of Being.* Peter Smith. New York. 1938.

Collectanea S. Congregationis de Propaganda Fidei seu Decreta Instructiones Rescripta pro Apostolicis Missionibus. Ex Typographia Polyglotta. Roma. 1907.

Comte, Auguste Comte. *Introduction to Positive Philosophy.* Hackett Publishing Company, Inc. Indianapolis. 1988.

Congar, Yves. *Tradition and Traditions.* Burns and Oates., Ltd. London. 1966.

-----------------. *Meaning of Tradition.* Ignatius Press. San Francisco. 2004.

Congregation for the Doctrine of the Faith. *Declaration on Certain Questions Concerning Sexual Ethics* as found in the official English translation of the Vatican by The Wanderer Press. 128 E. 10th St. St. Paul, MN. 1975.

Copleston, Frederick. *A History of Philosophy* Image Books. New York. 1974.

Cornelius a Lapide, *Commentaria in Scripturam Sacram.* Louis Vivès. Paris.

1859.

Croiset, John. *Devotion to the Sacred Heart of Jesus: How to Practice the Sacred Heart Devotion.* TAN Books and Publishers, Inc. Rockford, Illinois. 1988.

Davis, Henry. *Moral and Pastoral Theology.* Sheed and Ward. New York. 1943.

Dawson, Christopher. *Progress and Religion.* Sheed and Ward. London. 1929.

Descartes, René. *Discourse on Method* (as contained in *René Descartes, Benedict de Spinoza, Gottfried Wilhelm von Leibniz, The Rationalists* [Garden City, N.Y: Anchor Books, 1974]).

Dungan, David Laird. *A History of the Synoptic Problem.* Doubleday. New York. 1999.

Fabro, Cornelio. *God in Exile: Modern Atheism from its Roots in the Cartesian Cogito to the Present Day.* Westminster, Md. Newman Press. 1964.

--------------------. *L'Avvenura dell Teologia Progressista.* Rusconi Editore. Milan. 1974.

Ferrara, Christopher A. and Woods, Thomas A., Jr. *The Great Facade: Vatican II and the Regime of Novelty in the Roman Catholic Church.* Remnant Press. Wyoming, Minnesota. 2002.

Feuerbach, Ludwig. *The Essence of Christianity,* trans. George Eliot. Harper Torchbooks. New York. 1957.

Franzelin, Ioannes. *Tractatus de Divina Traditione et Scriptura.* Ex Typographia Polyglotta. Roma. 1896.

Gamber, Monsignor Klaus. *The Reform of the Roman liturgy: Its Problems and Background.* Una Voce. San Juan Capistrano, California. 1993.

Gannon, P.J. *The Rule of Faith: Scripture and Tradition.* The Catholic Truth Society of Ireland. Dublin. 1946.

Garrigou-Lagrange, Reginald. *Three Stages of the Interior Life.* TAN Books and Publishers, Inc. Rockford, Illinois. 1989.

Gihr, Nicholas. *The Holy Sacrifice of the Mass; Dogmatically, Liturgically and Ascetically Explained.* B. Herder Book Co. St. Louis, Missouri. 1935.

Gilson, Etienne. *Thomist Realism and the Critique of Knowledge* Ignatius Press. San Francisco. 1986.

Guardini, Romano. *The Humanity of Christ: Contributions to the Psychology of Jesus.* Pantheon Books. New York. 1964.

Hegel, G.W.F. *Introduction to the Philosophy of History.* Hackett Publishing Company. Indianapolis. 1988.

Hervé, J.M. *Manuale Theologiæ Dogmaticæ.* Berche et Pagis. Paris. 1929.

Homiletic and Pastoral Review. Ignatius Press. San Francisco, California.

Jones, E. Michael Jones. *Libido Dominandi - Sexual Liberation and Political Control.* St. Augustine's Press. South Bend, Indiana. 2000.

Kant, Immanuel. *Critique of Pure Reason.* Willey. New York. 1943.

Leen, Edward. *Progress through Mental Prayer.* Arena Lettres. New York. 1935.

Ligouri, St. Alphonsus. *Theologia Moralis.* Typis Polyglottis Vaticanis. Roma.

1905.

Louis Marie de Montfort, *True Devotion to the Blessed Virgin*. Montfort Publications. Bay Shore, New York. 1980.

Maritain, Jacques. *Three Reformers: Luther, Descartes, Rousseau*. Charles Scribner's Sons. New York. 1929.

----------------------. *Integral Humanism: Temporal and Spiritual Problems of a New Christendom*. Charles Scribner's Sons. New York. 1968.

Marquis de Condorcet. *Esquisse d'un tableau historique des progrès de l'espirt humain; suivi de Réflexions sur l'esclavage des ègres*. chez Masson et fils. Paris. 1822.

Nicene and Post-Nicene Fathers. Hendrickson Publishers. Peabody, Massachusetts. 2004.

Ott, Ludwig Ott. *Fundamentals of Catholic Dogma*. TAN Books and Publishers. Rockford, Illinois. 1974.

Palm, David. "A Question of Novelty: Why Tradition Rejects it" in *The Remnant:* http://ourworld.compuserve.com/homepages/remnant/palm.htm as of July 7, 2004.

Parente, Pietro. *Dictionary of Dogmatic Theology*. The Bruce Publishing Company. Milwaukee. 1951.

Peterson, Karen S. "Studies Shatter Myth about Abuse," originally found at http://www.usatoday.com/news/health/2003-06-22-abuse-usat_x.htm.

Pius X, Pope St. *An Exhortation on Catechetics to Catholic Parents and Teachers*. As found in *Catechism of Christian Doctrine*. Eugene Kevane, ed. Center for Family Catechetics. Arlington, VA. 1980.

--------------------. *Pascendi Dominici Gregis*. 1907.

Pius XII, Pope *Humanae Generis*. 1950.

Podradsky, Gerhard. *New Dictionary of the Liturgy*. Geoffrey Chapman Ltd. 1966.

Rahner, Karl. *Sacra Scrittura e Teologia* in *Nouvi Saggi I*. Ed. Paoline. Roma. 1968.

-----------------. *Foundations of Christian Faith: An Introduction to the Idea of Christianity*. The Seabury Press. New York. 1978.

Ratzinger, Joseph. *Revelation and Tradition*. Burns and Oats, Ltd. London. 1966.

Romanae, D. E. "The Incommutability of Ecclesiastical Tradition" originally located at: http://www.diocesereport.com/column/romanae/011802_incommutability.shtml.

Schleiermacher, Friedrich. *On Religion*, trans. John Otto. Harper and Row. New York. 1958.

Siri, Joseph Cardinal, *Gethsemani: Reflections on the Contemporary Theological Movement*. Franciscan Herald Press. Chicago. 1981.

Tanquerey, Adolphe. *Synopsis Theologiae Dogmaticae*. Desclée et Socii. Roma.

1927.

------------------------. *The Spiritual Life.* Belgium. 1930.

The Catechism of the Council of Trent. TAN Books and Publishers, Inc. Rockford, Illinois. 1982.

The Catholic Encyclopedia. The Encyclopedia Press, Inc. The Gilmary Society. New York. 1913.

Thomas Aquinas. *Thomae Aquinatis Opera Omnia.* Issu Impensaque Leonis XIII. edita, Roma: ex Typographia Polyglotta et al. 1882.

van den Aardweg, Gerard J.M. *Battle for Normality: A Guide for (Self-)Therapy for Homosexuality.* Ignatius Press. San Francisco. 1997.

Vincent of Lerins, *Commonitorium.* Migne. Patrologia Latina.

Wilhelm, Joseph and Scannell, Thomas. *A Manual of Catholic Theology.* London. Kegan Paul, Trench, Trübner & Co. Ltd. 1908.

Wuellner, Bernard. *A Dictionary of Scholastic Philosophy.* Milwaukee: The Bruce Publishing Company. 1966.

Made in the USA
San Bernardino, CA
13 January 2018